FLOWER TYPES

SPIKE RACEME CORYMB PANICLE UMBEL CYME

COROLLA SHAPES

ROTATE CAMPANULATE FUNNELFORM URCEOLATE SALVERFORM

TREE AND SHRUB SHAPES

LOW TRAILING ROUND COMPACT HORIZONTAL SPREADING

ERECT ARCHING UPRIGHT

CONE COLUMN WEEPING GLOBE FASTIGIATE

THE AMERICAN GARDEN GUIDES

dry climate
gardening
WITH SUCCULENTS

Consultants
Carol Bornstein, Santa Barbara Botanic Garden
Ernest de Marie, PhD.,The New York Botanical Garden
Mark Dimmitt, PhD., Arizona Sonora-Desert Museum
Virginia Hays, Ganna Walska Lotusland, Santa Barbara
James Henrich, Denver Botanical Garden
Mary Irish, Desert Botanical Garden, Phoenix, Arizona
Gary Lyons, horticulturist and landscape designer
Kurt Zadnik and Sean Hogan, University of California Botanical
Garden, Berkeley

Enabling Garden Consultant: Eugene Rothert, Chicago Botanic
Garden

dry climate gardening
gardening
WITH SUCCULENTS

The Huntington Botanical Gardens

By
Debra Brown Folsom, Ph.D.
RESEARCH BOTANIST

John N. Trager
CURATOR OF DESERT COLLECTIONS

James Folsom, Ph.D.
DIRECTOR OF THE GARDENS

Joe Clements
CURATOR OF THE DESERT GARDEN

Nancy Scott
SUCCULENT PLANT GROWER

Series Editor: Elvin McDonald
Principal Photography by John N. Trager

Pantheon Books, Knopf Publishing Group
New York
1995

Acknowledgments
This book was created with the help, expertise, and encouragement of a
great many people. We would like to thank all the consultants who con-
tributed so much to it, and the entire staff of Huntington Botanical
Garden, including Kathy Musial, Felipe Villar, Faustino Benitez-
Quintero, Carla Parkinson, Danielle Rudeen, Martin Coronado, and
Manuel Montero. We also appreciate the efforts of Kathy Grasso, Susan
Ralston, Amanda Gordon, Altie Karper, Alison Sowden, Roy Ritchie,
Bob Carr, Dave Ellis, Boyd and Mary Walker, Jerry Barad, John
Greenlee, Steve Lelewer, Doreen von Drach, Alan Kellock, David Prior,
Susan Kilpatrick, Marlin Hardeo, Doug Jensen, Jaime Gutierrez, Jay
Hyams, Avigal and Ilana Stein, Chani Yammer, Etti Yammer, Michelle
Stein, and Deena Stein.

Project Director: Lori Stein
Book Design Consultant: Albert Squillace
Editorial Director: Jay Hyams
Associate Art Director: Chani Yammer

Library of Congress Cataloging-in-Publication Data
Folsom, Dr. James
Dry climate gardening with succulents / writers, Debra Brown Folsom,
Ph.D. and John N. Trager
    p.   cm.   -- (The American Garden guides)
"Huntington Botanical Gardens."
Includes index.
ISBN: 0-679-75829-1 : $25.00 ($33.50 Can.)
1. Xeriscaping--United States. 2. Xeriscaping--Canada.
3. Succulent plants--Pictorial works. 4. Drought-tolerant plants--
Pictorial works. !. Folsom, Debra. II. Huntington Botanical Gardens. III.
Title. IV. Series
SB439.8.F65 1995
635.9'52--dc20   94-29986
                                                           CIP

Manufactured in Singapore

First Edition

9 8 7 6 5 4 3 2 1

The Desert Garden at The Huntington Botanical Gardens

contents

Mammillaria compressa

Aloe 'Tangerine'

Echeveria in strawberry pot.

3. Garden Design 162

4. Techniques 176

5. Special Conditions 200

the american garden guides

The network of botanical gardens and arboreta in the United States and Canada constitutes a great treasure chest of knowledge about plants and what they need. Some of the most talented, experienced, and dedicated plantspeople in the world work full-time at these institutions; they are the people who actually grow plants, make gardens, and teach others about the process. They are the gardeners who are responsible for the gardens in which millions of visitors exclaim, "Why won't that plant grow that way for me?"

Over thirty of the most respected and beautiful gardens on the continent are participating in the creation of The American Garden Guides. The books in the series originate with manuscripts generated by gardeners in one or several of the gardens. Drawing on their decades of experience, these originating gardeners write down the techniques they use in their own gardens, recommend and describe the plants that grow best for them, and discuss their successes and failures. The manuscripts are then passed to several other participating gardens; in each, the specialist in that area adds recommended plants and other suggestions based on regional differences and different opinions.

The series has three major philosophical points carried throughout:

1) Successful gardens are by nature user-friendly toward the gardener and the environment. We advocate water conservation through the precepts of Xeriscaping and garden health care through Integrated Pest Management (IPM). Simply put, one does not set into motion any garden that is going to require undue irrigation during normal levels of rainfall, nor apply any pesticide or other treatment without first assessing its impact on all other life—plant, animal, and soil.

2) Gardening is an inexact science, learned by observation and by doing. Even the most experienced gardeners often develop markedly dissimilar ways of doing the same thing, or have completely divergent views of what any plant requires in order to thrive. Gardeners are an opinionated lot, and we have encouraged all participants to air and share their differences—and so, to make it clear that everyone who gardens will find his or her own way of dealing with plants. Although it is important to know the rules and the most accepted practices, it is also important to recognize that whatever works in the long run for you is the right way.

3) Part of the fun of gardening lies in finding new plants, not necessarily using over and over the same ones in the same old color schemes. In this book and others in the series, we have purposely included some lesser-known or underused plants, many of them native to our vast and wonderful continent. Wherever we can, we call attention to endangered species and suggest ways to nurture them back to their natural state of plenty.

This volume was originated by the staff at Huntington Botanical Garden–Jim Folsom provided the introduction and design chapters, Deb Folsom wrote the plant portraits, which were reviewed by John Trager and Joe Clements; John Trager provided most of the photographs in the book. Nancy Scott contributed the chapter on techniques, and Gary Lyons added a page on history. Mary Irish at Desert Botanical Garden, Kurt Zadnik and Sean Hogan at University of California Botanical Garden, Berkeley, Virginia Hays at Ganna Walska Lotusland, Carol Bornstein at Santa Barbara Botanical Garden, Dr. Mark Dimmitt at Arizona-Sonora Desert Museum and Dr. Ernie de Marie at The New York Botanical Garden each reviewed the manuscript, adding comments throughout; Sean Hogan added information on hardiness on page 24, and Ernie de Marie provided the chapters on indoor gardening with succulents and on gardening with succulents in the North.

Elvin McDonald
Houston, Texas

Director's preface

The Huntington is quite a diverse institution, with a major research library, three art galleries, and public gardens covering nearly one-hundred-fifty acres. Its mission, as determined by founder H.E. Huntington, is to build collections, conduct research, and to be of educational value to the public. Because of the southern California climate and the historical direction of the gardens, we have built large plant collections displayed in various themed landscapes.

For nearly ninety years, The Huntington has been cultivating a twelve-acre Desert Garden. Due to its extensive holdings and remarkable visual impact, it is not only a most popular attraction but also our most botanically significant collection. When visitors explore the Desert Garden, they see the horticultural efforts of people who love plants and gardens, who are dedicated to spreading botanical knowledge and horticultural enthusiasm.

We hope that you will share our unabashed enjoyment of succulents and the desire to discover more about them. With missionary zeal, we bring this topic to you, hoping enthusiasm is infectious!

We believe this book is not only unique and informative, but timely. With gardeners around the country attempting to reconcile their varied passions and concerns—a love of the exotic, the need for beautifully built environments in urban settings, the desire to protect native habitats, a care to avoid environmental pollution, a wish to reduce expenses and conserve dwindling water and energy resources, and true concern for plant conservation—it is time we let them in on the secret about succulents and landscapes. You can achieve all those seemingly disparate goals with these plants and gardens. It is a message The Huntington is delighted to deliver.

James Folsom, PhD
Director of the Gardens

INTRODUCTION 1

For those who think succulents are only simple columnar shapes, a whole new world of texture, color, and shape is about to open.

Succulent plants are not different just because they have extraordinarily fleshy leaves, stems, or roots; their many advantageous features give the home gardener entirely new options and freedoms to create wonderful landscapes. People who have dedicated their time and garden space to standard shrubs, temperate herbaceous perennials, and tropical annuals will find renewed beginner's joy in the characteristics of succulents–from their tough-love lifestyle to the sculptural elegance of their line and form. In this book, we invite gardeners, both novice and experienced, to consider this entirely different path to gardening delight, a path of great texture, color, diversity, and drama.

WHAT IS A SUCCULENT PLANT? The boundaries of the group of plants that plants-people consider to be succulents can be surprising. To a botanist, succulence is a condition seen in many kinds and parts of plants, from the thick, fleshy leaves of *Sedum* to the juicy sweet fruit of a grape vine. To a horticulturist, and in this book, "succulents" are plants with thickened, fleshy vegetative parts (leaves, stems, and/or roots). We automatically associate these conditions with plants from deserts, but many succulents are native to forests and seashores. A more accurate statement would be that succulence is usually a storage adaptation of plants that have evolved in situations where fresh water is at a premium and must be conserved–from a desert, where rainfall may not reach five inches per year, to a seashore where available water is saline, to the canopy of a tropical forest where epiphytes (such as orchids, bromeliads, some cacti, peperomias, and others) may grow using only the water they may capture as rain runs down the tree branches. In practice, the category "succulent" is even broader, including almost any plant that will grow under the same horticultural conditions and has an interesting, fleshy texture, regardless of its native habitat. Moreover, the specialists devoted to succulents have given honorary status to a host of companion plants that grow well and look good alongside bona fide succulents, such as puyas, veltheimias, and other bulbs, and just about any tree or shrub with a swollen trunk.

Very different kinds of plants qualify as true succulents; exactly which plant part is fleshy gives us a simple classification scheme, grouping plants as either stem-succulents, or leaf-succulents. Practically all cacti have very succulent stems, while most members of the related iceplant family have fleshy leaves and/or stems. Many relatives of the lilies, from the giant yuccas, aloes, and agaves, to smaller haworthias have very fleshy leaves with the stems being more or less thickened. Various desert shrubs and trees (as well as those from other exteme habitats), such as burseras, pachypodiums, and fouquierias form swollen trunks that qualify them as caudiciforms (woody stem succulents).

Most of these plants share remarkable qualities of endurance; the abuse they can sustain is legendary. In November of 1993, a Huntington construction trenching project required us to remove a large bed of aloes, during which time the aloes were simply bare-rooted and set in partial shade. At about the same time, the Garden's staff shipped several boxes of succulents to Italy. Both projects were delayed. In May of 1994, the trench was closed and the aloes, in perfect condition, were replanted. They had actually formed new, thick roots that penetrated the hard-packed construction-area soil. By June, the Italy-bound plants were returned in their unopened boxes. Many survived this mobile long-term storage and could be replanted. How different—and how much more forgiving—these plants are compared to your everyday delphinium, coleus, or azalea!

And so it is with many succulents—a well-rooted specimen carefully transplanted is not so necessary due to the phenomonal capability of such plants to reroot and establish following disturbance. Cacti are great examples of this growth habit. A cutting can reman without roots for weeks, even months. Once planted in warm soil and given sufficient moisture, new roots are quickly formed. The same process occurs in nature. During severe dry spells, cactus roots may wither back to main branches, with the plant toughing out that period completely utilizing stored water. Given the first rain, new roots quickly appear to re-establish growth and take advantage of the temporary boon.

Because plants that are succulent come from many different groups (cacti, lilies, euphorbias), a succulent landscape is not a question of one lump or two. The variety of textures, colors, and flowering behaviors is splendid. All differing groups provide wonderful forms and textures, bringing a sculptural quality

HISTORICAL NOTES

Since prehistoric times succulents were used for medicine, food, drink, fiber, and shelter. The earliest known succulent is *Aloe vera;* its use for healing wounds is documented from late Sumerian times. *Aloe vera* is also the first succulent illustrated and the illustration survives in the sixth century codex *Aniciae Julianae,* a compendium of the writings of the Greek herbalist-physician, Dioscorides.

The Greeks and Romans used Dragon Tree resin to treat wounds. Arabs traded *D. cinnabari* in Egypt and in the ancient Mediterranean world. From the Canary Islands also came a dragon's blood that in Renaissance times was used to treat gum diseases. The dried resin was used as a wood stain for musical instrument, most notably Stradivarius violins.

In the Middle Ages, Europeans used native sedums and sempervivums to treat wounds and minor infections. But upon the discovery of America, sailors and conquistadores brought back strange prickly plants, the likes of which had never been seen in Europe. Nicolas Monardes, the sixteenth century Spanish physician, pointed out the major difference in his *Joyfull Newes out of the Newe Founde Worlde* (1577): ". . . for that one of the Thornes that it hath, did pricke me, it seemeth to be a straunge hearbe." Herbalists like Gerard and Parkinson happily described those new finds in their herbals but were puzzled as to their medicinal virtues. They did give them quaint names that bear little resemblance to modern equivalents; e.g., Melon Thistle (*Melocactus*). Torch Thistle (*Cereus*), and Prickly American Aloe (*Agave*).

Succulents were not studied botanically until the seventeenth century exploration of South Africa, which, coincidentally, coincided with the rise of ornamental gardening in Europe. From the Dutch colony at Cape Town numerous expeditions trekked inland with instructions to make careful descriptions of any unusual plants and animals. Among the plants were numerous species of *Aloe, Euphorbia,* and *Crassula,* which were described and illustrated by Dutch botanists.

Richard Bradley, an early eighteenth century English horticulturist, was the first to popularize succulents. In his *History of Succulent Plants,* he speaks of their attractiveness as novelists for the "stove" (glasshouse). Without the introduction of cheap glass at this time, the introduction of exotic succulents and tropicals to Europe would not have been possible.

One of the legacies of Linnaeus' epochal natural history works (the most important one for our purposes being his *Species Plantarum,* published in 1753) was that they inspired the early nineteenth century exploration of South America by Alexander von Humboldt followed by Darwin's famous voyage of the Beagle. These pioneering explorations opened a new era of plant exploration and spawned the Victorian natural history craze, which included the amassing of large collections of succulents form all parts of the world. Popular books, such as H. Allnutt's *The Cactus and Other Tropical Succulents*, were written for the home gardener, giving care instructions and directions for glasshouse construction. A growing nursery trade combined forces with botanic gardens like Kew, which had an enormous succulent house where special displays became Victorian media events. One such occurrence was the showing in 1845 of a "Monster Cactus", hauled by wagon from the wilds of Mexico and shipped to London from Vera Cruz. It was a giant barrel cactus (*Echinocactus ingens*) over ten feet tall and weighed more than one ton!

In the mid 1800s, the United States conducted transcontinental railroad and boundary surveys that contained vivid accounts of previously unknown cacti and other succulents native to the Southwest. From these surveys we learned of the existence of the saguaro cactus, ocotillo, and Joshua Tree. Soon, these plants appeared in specialty catalogues and were incorporated into the collections of the cactus-crazed.

At the beginning of the twentieth century, the emergence of a new urban living style in the Southwest, particularly Southern California, helped liberate succulents from their Victorian glasshouses and formal displays Much earlier, Spanish missionaries brought their traditions of Mediterranean gardening, along with plants, from Mexico and South America. By the turn of the century, Los Angeles had spectacular cactus landscapes in its public parks and cactus dealers, like Lyon and Cobb of Hollywood, sold specimens to local homeowners. *Agave, Aloe,* barrel cactus, *Cereus,* prickly pear, and *Yucca,* formed important components of residential landscaping. Both large and modest homes had on view showy specimen succulents, originally grown in a local nursery or plucked from a nearby desert.

However, one California resident was neither cactus collector nor landscaper. Luther Burbank was a self-taught plant breeder who claimed to have developed a spineless prickly pear cactus that would be eaten by cattle. The idea caught on and Burbank sold lots of plants. But it was unclear whether or not the cattle would actually eat them. It turned out that the cattle would not cooperate and today the plants survive only in local gardens. The Burbank Spineless Cactus may not taste good, but it looks good.

Many succulents provide unusual sculptural effects, such as the yuccas, aloes, and agaves at left. Brilliantly-colored flowers, like the ice plants above (*Drosanthemum* and *Lampranthus*) add another dimension to the landscape.

A BRIEF LESSON IN BOTANY

The particular botany of succulent plants expands greatly on an understanding of more typical plants. A discussion of succulents, therefore, concentrates on aspects of their unique biologies, all of which have to do with the evolutionary adaption to dry, often harsh circumstances. Deviations from standard textbook botany range across the many modes of adaption a plant can demonstrate, expressed in physical form (morphology) and internal structure (anatomy), detectable in its nutritional, water-handling, and chemical interactions (physiology), and observable in its biological interactions with other plants and animals (ecology).

Most obvious to the novice are the straightforward differences between the way succulent plants are built and the more familiar forms of typical landscape material. Start with something standard: a rose, holly, or impatiens plant. Each has stems bearing leaves that are broad and more or less thin and flat. The blade of the rose leaf is broken into parts attached to a stalk (the petiole) and bearing little flaps of leaf tissue (the stipules) where it is attached to the stem. Moreover, the rose has prickles (not thorns), which are spinelike growths that are produced by the same process a plant would normally use to produce bark. The leaf of holly is more simple, with its blade not divided into several pieces. Holly leaves, however, often do bear spiny projections from the leaf margins. Both the rose and the holly have woody stems and shrubby growth form. The impatiens, on the other hand, is not woody, and therefore doesn't qualify as a shrub; botanically it is an herb. The above-ground stems of herbs lack the ability to add layers of wood each year (to make secondary growth) and the stems do not normally persist from season to season in temperate gardens (although the roots may persist and resprout when conditions are right). (In the tropics our definitions run into trouble, for soft-stemmed herbs can often make shrubs and grow for several

years, producing the need for the term "subshrub.") Though the impatiens leaf seems about as normal as a leaf can be, its stem is suprisingly succulent, reminding us that many plants from various habitats have soft fleshy tissues, though they cannot survive in desert habitats and do not normally fall within the sanction of "succulent."

For a tea rose, an American holly, or a garden impatiens to survive in a desert climate, some serious adaptations would be in order. Something would have to be done about those leaves. Leaves are the major site of water loss in a plant, with thousands of tiny pores (called stomata) usually found on the lower leaf surface, that allow large quantities of water vapor to escape each day. Either the leaf must be better protected from water loss, or it must go. Evolutionarily, this is what has happened to plants in dry areas. Succulents from desert regions either lack foliage altogether or bear leaves that are well-protected from water loss. Most cacti have evolutionarily delegated the green-scheme responsibiity of photosynthesis to stems, which are intrinsically better shielded from water loss than leaves. The true "leaves" of cacti are the spines that arm and adorn them. Agaves and aloes, on the other hand, have fortified their leaves through millions of years of evolution; their foliage is succulent, waxy, and even stemike.

Cacti, agaves, and aloes are very common in the succulent landscape, but they represent only two of myriad evolutionary responses to the desert leaf dilemma. Take for examples the lithops and certain haworthias, plants that produce succulent leaves tucked neatly into their native soil with only a lens of tissue exposed to the dry air so that sunlight can be conveyed to photosynthetic tissues. Or consider the very different behavior of desert shrubs, which may produce fairly normal looking leaves, though often of small or fractured size. The response of such plants may be that of protection, such as that found in creosote bush, with leaves stickily plastered by resins or may well be more escapist, with leaves present during moist seasons but deciduous (falling seasonally) during dry times.

Returning to our standard plants, the rose, holly, or impatiens exposed gradually to desert conditions over a million years or so would have to evolve new ways of making water available, since water is the internal support system for plant cells, provides the stream of nutrients that tissues require, and is critical to photosynthesis and other chemical reactions. Merely cutting down on water loss may be an insufficient response to a desert habitat, which is characterized by less than five inches of precipitation each year, so adaptations for more efficient water collection, water use, and

---

SCIENTIFIC NOMENCLATURE
Botanists and horticulturists use a binomial, or two-name system, to label the over 250,000 species of living plants. Because the names are in Latin form, this system crosses time and language barriers and allows people all over the world to communicate about plants. Occasionally, a scientific name will be changed by scientists to reflect additions to our knowledge about the plant.

A scientific species name is made up of the genus and the specific epithet, as in *Agave americana*. The genus is always first and is always capitalized. The specific epithet follows and is not capitalized. If another Latinized name follows the species, it denotes a subspecies or forma.

Cultivated plants are often selected for a particular attribute, such as leaf or flower color or resistance to disease. These selections are given a cultivar, or cultivated variety, name in addition to the species. Cultivar names are capitalized and in single quotes, such as 'Volcanic Sunset' or 'Opalina'. Hybrid plants resulting from sexual reproduction between two different kinds of plants may be denoted by an x, such as *Sedum xrubrotinctum*.

PROTECTIVE ADAPTATIONS
Protective adaptations for plant surfaces (leaf, stem, etc.) appear endless. Plants can exude substances that are deposited on external surfaces; if they are sticky oils and terpenes, the surface is resinous; should the compounds be waxy, the surface can be very glossy or may be whitened (in botanial jargon, glaucous). The epidermal cells may grow in ways that create long protrusions which to us look like papillae, hairs, or scales. There are scores of terms to describe various levels of hairiness or scaliness, from glabrate (having a few scattered hairs) to hirsute (with short, stiff hairs) to lanate (wooly). A surface that is scabrous, for example, has stiffer hairs than one which is merely hispid.

water hoarding would be necessary. In desert plants, every aspect of plant biology is brought into play to cope with low available water, from the leaf adaptations to storage of water in succulent tissues, to root specializations that deal with infrequent and short-lived precipitations, to physiological reactions that conserve water, to ecological aspects such as seed germination, season of growth, and water storage capabilities.

Just studying a natural desert landscape, one knows the overall look (the physiognomy that defines the desert biome) is radically different from that of a forest in the tropics, the Appalachians, or the Pacific Northwest. Plants are much more scarce, there are relatively few of tree proportions, certainly not enough to create a canopy. Plant forms are less leafy, harder, more compact. There is much barren terrain, though not much soil—for soil-making is a process that requires plant cover with the leaching action of percolating water and humic acids. Unless a desert area was anciently a wetter climate with a different flora, real zoned soil has never developed. Indeed the sporadic nature of rainfull may have produced caliche or surface deposits of intense carbonates or salts. Decorating the land are scattered, individual plants or small clusters. There may be desert shrubs petticoating a host of other plant species. In some deserts there will be a faint carpet of narrow grasses and other herbs.

The exact makeup varies with geography and exact climate but we still find plants of these areas falling into certain categories of "life forms," an established system of comparison that botanists find convenient. Deserts are short on large, treelike plants, populated more with those of smaller stature. The surprising fact, though, is that most of the diversity present in a desert is normally not the succulents and desert shrubs we discuss in this book. They are important, and most of the year they are the "aspect dominants" (the plants that appear to dominate the landscape). It is, however, the desert annuals, those plants that live much of the year as seed in the soil, which often predominate from the perspective of sheer diversity. As much as seventy percent of the total kinds of plants found growing in a desert may be of this persuasion, thus yielding both a false understanding if viewed in dry seasons and a completely new perspective if seen at a time when, because of favorable rainfall, the desert is "in bloom" due to the rapid germination and maturation of representatives of the normally invisible gene pool.

That knowledge also completes our list of general physical categories in which desert plants fit;
•"annuals": plants that exist during harshest times as part of the seed pool;
•desert shrubs and trees: plants that normally have green bark and small leaves that are either well-protected or deciduous;
•stem succulents: plants that store moisture and have reduced, modified, or absent leaves;
•leaf succulents: plants with thickened, well-protected leaves, often borne in rosettes, sometimes growing as ground covers.

Beyond the readily observable, we discover that the beauty of succulent plants is much more than skin deep. There are fascinating lessons about how metabolism and structure can work together to open stomata during darkness only with the consequent reduction in water loss (CAM, Crassulacean Acid Metabolism). There are examples of seed that require a given amount of rainfall to leach self-produced growth inhibitors from the seed coats, thus insuring germination during a time of adequate moisture. One discovers that desert plants are rife with powerful chemicals that may yield as much defense against herbivores as more obvious spines. Take, for example, peyote, a cactus that for all the world looks to be a defenseless vegetable treat for any desert animal. Lacking spines, this plant more than makes up the loss through production of toxic alkaloids. And then there are fascinating accounts of pollination ecologies and reproduction biologies, such as the fly pollination of asclepiads, that parallel the high degree of specialization one begins to associate with other aspects of succulents.

Looking at the lives of desert plants, how finicky the rose, the holly, and the impatiens seem. These more standard garden plants have their own fascinating beauties, but by comparison they require so much attention—soil, water, constant care. They are certainly not prepared for life in the desert. Succulents, on the other hand, have spent their time in the wilderness, they have been through the plant world's own version of Outward Bound. Unshaven and hardened they come to the dainty world of gardening with unappreciated style and vigor. These plants have biologies that perfectly match many situations. They truly merit a place in the sun.

Many succulent gardeners collect unusual plants–not hard to find in the succulent field. *Above: Borzicactus celsianus* var. *hendriksenianus,* and a monstrose form of *Euphorbia ingens.*

to landscapes unequaled outside topiary and giant sequoias. This may not be so obvious as you consider a single cactus, but a visit to any well-designed display garden or competent succulent nursery will dispel the notion that all succulents are merely lookalikes for saguaros or opuntias. Add to this diversity the companion bulbs, herbs, shrubs, and small trees, and one finds that the range of textural types and plant shapes available for a succulent landscape is as rich as that for any normal perennial or woodland garden.

Moreover, succulents grow and change with the seasons more rapidly than one would think from an occasional pedestrian glance. Many bring the added bonus of exotic and plentiful flowers. Not to be missed in our own region of southern California is the midwinter bloom of aloes, hitting all the bright colors from yellows to oranges to fiery reds. In spring and summer the iceplants make a spectacle from Santa Barbara south, blanketing entire slopes with the most fluorescent of purples, pinks, reds, and yellows.

The power and combinations of these colors seem improbable; for anyone trying to compare the colors of cactus and ice plant flowers to other types of plants runs headlong into the quiet fact that coloration for these flowers is based on a totally different set of chemical compounds. The betalains, first characterized from beets, are responsible for the floral brilliance of cacti and their relatives as compared to other garden plants. As you learn even more about these plants, it will become apparent how much there is beyond the fascinating exterior–biologies, chemistry, history enough to nourish your intellectual curiosity just as the plant forms give aesthetic dividends.

These succulents are great. They deliver on all promises, bringing as much pleasure as the most delicate orchid or flower-encrusted peach. Moreover, you will discover how ridiculously easy they are to grow, how forgiving they are to people who travel or get caught up in other activities, how little water and special treatment they need. They may be just the plants you've been wondering about, the ones that suit your lifestyle.

PLANT REQUIREMENTS One of the very reasons The Huntington has a desert garden appears to be that the first curator, William Hertrich, thought the thin, poor quality of the soil layer in the southeastern corner of the estate would support little more than a display of cacti. The resulting exuberant garden heartily denies such a negative beginning. That history coincides with what people in the "desert southwest" (from El Paso to Tucson to Los Angeles) have learned to expect: succulent plants bring greater dividends than simple tolerance of harsh circumstances. For here, most people who garden meet the growth requirements of these plants by merely having a square yard of free space. The climatic default value in many areas of this region yields conditions of temperature, aridity, and high insolation (bright sunlight) that can naturally support growing succulents.

But the large area we call the Southwest embraces many climate patterns; what are the limitations in real terms? To garden successfully with a wide range of succulents, your site should have bright light with or without some tree- or shrub-shaded areas for plants with special requirements. The temperature should be moderate to subtropical (most plants discussed here can be exposed to 25° F. for short spells, though some cacti and plenty of stonecrops and their relatives can withstand freezing to 0° F.) The soil can be of varying character, but must provide for good drainage.

Irrigation and the use of added soil amendments and fertilizers will depend on the specific site and what you want to accomplish. At The Huntington, we always amend soil with humus prior to planting or replanting a bed, figuring the better the soil, the better the growth. On the other hand, plants just placed in almost any normal soil will grow. Here, we water most areas in the desert garden about once a week, in addition to our annual rainfall, which averages between ten and fifteen inches (and falls in the cool season from September through April). Though we could stretch that, and in non-public areas have succulents that get watered less than five times a year, the plants look better with more attention. The same is true for added fertilizer. More water and better levels of application yield more handsome specimens and a more lavish garden.

Yet these plants are among the brightest stars of the xeriscape firmament. A succulent corner at the Director's home on The Huntington property receives no added water throughout the entire year, and still looks fine. Realizing that in this climate, six to nine months may pass with summer heat but not a drop of rain, one has to appreciate the powerful capacity of succulents to survive without irrigation. This, indeed, is the final test of what is called a xeriscape–a garden that thrives on annual precipitation. In reality, since xeric refers to very dry habitats (from prairie to desert), the term is botanically difficult. A "xeriscape" in Appalachia, Victoria, B.C. or southern Florida becomes a perplexing concept. The default landscape in those regions produces lush forests of giant trees, which by any stretch of the imagination are far from xeric. In these wetter regions, researchers only talk about xeric sites as special circumstances, places with sunny exposures and thin or very sandy soils that will not support the expected verdure. What people are really talking about when they "xeriscape" is better termed ambient gardening, growing plants that will thrive given the normal local climate, given the logic that using large quantities of a resource to maintain a landscape is not thrifty, therefore not environmentally sound. In the Southwest, that limiting resource is frequently water.

For gardeners in more humid or colder parts of North America, the creation of a succulent landscape presents different, even greater challenges, but is often easier than you would imagine. Good plant selection can support beautiful outdoor rockeries of succulents from New Jersey to even colder areas such as mid-Missouri (the handsome succulent planting at The Missouri Botanical Garden) and Denver (the magnificent Alpine rockery at Denver Botanical Garden). Of course, if you have a south-facing window, a bright atrium or an abandoned greenhouse, succulents can provide the best return for investment of time, money, and heating/cooling resources.

Whatever your climate, situation, or goals, there is a niche for succulents.

For the uninitiated, some words associated with succulents are bewildering. Here are definitions of some terms used throughout this book; for a more complete list of definitions, and more complete definitions of these terms, see the glossary on page 215.

Agave parviflora forms a rosette of acuminate (gradually tapering) leaves, each with an apical (at the tip) spine.

Aloe plicatilis bears flowers in racemes (unbranched stalks bearing numerous flowers, each borne on an individual pedicel [stem]).

Aloe spectabilis bears flowers in a panicle, a loosely branched, pyramidal flower cluster. Its glaucous (waxy bluish gray to bluish white) leaves form a rosette.

Bromelia balansae produces a terminal (growing at the tip) panicle from a rosette of serrate (saw-toothed) leaves.

Coryphantha missouriensis bears areoles (structure from which spines and flowers are produced) at the apexes of tubercles (knoblike projections).

Dioscorea elephantipes forms twining stems atop a caudex (woody or fleshy basal stem) covered with woody tubercles.

The enjoyment of growing, studying, and living with these beautiful and fascinating plants only increases from the moment they first come into your hands.
Their singularly exotic and expressive nature will carry you through every gardening drought.

ABOUT THE AUTHORS

THE HUNTINGTON, located in San Marino, California, is the former home of Henry
E. Huntington. It houses world-class botanical gardens, eighteenth and nineteenth century art, and rare books and manuscripts. Among its most famous
artworks are Lawrence's "Pinkie" and Gainsborough's "Blue Boy". The collections cover over one-hundred-twenty acres, including gardens of roses, tropical
plants, Australian plants, camellias, Asian plants, and herbs. The Huntington
Desert Garden covers twelve acres and includes over five thousand different
kinds of cacti and other succulents as well as companion plants.

Dr. James Folsom, Director of the Gardens, has been at The Huntington for over
ten years. He received his Ph.D in botany from the University of Texas at
Austin and has gardened in many areas of the South and Southwest.

Dr. Debra Folsom also received her Ph.D. in botany at the University of Texas at
Austin and is Research Botanist and Curator of the herbarium at The
Huntington. A native of Pennsylvania, she now lives on the grounds of The
Huntington with her husband, Jim Folsom.

John Trager is Curator of the Desert Collections and manager of the
International Succulent Introductions, the Huntington's plant introduction
program. He is known for his photography, which has appeared in numerous
horticultural publications, including this book.

Joe Clements, holds a bachelor's degree in Geology from Whittier College and is
Curator of the Desert Garden at The Huntington. He is responsible for design
of new plantings as well as the day-to-day maintenance of the garden.

Nancy Scott is a wife and mother whose love of plants was instilled in her by her
own mother. She hold a bachelor's degree in Agricultural Biology from
California State Polytechnic University, Pomona, and was formerly plant prop-
agator at The Huntington.

Agave parryi var. *huachucensis,
Echeveria albicans, Kalanchoe.*

Varieties are arranged alphabetically, according to their Latin names; listings for all companion plants follow the list of succulents. (See the index or contents page for translations of Latin names.)

Though gardening is essentially a hands-on endeavor, some of its greatest pleasures are vicarious: for most gardeners, nothing surpasses the joy of discovering a new plant. And since more than five thousand different succulents and companion plants are currently under cultivation–and nurseries, botanists, and private gardeners the world over are dedicated to finding and introducing more–there will never be a shortage of horticultural treasures from which to choose.

This chapter is designed to help you sift through those treasures and make a choice. The staff at Huntington Botanical Garden has selected more than one hundred and fifty plants that work well for them, mixing common, easy-to-find varieties with others you might not know about, but should; experts from other botanic gardens around the country then added plants that thrive in their own regions. Because most of the gardeners couldn't bear to leave out their favorites, we've included additional recommended plants at the end of many of the entries; and a brief description of many other shrubs at the end of the chapter.

The first part of the Plant Selector lists the included varieties according to their size and shape. Following that is the main portion of the chapter–detailed "plant portraits" describing the best conditions for the plants, routine care, propagation, pest and disease tolerance, and uses in the landscape. Two hundred of the recommended plants are illustrated, with captions noting their size and climate zone.

There are only a few keys to successful gardening; choosing the right plant is among them. If a well-tended plant refuses to thrive or succumbs to disease, it probably doesn't belong in its present site. Before deciding on a plant, you need to understand the special conditions of your own garden. Is it sunny, shady, or a combination of both? Is rainfall abundant, or nearly nonexistent? Is the soil sandy, loamy, heavy, well or poorly drained? What is your soil's natural pH? Information on how to answer these questions is located in Chapter 4; your local nursery, botanical garden, or agricultural extension can also help. But don't forget that your site is unique, with a microclimate of its own created by the contours of the landscape, shade, and natural barriers; it may be different from those next door, let alone at a nursery ten miles down the road.

Sean Hogan of the University of California Botanical Gardens at Berkeley has studied plant hardiness for many years. He has contributed the following notes.

Climates as well as plants can be fickle. The temperature tolerances on the following pages and the zone map on opposite page are meant for use as reference only; they can't be depended upon under all circumstances. If anything, most plants are hardier than one might expect, especially if given the right place in the garden. The climates of the Southwest vary from the benign year-round paradise of coastal southern California to the severe winters and summer of the high Great Basin. As discussed in Chapter 5, suitable plants can be found for almost any range.

In general, USDA Zones nine and ten are close to the water or at the very lowest elevations inland including southern Texas and southern Arizona. The Pacific coastal components experience the least fluctuations allowing an astonishing variety of plant life to be grown. Lack of heat in summer can be a small hindrance, especially in coastal California an Oregon. In the low-elevation deserts of California and Arizona or near the Gulf of Mexico, lack of heat is certainly no problem and heat-loving plants are at their best. In that region, it's not a question of finding a plant that can be grown, but of of how many will fit out of the overwhelming choice.

Zones seven and eight are, as one might expect, further north and inland, and higher in elevation. Winter cold snaps can have some bite and careful consideration and experimentation are necessary. South central Texas, southern New Mexico, the Southwest's medium-elevation deserts and much of the coastal Northwest are covered here. Repeated frosts are the winter norm and occasional "big freeze" culls what can be grown. It is in Zone 6 and below that the most care must be taken. Still, even here, where the ground often freezes, a surprising number of succulents can be grown (see Chapter 5). The amount of snowcover or other protection is of paramount importance. Areas covered are all interior or high elevation sites, and areas subject to dramatic temperature fluctuations diurnally and seasonally. The interior Northwest, much of the Great Basin, and the southern high deserts lie here.

The map below was created by the United States Department of Agriculture. It divides the United States into climate zones. Most nurseries (and this book) use these classifications to advise where plants will be hardy. Although this is a useful system, it is not foolproof; it is based on average minimum temperature, and a particularly cold winter might destroy some plants that are listed as hardy in your climate zone. More often, you will be able to grow plants that are not listed as hardy in your zone, particularly if they are in a sheltered area. There are other climate-zones classifications; the Arnold Arboretum's is also used quite often. The climate zones referred to in this volume are those of the USDA.

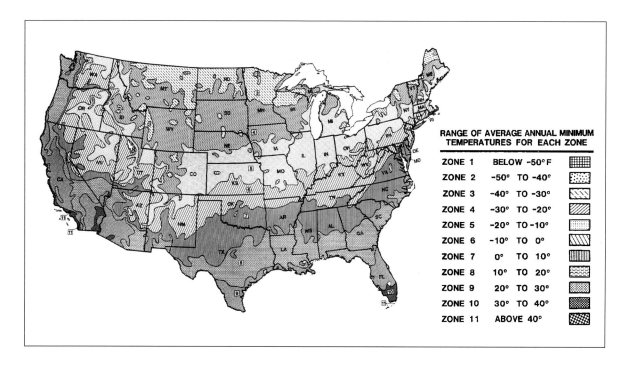

RANGE OF AVERAGE ANNUAL MINIMUM TEMPERATURES FOR EACH ZONE	
ZONE 1	BELOW -50° F
ZONE 2	-50° TO -40°
ZONE 3	-40° TO -30°
ZONE 4	-30° TO -20°
ZONE 5	-20° TO -10°
ZONE 6	-10° TO 0°
ZONE 7	0° TO 10°
ZONE 8	10° TO 20°
ZONE 9	20° TO 30°
ZONE 10	30° TO 40°
ZONE 11	ABOVE 40°

Climates vary considerably even within single map zones. The temperatures indicated for a particular region represent average highs and lows over a several-year period and rarely distinguish microclimates or lengths of time at the estimated low temperature. A low of 20 F in Tucson may last only a short period of time and rise to 60 F. the same day. The same low in Amarillo might not recover to the freezing point, allowing deeper freezing of plant tissue and soil. The same freeze in Portland might come after a soaking rain, thereby freezing the soil more deeply and causing damage to the center of rosette-forming succulents that have residual moisture between the leaves. As well, leaves or stems that are full of water rupture more easily. Topography plays one of the most important parts in the determination of microclimate. A location on a sunny slope above a valley where cold air can pool might raise the local temperature several degrees, even into another zone or two. Protection from the dessicating effect of wind is also helpful, especially when temperatures are below freezing.

Factors such as the amount of rainfall and in which season it falls are important to the growth of plants as well. Many desirable cacti, other succulents, and accompanying desert plants occur naturally in areas of dry winters and warm monstrously moist summers; this means that the plants need supplemental watering on the Mediterranean west coast. They appreciate the warmest positions possible where temperatures are cooled by marine influence. For the same plants, excess moisture during the winter dormant period can lead to rot or freeze at temperatures the plants might easily tolerate while dry. For those native to winter rainfall areas such as coastal Chile, western South Africa, or the immediate west coast of North America (from Oregon to Baja California), the heat of summer coupled with unaccustomed moisture can turn a favorite Dudleya into instant compost. Plants suited to these areas relish the cool rains of winter but prefer to spend the summer with only minimal attention.

Important steps in beginning a succulent or xeric garden include knowing one's local climate and learning as much as possible about desired plants in their native habitats. Finding or creating the various niches in one's landscape are also important, so plants can be grouped for both effect and culture. Protecting plants from the elements via a temporary winter cover, for example, or changing such things as soil or light exposure are much more easily accomplished if plants of similar requirements are together.

Most publications–including this one—err on the side of conservatism when assigning climate zones to plants. If a plant seems marginally hardy to your area, talk to people in your area, and see what success they've had. Consider what kind of protection you could provide, and what factors, other than average temperature, are in your favor.

The following lists group cacti and other succulents by their uses in the landscape. Heights can be controlled by pruning, and plants grow to different heights according to their situations. See page 213 for information on growing succulents in shade. These lists are not complete–you will find many more plants on the following pages for each situation.

Succulents for groundcover

Abromeitiella
Aloe brevifolia
Aptenia
Cephalophyllum
Crassula pubescens ssp. radicans
Delosperma cooperi
Dorotheanus
Lampranthus
Nolina palmeri
Nolina bigelovii
Ruschia granitica
Sedum dasyphyllum
Sedum spurium
Senecio rowleyanus

Treelike succulents

Agave species
Aloe ferox
Aloe marlothii
Aloe spectabilis
Aloe bainesii
Aloe dichotoma
Beaucarnea
Crassula arborescens
Cyphostemma juttae
Dasylirion texanum
Dracaena draco
Fouquieria columnaris
Nolina longifolia
Pachypodium geayi
Pachypodium succulentum
Pereskia grandiflora
Portulacaria afra
Puya chilensis
Uncarina
Yucca brevifolia

Shrubby succulents

Aeonium species
Aloe ciliaris
Cotyledon species
Crassula species
Dasylirion wheeleri
Euphorbia canariensis
Fouquieria splendens
Pereskia aculeata
Sedum dendroideum
Yucca filifera
Yucca whippiei

Low-growing cacti

(usually under three feet)
Acanthocalycium
Arthrocereus
Astrophytum
Borzicactus
Cleistocactus chacoanus
Coryphantha missouriensis
Echinocereus triglochidiatus
Echinocereus viridiflorus
Echinopsis
Gymnocalycium denudatum
Mammillaria compressa
Mammillaria geminispina
Notocactus leninghausii
Opuntia compressa
Stenocereus eruca

Tall cacti

(usually over five feet)
Carnegiea gigantea
Cephalocereus
Cereus peruvianus
Cleistocactus strausii
Ferocactus wislizenii
Lophocereus schottii
Myrtillocactus geometrizans
Opuntia ficus-indica
Pachycereus marginatus
Pilosocereus
Stetsonia coryne

Succulents for hanging baskets

Aporocactus
x *Aporophyllum*
Crassula rupestris
Epiphyllum
Hylocereus
Kalanchoe synsepola
Rhipsalis
Schlumbergera
Sedum burrito

Succulents that form rosettes

Aeonium decorum
Agave
Aloe
Dudley virens
Dyckia
Echeveria
Gasteria
Graptopetalum
Haworthia attenuata
Sedum

Succulents with sword-shaped leaves

Aeonium
Agave
Aloe
Beaucarnea
Cotyledon tomentosa
Cotyledon orbiculata
Hesperaloe parviflora
Pelargonium species
Pereskia species
Sedum dendroideum
Senecio medley-woodii
Uncarina
Yucca species

Succulents for containers

Acanthocalycium glaucum
Agave victoria-reginae
Astrophytum ornatum
Borzicactus
Cephalocereus senilis
Cleistocactus
Coryphantha
Cotyledon species
Crassula perfoliata var. falcata
Echinocactus
Echinopsis
Ephiphyllum
Gymnocalycium
Kalanchoe blossfeldiana
Mammillaria geminispina
Notocactus
Opuntia
Pachycereus

plant selector

Top: Abromeitiella brevifolia.
Above: Even small plants less than one inch tall can produce the dramatic two-and-one-half-inch blooms of *Acanthocalycium glaucum.*

ABROMEITIELLA *Bromeliaceae*

Abromeitiella is a dwarf, mat-forming succulent from Argentina and Bolivia. Its small, dense, one- to two-inch rosettes of lance-shaped to triangular stiff, fleshy, leaves proliferate via offsets to form a compact cushion up to six feet across. Inconspicuous green flowers are borne on short inflorescences. **A. brevifolia,** distinguished by its relatively smooth leaf margins, has both a large and a small form, the latter sometimes sold under the synonym *A. chlorantha.* **A. lorentziana** is a slightly larger plant with spiny leaf margins and a silvery epidermis. Abromeitiellas, hardy to Zone 9, are propagated by seed or division and grow well in full sun or partial shade.

ACANTHOCALYCIUM *Cactaceae*

Acanthocalycium glaucum, native to the higher elevations (3,000 feet) of northern Argentina, is generally grown for its showy, large golden yellow or orange flowers. The stems are pale bluish gray, globular to about three inches in diameter, but becoming elongated in age. Spines are brown to black, about an inch long.

Inland or in the low desert, *A. glaucum* should be grown in part shade to prevent scorching, especially during the seedling stage. It should receive ample water in spring and at least some supplemental water in summer. Plants can withstand cool conditions but should be kept on the dry side with excellent drainage in winter.

A. glaucum is propagated only from seed, but seedlings are readily available in the nursery trade. Well-grown seedlings are fast-growing with fungal-resistant root systems and thus do not require grafting or any other special care.

Acanthocalycium violaceum is also recommended; its pale pinkish violet flowers are very attractive.

ADENIUM *Apocynaceae*

Adenium obesum, the "desert rose," is native from East Africa to southern Arabia. It was introduced into cultivation in England in 1846 and has been a popular greenhouse plant ever since. Considering its ease of cultivation and showy flowers, it is amazing how few adeniums have infiltrated arid landscape design as ideal patio container plants. Adenium is typically either a low, caudiciform shrub with a gnarled trunk or a small, erect, succulent-stemmed tree, eventually to about six feet tall (smaller in containers), usually tapering to a few thick branches. The trunk is smooth with grayish brown bark; roots often form swellings which can be elevated above ground level when transplanting. Leaves are leathery and glossy green, about three to five inches long, and mainly clustered at the ends of branches in loose rosettes. Leaves are typically deciduous, dropping when the air temperature falls below 50° F. Plants can retain their leaves and produce flowers year round if ambient temperature permits. If it is cold enough to induce leaf drop, it is best to allow dormancy, and be spare with water in winter; overhead frost protection is beneficial.

The flowers are funnel-shaped and are produced throughout the season. Colors vary from pale pink to cherry red, often paler toward the center. A

ABROMEITIELLA BREVIFOLIA Dwarf, mat-forming plants with one- to two-inch rosettes of stiff lance-shaped to triangular leaves, inconspicuous green flowers in spring. Full sun or part shade. Slow growing, but can be hastened with fertilizing. Zones 9-10.

ACANTHOCALYCIUM GLAUCUM Globular stems to three inches tall bear brown to black spines and large golden yellow or orange flowers throughout the growing season. Part shade; tolerates cool conditions. Moderately fast growing. Zones 9-10.

ACANTHOCALYCIUM VIOLACEUM Flattened globular stems covered with slender brown spines and with pinkish-violet flowers borne throughout the growing season. Part shade. Fast growing. Zones 9-10.

ADENIUM X ARIZONA (DESERT ROSE) Either a low, gnarled shrub or small succulent-stemmed tree growing to six feet. Leathery leaves are glossy green; pale pink to cherry-red flowers are funnel-shaped. Flowers throughout the growing season. Full to partial sun; warm conditions. Vigorous. Zones 9 (with protection)-10.

PROPAGATING ADENIUM

To propagate your own *Adenium,* place fresh cuttings into a well-aerated medium under high humidity at 80-90° F. Expect moderate success in two to six months. Mark Dimmitt, noted *Adenium* hybridizer finds that six- to eight-inch tips root in two to three weeks at 90° F. under mist; they must not be allowed to wilt. Woodier cuttings take a few months, but are less likely to rot. Fresh seed (reported to be viable for two to four months, though some gardeners have had success with seed over two years old) should be sown shallowly in sand in spring and kept at 80-90° F. with good air circulation. Both seed-grown and cutting-grown plants are typically vigorous, flowering in only eight to twelve months. Viable seed typically germinates quickly and seedlings will form caudexes within three months.

Some sources suggest that *Adenium* cuttings should be allowed to dry for several days to allow callus formation before being rooted. This is certainly not recommended for tip cuttings, which should not be allowed to wilt. It will not harm woodier cuttings, but is not necessary.

number of cultivar selections are available, some of them hybrids of other species: **'Crimson Star'**, which produces solid red flowers, **'Volcanic Sunset'**, a more compact, densely branched form, and **'Asha'**, with immense pink flowers, five inches across. Flowers last two to five days, with an individual specimen being literally covered with blooms over a period of months.

Zone 10 is the climatic limit for growing *Adenium* outside year round. Dieback of branch tips may occur below 40° F., and frost may kill the plant outright. In inland southern California (Zone 9), more mature adeniums in pots can be left outside in a protected area year round with only minor damage.

Adeniums thrive best when grown in a rich, very well-drained soil in full sun (part shade in very hot climates), at temperatures above 80° F. It is critical to fertilize regularly during active growth periods in order to achieve the most glorious bloom and the healthiest growth. Ample water is necessary when the plant is blooming or leafed out; even when dormant, adeniums should not be allowed to dry out completely. However, avoid watering if cold weather is expected. Pruning is not necessary (except to shape spindly plants), and plants either in pots or in the ground should receive only the most shallow of weeding to avoid disturbing the surface roots. If damaged, the plants exude a thick, gummy sap that is toxic.

One- to four-year-old seedlings are the most readily obtainable adeniums. (Some taxonomists recognize up to eight taxa of *Adenium*, while others group all variable forms into *A. obesum*. Therefore, considerable variation in plant form may be expected under this name.) If adenium shopping in the nursery, check dormant plants for developing flower buds and make sure all branches are firm and "filled-out" looking. In actively growing plants, look for healthy-looking, glossy green leaves and make sure the specimen is free of insects. Check the base of the plant as well; overwatered adeniums often rot from the base up and may have some leaves and firm branches even though the roots are rotted.

Fungal and bacterial rot encouraged by dampness in cool weather are the greatest threats to *Adenium*. Good drainage and adequate air circulation will help prevent these problems. A well-aerated environment is also the best prevention for insect pests (mealybugs, aphids, and spider mites) as well. If these do appear, frequent spraying with water or insecticidal soap will usually cure the problem.

AEONIUM *Crassulaceae*

A number of *Aeonium* species make excellent garden plants, some as groundcovers and others as individual specimen plants. Native to Morocco, **Aeonium arboreum** forms a shrub to three feet tall, with rosettes of two- to three-inch leaves. A popular cultivar of this species is **'Zwartkop'**, a selection originally made in Holland. Foliage color in 'Zwartkop' varies according to ambient light conditions and growing season. In winter, the new growth is green but soon darkens to a deep maroon, appearing almost black during summer dormancy. Inflorescences are typically seen only in relatively mature plants; each is an eight-inch-long, pyramidal panicle of bright yellow flowers borne in winter. 'Zwartkop', like all aeoniums, is propagated quickly and efficiently from stem cuttings. Recently, the noted hybridizer John Catlin has been working to create other dark foliage *Aeonium* hybrids. Three current introductions are **'Zwartkin',** featuring dusky purple, matte-finished leaves; **'Garnet',** with glossy purple-red leaves; and **'Cyclops',** which forms huge, solitary rosettes.

   A. decorum, native to the Canary Islands, is a spring blooming species. Flowers are white with some pink variegation. The cultivar **'Sunburst'** grows to about one foot tall; stunning leaf rosettes are variegated green and yellow with red-tinged, ciliate leaf margins.

   ***A. undulatum* 'Pseudotabuliforme',** the saucer plant, is of uncertain horticultural origin. Its short stems sucker at the base. Leaves are bright, glossy green and four to six inches long; rosettes are dramatically flattened and always attract attention. Although rarely formed, inflorescences are about one foot long with the typical pyramids of bright yellow flowers.

   Many other *Aeonium* species are available for garden use. ***A. percarneum,*** a shrub to four feet, is one of the few species within the genus that is grown primarily for its floral show: ten-inch cascades of pale pink flowers produced in winter or early spring. ***A. castello-paivae,*** with gray, glaucous, somewhat limp

Above: Aeonium arboreum 'Zwartkop'. *Left: Aeonium percarneum,* one of the few aeonium species grown for its flowers; shown here with *Aloe* and *Lampranthus aurantiacus* 'Gold Nugget'.

ADENIUM OBESUM V. MULTIFLORUM Similar to *A. obesum*, but flowers with a pale throat with red lines and dark-edged petals. Full to partial sun. Vigorous. Zone 10.

ADENIUM SWAZICUM Pink flowers. Full to partial sun. Vigorous. Zone 10.

AEONIUM ARBOREUM 'ZWARTKOP' Shrub to three feet with rosettes of green to deep maroon leaves. Bright yellow panicles appear in winter. Full sun to partial shade; established plants hardy to the mid-20s F. Moderately fast winter grower. Zones 9-10.

AEONIUM DECORUM 'SUNBURST' Shrub with green, pink, and yellow variegated leaf rosettes and spring-blooming white flowers; grows to one foot. Full sun to partial shade; established plants hardy to the mid-20s F. Moderately fast winter grower. Zones 9-10.

leaves and greenish white flowers, is preferred if the planting area in question is in full shade. **A. haworthii,** with blue-green leaves and creamy yellow or pale pink flowers, has a particularly compact, rounded growth habit when grown in full or partial sun, making a mound about two feet tall.

Many aeoniums become somewhat leggy over the course of three to five years. To preserve a uniform appearance for bedding purposes, aeoniums are often cut and replanted periodically. If that method is followed, plants will rarely if ever reach blooming size.

Aeoniums will tolerate partial shade inland, although full sun is preferable along the coast. All of the above species are hardy to the mid-20s F. once established.

AGAVE *Agavaceae*

The genus *Agave* includes some of the finest landscape succulents available. All form basal rosettes of leaves ranging from a massive ten feet across to a diminutive four inches. They are solitary or branch from the base, sometimes forming large clumps. Agaves are vigorous, resistant to most pests, and require no special care.

Agave americana, the century plant or maguey, is a grand example with its massive rosettes reaching ten feet in both height and spread; unfortunately its size limits its use to large yards or gardens. Succulent, fibrous leaves, up to six feet long, are grayish green to bluish green, about ten inches wide, with sharp terminal spines and toothed margins. The century plant is rather slow growing in its native habitat of Mexico, but provided with supplementary water during the summer, it will make quite rapid growth. Awesome inflorescences, up to forty feet high, are dense panicles of pale yellow flowers, each about

Above: Greenovia, another Canary Island genus of succulents related to *Aeonium.* Its basal rosettes fold into a chalice shape during summer dormancy when only light watering is required. It grows best in full shade to partial shade, is moderately vigorous and is hardy in Zones 9 to 10.

Agave americana 'Variegata'.
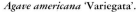

AEONIUM UNDULATUM 'PSEUDOTABULIFORME' (SAUCER PLANT)
Short stems bear bright, glossy leaves in flattened rosettes
and, rarely, yellow pyramidal flowers. Full sun to partial
shade; established plants hardy to the mid-20s F.
Moderately fast winter grower. Zones 9-10.

AGAVE AMERICANA 'VARIEGATA' (CENTURY PLANT) Rosettes of
bluish green leaves sport yellow marginal stripes; yellow
panicles appear on mature plants. To ten feet across. Full
sun; warm conditions. Vigorous if watered in summer.
Zones 9-10.

AGAVE VICTORIAE-REGINAE Incurved leaves in blunt, one-foot
basal rosettes are dark green with white bands; flowers are
borne in thirteen-foot pale green to cream panicles. Small
terminal spines. Needs full sun, good drainage.
Slow growing. Zones 9-10.

AGAVE GUADALAJARANA Gray leaves with spiny margins bear
attractive imprinting on their surfaces. Grows to two feet
across. Full sun. Moderate growth rate. Zones 9-10.

three inches in diameter. Inflorescences typically do not form until the plant is at least ten years old, and their appearance signals the demise of the parent plant. After blooming, remove the dead central plant and allow some of the prolific offsets that have formed at maturity to replace the original specimen.

A. americana grows best in full sun in well-drained soil. Keep in mind when planting that *A. americana* will eventually reach a diameter of ten feet and needs space to develop a good, symmetrical shape. Also, the terminal leaf spines are dangerous if planted too near pathways. *A. americana* withstands very high temperatures with ease. It can survive without any irrigation in areas with annual rainfall of at least ten inches, but moderate watering during the hottest months will keep the leaves looking plump. Established plants can survive occasional temperature dips into the low teens, but may suffer frost damage after prolonged temperatures around 20° F. They are slow to recover from frost damage.

A. americana may be propagated from seed, but seed set in garden situations is often hybridized. Offsets from older plants are easy to establish when available. Old, lower leaves can be removed as they wither and turn brown. Agaves in the Southwest have been plagued by yucca weevils in recent years. Scattering granular insecticide around the base in spring should control them. (Most species are resistant in their native ranges.) Other cultivars of interest are **'Marginata'** with yellowish white to deep yellow leaf margins; **'Aureo-marginata-monstrosa'**, with small (two-foot), slightly contorted rosettes and leaves with broad yellow margins; **'Variegata'**, (synonym: *A. americana* var. *picta*) with yellow margins and the occasional drooping or twisted leaf; **'Medio-picta'** with leaves having wide yellow central stripes; and **'Medio-picta-alba'**, with cream-colored central striped leaves and a smaller, more refined habit (four-foot rosettes). **'Striata'** has leaves striped with yellow or white. Variegated forms are typically less cold hardy.

A. americana is not the only large agave worthy of landscape use; indeed, it is one of several excellent candidates for large spaces. **A. tequilana,** from Jalisco, Mexico, has stiffly projecting, thin, leathery leaves that emerge from ground-level to form a five-foot rosette. Inflorescences up to twenty feet tall bear three-inch flowers. *A. tequilana* is propagated from seeds or offsets. **A. attenuata,** from Hidalgo, Mexico, has a trunk to five feet tall with smooth, elliptic, two-foot-long, light green leaves, ten inches wide, without marginal or terminal spines and forming three- to four-foot rosettes. Inflorescences are dense, drooping racemes that reach ten feet in height and bear greenish white flowers about two-and-one-half inches long. Bulbils are produced in abundance. *A. attenuata* is propagated from seeds or bulbils. It is frost sensitive but is sufficiently shade-tolerant to thrive with protection in Zone 9. **'Nova'** is a superior selection with attractive glaucous blue leaves and straight inflorescences. **A. atrovirens,** from central Mexico, forms massive basal eight-foot rosettes of seven-foot-long, gray-green leaves, each a foot wide. Inflorescences tower over thirty feet, with twenty to thirty umbels of reddish, three-inch flowers. **A. franzosinii,** another mammoth, has ten-foot rosettes of eight-foot-long leaves that

Agave parryi with *Echeveria albicans* and *Kalanchoe tomentosa*.

During the several years that man and *Agave* lived together, *Agave* has been a renewable resource for food, drink, and artifact. As man has settled into communities, *Agave* became fences, marking territories, protecting crops, providing security, and ornamenting the home. As civilization and religion increased, the nurturing *Agave* became a symbol, until with its stimulating juice man made it into a god. The religion and the god have gone, but *Agave* still stands as a donor species of the first order. Among the world's crops, are there others that have played a more useful and bizarre role? If we are to ask more of the *Agave*, we must give it more attention and growing room.

HOWARD SCOTT GENTRY.
FROM *AGAVES OF CONTINENTAL NORTH AMERICA*, 1982.

typically arch; each white-gray to blue-gray leaf is about six inches wide at the center with small, spiny black teeth. Inflorescences of three-inch yellow flowers reach up to thirty-five feet.

Slightly smaller but still formidable are **A. ferox** and **A. vilminiana.** *A. ferox* produces basal six-foot rosettes with dark green, glossy three-and-one-half-foot flat leaves. Leaf margins have black-brown teeth up to one inch long. Its inflorescences, also to thirty feet tall, bear yellow, three-and-one-half-inch flowers. *A. vilmoriniana* leaves, more fleshy in texture and smooth-margined, are about three feet long and arranged in looser five-foot rosettes. It bears an unbranched, giant pipe-cleaner-like inflorescence of yellow flowers.

Beautiful, smaller agaves are also readily available. **A. guadalajarana,** from Jalisco, Mexico, has gray leaves with spiny margins and attractive imprinting on leaf surfaces resulting from the overlapping of leaf margins in the tightly compressed buds. **A. parryi var. truncata** (commonly called mescal in some areas; in other areas, mescal is a common name for any agave) is native to the southwestern U.S. and Mexico. Leaves are stiff and incurved, about one foot long and four inches wide, forming a compact, artichokelike two-foot rosette. They are light gray with a one-inch-long, black terminal spine and marginal teeth, often recurved. *A. parryi* generally blooms after about twenty years, forming fifteen-foot panicles of small, creamy yellow flowers that appear orange in bud. *A parryi* is well-suited to container growing or rock gardening. It is hardy to at least the mid-20s. **A. deserti** is another gray-leaved species that eventually forms a many-leaved two-and-one-half-foot rosette, offsetting to form clumps. **A. macroacantha** also clumps but has spherical one-foot rosettes of slender gray leaves. **A. colorata,** from Sonora, Mexico, has short stems and rosettes with only a few two-foot-long, seven-inch-wide leaves. These basically glaucous leaves are often cross-banded and red-tinted, typically with attractive bud imprints like those seen in *A.guadalajarana.* Yellow three-inch flowers are borne on ten-foot panicles. For a more hardy species, **A. utahensis** is recommended. It forms six- to twelve-inch basal rosettes, usually with offsets, of glaucous leaves, just over an inch wide, with small, marginal teeth. Inflorescences are about eight feet tall bearing short-stalked yellow flowers one-and-one-half inch in diameter.

A. parviflora, native to Arizona and northern Mexico, forms an attractive, four- to six-inch rosette. Leaves are stiff, one-half inch wide or less, and dark green with many white markings on the upper surface. Leaf margins bear short white threads and a few basal teeth. Inflorescences are five-foot-tall panicles with small yellow or greenish yellow flowers borne in pairs or foursomes. *A. parviflora* is propagated from seed or offsets. Mary Irish of the Desert Botanical Garden considers **A. toumeyana** and its minute subspecies **A. t. bella** to be among the loveliest of the small agaves; they are quite coldhardy, tolerate full sun or partial shade, and are superb for a small area.

A. victoriae-reginae, another central Mexican species, has ten-inch-long, two-inch-wide stiff, incurved leaves arranged in a blunt, basal one-foot rosette. Leaves are usually dark green with white bands and other markings. The terminal spines are small, and the white leaf margins do not have teeth.

A. parviflora

A. parryi var. *truncata*

A. ocahui (with *Euphorbia xantii*)

A. stricta 'Nana'

A. macroacantha

A. victoriae-reginae

A. franzosinii

A. deserti

A. stricta

AGAVE FILIFERA One-foot rosettes of green to purplish leaves, marked with brown lines and marginal white threads. Six-foot flower spikes change from green to maroon with age. Full sun. Moderate growth rate. Zones 9-10.

AGAVE MURPHEYI Two-and-one-half-foot rosettes of bluish leaves, here attractively variegated with yellow stripes. Twelve-foot panicles of waxy-green purple-tipped flowers often bear bulbils. Full sun to partial shade. Moderate to fast growing. Zones 8-10.

AGAVE COLORATA Short stems bear one- to two-foot rosettes of glaucous two-foot leaves, often cross-banded and red-tinted; yellow flowers appear in ten-foot panicles. Full sun. Moderate growth rate. Zones 8-10.

AGAVE ATTENUATA 'NOVA' Trunk, growing to five feet tall, bears smooth, elliptical two-foot glaucous blue leaves in three- to four-foot rosettes and straight spikes of greenish white flowers. Full sun, though partial to full shade enhances the bluish color. Fast growing. Zone 9 (with protection)-10.

Inflorescences are thirteen-foot panicles of pale green to cream two-inch flowers usually borne in threes. *A. victoriae-reginae* is propagated from seeds or occasional offsets.

A. filifera has one-foot rosettes of green to dark green or purplish leaves marked with brown lines and with marginal white threads. Inflorescences are six-foot spikes with two-inch flowers that start out greenish but turn maroon with age.

A. horrida, native to Morelos, Mexico, forms basal one- to one-and-one-half-foot rosettes with no offsets. Glossy dark green leaves are up to one foot long and three inches wide with horny margins and large, hooked teeth. It is a bit tender at Desert Botanical Garden.

A. murpheyi, from Arizona and northern Mexico, forms basal two-and-one-half-foot rosettes and offsets. Leaves reach up to twenty-six inches long and over three inches wide; they are typically light bluish green to yellow-green and sometimes are cross-banded. Leaf margins have small teeth. Inflorescences are twelve-foot panicles, often bearing bulbils, displaying pale, waxy green three-inch flowers with purplish tips. There is a particularly handsome variegated form occasionally available. This plant is edible and has long been cultivated. Nearly extinct in the wild, the few known populations are found in ancient agricultural fields.

A. pelona and **A. ocahui** are both non-offsetting species with rosettes of many straight, narrow leaves lacking marginal teeth; their aspect is that of a very symmetrical starburst. *A. pelona* has leaves of dark to purplish green with a reddish margin; *A. ocahui* has lighter green leaves. Their rosettes attain a spread of two to four feet. Both have spicate inflorescences; *A. ocahui* has yellow flowers while those of *A. pelona* are deep maroon. Both species are hardy to at least 15° F. and are tolerant of desert heat.

For a different presentation in the garden, clump-forming agaves may be desirable. **A. stricta,** the hedgehog agave of central Mexico, has thick stems that branch with age to develop many heads. Erect, slightly incurved green leaves

Sedum pachyphyllum, Agave attenuata, Aloe.

Aloe dawei, above, is somewhat unusual among aloes for its horizontally spreading flowers. As a result, each bud holds a droplet of winter rain, especially appealing when backlit.

are long, narrow, and tapering, about fourteen inches long and one-quarter inch wide, terminating in very sharp, one-inch spines. These are arranged in one-foot rosettes which can form clumps to eight or more feet across. Inflorescences reach eight feet in height and bear one-inch white flowers. **A. shawii,** from southern California and Baja, has short, branching stems that form clumps of two-foot rosettes with one- to two-feet-long, five-inch-wide, dark green leaves. Hooked red marginal teeth and curved terminal spines are characteristic of the species, though smooth-margined forms also occur. Greenish yellow flowers, three-and-one-half inches across, are borne on ten-foot-tall inflorescences. *A. sebastiana* is similar to *A. shawii,* but has glaucous gray leaves and short, flattened inflorescences. Both are adapted to cool, maritime climates and are hardy to Zone 9. **A. univittata** is an offset-forming species with one-foot rosettes of one-foot-long, sword-shaped leaves, each two inches wide, that are dull green with lighter central stripes. Margins are horny and bear hooked teeth. Pale green flowers, two inches long, are borne on ten-foot spikes.

ALOE *Liliaceae*

Encompassing a wide range of size, color, and growth habit, the Old World genus *Aloe* has long provided some of the most popular succulents for landscaping. In southern California, aloes are ubiquitous elements of both private and municipal gardens. Regardless of how much space a gardener can devote to aloes (and there have been whole estates devoted to the genus), there is certain to be a selection, either clump-forming or solitary, that is well suited to the site. They tolerate a wide range of soils. Most require full sun, but a few perform well in shade as well. Those treated here are generally hardy to Zone 9 and provide spectacular floral displays in winter when little else is in flower.

Among the diminutive species which clump only sparingly are **A. dorotheae, A. erinacea,** and **A. variegata.** These can be used as lone accents or massed to good effect. *A. dorotheae* is a variable species, but the form described here offsets sparingly and produces ten-inch rosettes of six-inch recurved fleshy leaves, one to one-and-one-half inches across with white-tipped spines along the scalloped margins. Inflorescences are two feet tall, bearing racemes of two-inch red flowers in winter. Its main attraction, however, is that the glossy leaves blush bright red in cool, sunny winter conditions. *A. dorotheae* can withstand temperatures in the upper twenties. *A. erinacea,* hardy to about 15° F., can produce solitary six-inch rosettes or occasional clumps of dense rosettes with lance-shaped to triangular gray-green leaves, each about four to seven inches long and one-and-one-half inches wide. Leaves characteristically have a few black-tipped white spines near the tip and several teeth on the undersides and along the margins. Inflorescences reach two to three feet in height and bear numerous crim-

ALOE PETRICOLA Glaucous-leaved, two-foot rosettes with bicolored red and white or orange and yellow inflorescences. Full sun. Moderate growth rate. Zones 9-10.

ALOE BAINESII Tree to thirty feet or more with thick swollen base and tapering branches terminating in two-foot rosettes. Flowers drab pinkish to orange. Full sun. Moderate growth rate. Zones 9-10.

ALOE VACILLENS Glaucous-leaved two-foot rosettes. Yellow or red flowers. Full sun. Moderate growth rate. Zones 9-10.

ALOE SPECTABILIS Three- to four-foot rosettes of glaucous, often spiny leaves on a trunk eventually to twelve feet. Orange to yellow flowers. Full sun. Moderate growth rate. Zones 9-10.

Above: A. suprafoliata. Right: A. virens.

son buds that open to yellow; flowering is rare in cultivation, occurring only after a dry summer period. The species is grown primarily for its boldly spined leaves. *A. variegata,* the partridge breast aloe, will produce a few offsets, but is most attractive as single, thick-leaved eight-inch rosettes. Leaves, arranged in three ranks, are dark green with transverse bands of white spots and white margins with small white teeth. Inflorescences are about one foot tall, bearing twenty to thirty one-and-one-half-inch flowers of scarlet to pink with green edges in spring and early summer. It is reliably hardy into the teens.

There are also small, clump-forming aloes, like **A. aristata, A. brevifolia, A. humilis, A. jucunda,** and **A. virens.** *A. aristata* forms compact clumps composed of up to a dozen four-inch rosettes. Leaves are green, flat, and incurving, with white bumps and spots and soft white teeth along the margins. Leaf tips may terminate in a bristle. Flowers are over an inch long, dull red, and borne on simple or branched one-and-one-half-foot-tall inflorescences in early summer. *A. brevifolia* is a stemless species that forms a dense carpet. Rosettes are about six inches in diameter, composed of glaucous green, one-inch wide fleshy leaves with white teeth along the margins. Flowers, one-and-one-half inches long, are orange, borne in sixteen-inch racemes in early summer. *A. humilis,* the spider aloe, forms dense clumps of three-inch rosettes, each composed of four-inch-long glaucous green leaves that are convex on both surfaces and covered with white teeth. Orange flowers, borne on fourteen-inch racemes in early spring, are quite large (over an

A. camperi 'Cornuta'

A. ciliaris

A. dorotheae

A. marlothii

A. plicatilis

A. berhana

A. aculeata

A. nobilis

A. dichotoma and A. camperi 'Cornuta'

Aloe virens with *Euphorbia mauritanica.*

inch long) in proportion to the small rosettes. *A. aristata, A. brevifolia,* and *A. humilis* are all hardy to Zone 9. *A. jucunda,* on the other hand, is more frost tender and requires protection outside Zone 10. This species has compact, ground-level rosettes, three to four inches in diameter. Spreading leaves have flat upper surfaces, dark green with pale spots above, and somewhat rounded and more speckled undersides. Twelve-inch inflorescences bear small, dull pink flowers. *A. virens* is another small clump-former with narrow lance-shaped leaves, about eight inches long, armed with white teeth. Bright red flowers, about one-and-one-half inches long, are borne on two-foot racemes. All of the smaller aloes are suitable for mass bedding or as rockery accents.

Handsome, medium-sized aloes include **A. broomii, A. camperi, A. microstigma, A. petricola, A. striata, A. suprafoliata, A. vera,** and **A. wickensii.** *A. broomii,* hardy to Zone 9, forms solitary two- to three-foot rosettes composed of one-foot long green, faintly lined leaves that taper to long dry points with apical spines. Leaf margins are scalloped in outline and dark reddish brown. Inflorescences, appearing in spring, are typically unbranched, to four feet tall, bearing large numbers of one-inch pale orange flowers that are partly obscured by prominent cream-colored bracts. Even before the flowers appear, the inflorescence is intriguing because of the snakeskinlike pattern of overlapping scales. *A. camperi,* hardy to the low 20s, is a variable species grown for its profuse orange flowers. Its one-and-one-half-foot stems branch from the base to form clumps two-and-one-half feet across. Terminal two-foot rosettes of very fleshy leaves produce one or more two- to three-foot tall, branched inflorescences in April or May. Flowers, one inch long, are typically darker in bud. **A. camperi** 'Cornuta' is an especially floriferous selection with spotted leaves and compact, densely flowered inflorescences produced in March. *A. microstigma* forms solitary two-foot rosettes or small clumps. Green leaves are usually spotted, with scalloped margins sporting reddish brown teeth. Red buds fade to greenish yellow as they open and are about one inch long, borne on three-inch racemes in winter. *A. petricola,* hardy to Zone 9, is attractive for its two-foot rosettes of gray-green incurved leaves and its bicolored inflorescences. Flowers are dull red in bud but open to greenish white or orange, and are borne in dense three-foot panicles in winter. *A. suprafoliata* seedings are desirable container plants because of their fan-shaped arrangement of leaves. In maturity, however, the glaucous leaves spiral to form ground-level one-foot rosettes. Inflorescences, several per rosette, reach three feet in height and bear two-inch coral red flowers with glaucous bluish tips in early winter. *A. striata* forms pinkish gray one-and-one-half foot rosettes of broad, gracefully incurved leaves with smooth pink margins. Flat-topped panicles of orange flowers appear in spring.

Although perhaps not as decorative a garden plant as those species list-

ALOE DAWESII Two-foot rosettes of green leaves and orange flowers. Full sun. Moderate growth rate. Zones 9-10.

ALOE FEROX Three- to four-foot rosettes of glaucous, often spiny leaves on a trunk eventually to fifteen feet. Orange flowers on erect brown peduncles. Full sun. Moderate growth rate. Zones 9-10.

ALOE ARBORESCENS Clumping shrub with many heads of gray-green leaves. Flowers in pyramidal racemes, red-orange or yellow. Full sun to partial shade. Moderate to fast growth rate. Zones 9-10.

A. WICKENSII Two-foot rosettes of blue-green leaves with bicolored red and yellow inflorescences. Full sun to partial shade. Moderate growth rate. Zones 9-10.

Above: Aloe vera has been valued for its healing qualities for over two thousand years; records of its use date back to Dioscorides, the Greek historian. Famous aloe-users in history include Cleopatra and Josephine, wife of Napoleon, who used it as a moisturizer. Aloe has also been used by African hunters to mask their human scent when stalking prey and by dermatologists as a cure for acne and dandruff. Aloe used alone can dry skin; it works best when mixed with vitamin E or other moisturizers. Another species, *A. ferox,* has been used to cure stomach ailments.

ed above, **Aloe vera** (synonym *A. barbadensis*) is a useful, medium-sized species familiar to many people and cultivated and often naturalized throughout the tropics and subtropics; it is reportedly hardy to Zone 8. This plant is the major source of the drug aloe, useful for easing the pain of minor burns. Some studies have suggested that aloe induces cell division, thus helping the body to regenerate damaged skin. *A. vera* has two-foot rosettes of glaucous green leaves armed with white teeth along the margins. Flowers are yellow, about one inch long. The common *A. vera* of commerce appears to be a hybrid of smaller stature which retains its juvenile foliage coloring, bright green with white spots, and bears bicolored inflorescences with orange buds opening to yellow.

A. *wickensii* forms two-foot rosettes of lance-shaped, blue-green leaves. Flowers are crowded in tight clusters along slender four- to five-foot tall branched inflorescences and are distinctly bicolored with red buds opening to yellow. *A. wickensii* var. *lutea* bears pure yellow flowers.

Among the larger aloes, **A. africana, A. ferox, A. marlothii, A. spectabilis,** and **A. thraskii** all make excellent more or less solitary specimens hardy through Zone 9. While several of them become treelike in age, they are basal rosettes for their first several years in the garden. *A. africana,* the spiny aloe, has stems that may reach twelve feet, often covered by dried old leaves. Branches terminate in dense three-foot rosettes of dull green leaves with spiny margins and undersides. Several inflorescences are produced by each rosette; two-foot racemes sport flowers, red in bud, opening to yellow-orange. *A. ferox,* the Cape aloe, produces unbranched stems to fifteen feet tall, clothed with persistent dried leaves. The new leaves, each about three feet long, borne in dense terminal four- to five-foot rosettes, are thick and sword-shaped dull green, sometimes with a reddish tinge. Leaf margins and sometimes both surfaces are armed with stout reddish teeth. Red or orange flowers are borne on erect panicles in late winter and early spring. *A. marlothii* constitutes one of the most imposing of landscape aloes, producing unbranched trees to eighteen feet tall. When not in flower, it superficially resembles *A. ferox.* However, in winter its orange to yellow flowers are closely packed on horizontally branched panicles three to four feet across; the effect is evocative of a windswept grass fire. *A. spectabilis,* another spiny-leaved species, has stems of six to twelve feet in height and three-foot-long, dark green leaves in four- to five-foot rosettes. Yellow to orange flowers are two inches long, borne on glossy dark green to almost black peduncles in striking contrast to the flowers. *A. thraskii* has unbranched stems of three to six feet clothed with persistent dead leaves; the massive, four- to five-foot terminal rosette has lance-shaped, five-foot-long, eight-inch-broad at the base, recurved dull green leaves with red or brown margins armed with thin reddish teeth. Panicles of yellow to orange one-inch flowers are borne in winter.

For larger, clump-forming species, try **A. arborescens, A. ciliaris,** or **A. plicatilis.** *A. arborescens,* the giant aloe or candelabra plant, forms a shrub to ten feet or more tall and wide. Branches terminate in one-and-one-half-foot rosettes of dull, gray-green, sometimes tinged red, two-foot-long leaves, each about two inches wide, with spiny margins. Flowers are scarlet to orange, about two inches long, and borne on dense pyramidal racemes about two feet long in spring. Each rosette typically produces several inflorescences. A less vigorous yellow-flowered form is sometimes available, as is an attractive variegated form with leaves striped in pale green and creamy yellow. *A. arborescens* grows best in full sun but will tolerate partial shade. It is very tolerant of drought, heat, and salt-laden sea breezes but will fare best with supplemental watering during the hottest summer months. *A. ciliaris,* the climbing aloe, produces climbing or scrambling stems, to fifteen feet or more; the last foot or two has evenly spaced six-inch-long slightly fleshy leaves with white teeth along the margins. When grown in the open, the stems of *A. ciliaris* mound up upon themselves to form a dense shrub to six feet tall and ten feet across. Flowers, about an inch long, are scarlet red and droop along the branches of one-foot racemes. *A. plicatilis,* the fan aloe, is a highly branched shrub or small tree to six feet tall, with the thick branches having a gnarled caudiciform quality. The leaves are strap-shaped, light blue-green, smooth-margined with rounded tips and about one foot long, arranged in fans at branch ends. Scarlet flowers are pendent, about two-and-one-half inches long, borne on twenty-inch racemes in winter. *A. plicatilis* is difficult to propagate but some percentage of cuttings will root.

A. bainesii and **A. dichotoma** are the most desirable of the truly tree-forming aloes. *A. bainesii* can reach heights up to sixty feet with venerable old specimens having trunks as much as nine feet across. Branching is dichotomous, with each bifurcation terminating in a dense two- to three-foot rosette of leathery green leaves. Flowers are pale pink with green tips, borne on one-foot inflorescences in winter. *A. dichotoma* forms a towering tree, to thirty feet tall, with a domed crown and a trunk three to four feet in diameter and many dichotomous branches. Leaves are about eight to twelve inches long, two inches wide near the base, and glaucous blue-green with yellow to brown teeth along the margins; they are borne in one-foot terminal rosettes. Flowers are bright yellow, just over an inch long, and borne on three-branched, one-foot-tall panicles in winter. *A. dichotoma* grows well in full sun or partial open shade. It is tolerant of most soils and thrives in intense heat. Occasional supplemental watering keeps the leaves succulent during dry seasons. It is absolutely hardy to about 25° F., but can survive somewhat lower temperatures though leaves may be damaged.

Above: Aloe 'David Verity', created by noted hybridizer David Verity, formerly a professor at UCLA's Mildred E. Mathias Botanic Garden, will be introduced by the Huntington Botanical Gardens within the next two years as part of the International Succulent Introduction (ISI) program, based at the Huntington. The aim of ISI is to propagate and distribute new or rare succulents to collectors, nurseries, and institutions. Selections are made from collections in the wild as well as newly created hybrids; the plants are then grown, evaluated, and propagated at The Huntington. New introductions are announced annually in the March/April issue of the *Cactus and Succulent Journal,* and distributed to interested parties. Over the past years, Huntington has introduced dozens of varieties. Among the most successful have been *Echeveria lilacina* and *Adenium* 'Crimson Star'.

Aporocactus flagelliformis produces attractive three-inch flowers.

APOROCACTUS *Cactaceae*

A native of the highland plateaus of Mexico, the epiphytic rat-tail cactus is widely grown outdoors as a hanging basket plant. Indoors, it has been cultivated in Europe as a window or conservatory plant since 1690. Pendent stems are thin, one-quarter to one-half-inch across, and up to five feet long, densely clothed in short, reddish to white, needle-shaped spines. The hummingbird-pollinated flowers, borne through March and April, are showy magenta and about three inches long. Typically, each lasts several days. Most plants grown from cuttings flower within two to three years, especially if somewhat pot-bound. The fruits are attractive, bristly red globes about one-half inch in diameter but rarely form without hand pollination.

Aporocactus thrives best in part shade; full sun will cause yellowing and stunted growth. *Aporocactus* will bear extreme heat if well-shaded and winter lows in the 30s if dry. Frost protection is necessary to prevent stem spotting and tip die-back. Preferred soil is loose, well-aerated, and rich, with a slightly acidic pH (5.5-6.5). This plant demands ample moisture in spring and summer, tapering off to only occasional watering during cooler seasons.

Aporocactus is typically propagated by shoot cuttings. When purchasing a rooted cutting in a nursery, look for one that has already begun to branch. Once established, the rat-tail is a rampant grower, especially if fertilized. Older stems may root adventitiously.

Aporocactus is susceptible to infestation by scale and mealybugs, so spraying with a mild systemic may be necessary occasionally.

Intergeneric hybrids, such as **x *Aporophyllum* 'Lawrence'** (an *Aporocactus- Epiphyllum* hybrid) are also popular. 'Lawrence' has larger, more profuse, brighter pink flowers borne on shorter stems.

APTENIA CORDIFOLIA *Aizoaceae*

Aptenia has gained a strong foothold in the horticultural trade in recent years due to its notable tenacity in harsh environments. Native to the eastern coastal deserts of South Africa, *Aptenia* is a trailing perennial used primarily as a fast-growing groundcover. Leaves are fleshy, bright green, and heart-shaped, about one inch across. Flowers are solitary, about one-half inch across, and magenta with many petals. Flowering begins in spring and persists through summer.

The cultivar **'Red Apple',** named for its bright red flowers, is thought to be a hybrid between *Aptenia* and a related ice plant, *Platythyra haeckeliana;* it is more vigorous than either species. The species are typically propagated from seed, but 'Red Apple' is perpetuated strictly from cuttings. Cuttings are taken in winter; they root quickly and easily.

Although *Aptenia* is extremely drought resistant, it will be both more lush and more floriferous if watered, especially when grown in full sun. In partial shade, less water will suffice, but flowering will also be reduced. Tolerant of both shade and drought, *Aptenia* makes a good underplanting for native dry land oaks in southern California.

APOROCACTUS FLAGELLIFORMIS (RAT-TAIL CACTUS) Thin, pendent stems, up to five feet long, bear short, reddish to brown spines. Crimson- to purple-pink flowers appear in early spring, followed by bristly red globular fruits. Part shade; bears high heat. Rampant grower. Zones 10.

xAPOROPHYLLUM 'LAWRENCE' A hybrid of *Aporocactus* and *Epiphyllum*. Stems are shorter and less spiny than Aporocactus. Partial shade. Vigorous. Zones 9-10.

APTENIA CORDIFOLIA 'RED APPLE' Groundcover with fleshy, bright green, heart-shaped leaves and bright red spring and summer flowers. Full sun to partial shade. Extremely vigorous. Zone 9-10.

ARTHROCEREUS RONDONIANUS Small erect-stemmed plant, growing to ten inches, with ribbed, bright green stems and golden-yellow to reddish-brown spines. Deep pink, fragrant flowers appear at night in late spring. Partial shade; warm conditions. Vigorous. Zone 10; select clones to Zone 9.

ASTROPHYTUM ORNATUM (STAR CACTUS) Globular to cylindrical plant, usually a foot or less in height (but up to five feet or more), with ribbed dark green stems and golden-yellow to brown spines. Satiny yellow flowers appear in summer. Full sun to light shade. Moderate to fast growing. Zones 9-10.

ASTROPHYTUM MYRIOSTIGMA Stems have smooth, rounded ribs and are densely covered in chalky white scales. Avoid scarring the scaley white surface. Full sun or light shade. Slow to moderate growth. Zones 8-10.

BEAUCARNEA RECURVATA (PONYTAIL PALM) Shrub to thirty feet with tufts of drooping leaves; plumes of tiny light yellow to white flowers appear on older plants. Full sun to partial shade; mature plants hardy to 18° F. Vigorous grower when planted in shade and given adequate water and fertilizer. Zones 8-10.

BORZICACTUS SAMAIPATANUS Bright green, upright-branching stems grow to five feet tall, bearing short golden spines and orange-red to pastel coral pink or purple flowers. Full sun to partial shade. Vigorous. Zones 9-10.

ARTHROCEREUS RONDONIANUS *Cactaceae*

This *Arthrocereus* species is a plant with erect cylindrical, bright green stems, one-inch in diameter, that reach about ten inches in height. Stems have thirteen to fifteen low, rounded ribs and are covered with fine, densely clustered, golden-yellow to reddish brown spines. Central spines in each cluster may be up to three inches long (but are usually shorter), each surrounded by forty to fifty shorter, more bristlelike spines. Flowers are large (usually about four-and-one-half inches long), deep pink, nocturnal, and fragrant, and open for more than one night.

Native to Brazil, *Arthrocereus rondonianus* is generally tender, but one reddish spined clone available in cultivation displays an uncommon vigor and hardiness into the mid-20s F. once established.

Plants thrive best in partial shade; full sun exposure can cause scorching of the stems as well as tip die-back.

Borzicactus aureispinus.

ASTROPHYTUM *Cactaceae*

Astrophytum ornatum, the star cactus of central Mexico, is widely considered to be the hardiest of its genus with established plants withstanding temperatures in the low 20s F. At Desert Botanical Garden, they have been damaged at 20° F., and are considered to be the least hardy. Typically it is seen as a short, spherical-stemmed plant–a small, green globe at ground level–but it will assume a more cylindrical shape with age as it can reach three to nine feet in height and eight to twelve inches in diameter. In pot cultivation, it rarely exceeds one foot in height. The stems usually have eight prominent ribs; the epidermis is dark green with bands of gray-white spots and one-inch-long golden-yellow to brown spines. Flowers are borne just below the top of the stem; often several are open at once. Under good growing conditions, the satiny, lemon yellow, three-and-one-half-inch flowers will be produced on and off all summer.

Astrophytum grows fastest in full sun with adequate supplemental watering and generous fertilizing during the growing seasons of spring and summer. Many succulent growers prefer to grow *Astrophytum* in light shade, however, so that the stem maintains a richer, darker green color. Plants may be grown easily from fresh seeds, which are large and germinate readily, usually within three to five days of sowing. One- to three-year-old seedlings are widely available at succulent nurseries.

A. myriostigma, with its smoother, more rounded ribs and dense covering of chalky white scales, is also attractive, though is has smaller flowers and is slightly less cold hardy (though at Arizona Sonora-Desert Museum it has survived undamaged down to 15° F.).

BEAUCARNEA *Agavaceae*

Beaucarnea is native to the dry regions of Texas and southeast Mexico. Often tagged "ponytail palm" in plant shops, it is not a palm at all, but rather a slow-growing member of the agave family. In the suburban landscape, *Beau-*

VIEWPOINT

CACTUS FLOWERS

Cactus flower best when they are well nourished with light, fertilizer, and water. They perform best when given as much light as they can stand without burning and generous fertilizer and water (though they should be allowed to dry out between watering). One plant I'd recommend for people who want surefire success is *Borzicactus samaipatanus*; it flowers profusely for a long time regardless of how it's cared for (though it will do even better with some attention).
JOHN TRAGER,
HUNTINGTON BOTANICAL GARDEN

Although It's hard to generalize about so large a genus, I find that many cactus flower more profusely after a cool and dry winter rest; a couple of good freezes also help. Some of our best flowering cacti are *Echinopsis,* which flower in great profusion but are ephemeral, and *Ferocactus wislizenii,* the fishhook cactus, which flowers for over two months.
DR. MARK DIMMITT,
THE ARIZONA-SONORA
DESERT MUSEUM

In our coastal area we find that a really hot spring and summer without fog are the best conditions for cactus flowering. We also found that the year after our five-year drought brought profuse flowers (though we did provide supplemental water throughout the drought). *Cereus peruvianus* presents a display of huge flowers reliably; *Notocactus leninghausii* and Trichocereus huascha are also wonderful.
VIRGINIA HAYS,
GANNA WALSKA LOTUSLAND

Cacti grown indoors have the same requirements as those grown outdoors: a dormant period with cool temperatures, preferably dropping at night. A few cacti, such as the Christmas cactus, are photoperiodic, but most need full light.
ERNEST DE MARIE,
THE NEW YORK BOTANICAL GARDEN

carnea is usually seen as a large shrub (perhaps six feet tall) but it will eventually stretch into a tree up to thirty feet tall with a tight head and a full trunk. A prominent feature of the genus is the characteristic bulbous base; though merely onion-sized in small plants, it will become enormous (up to six feet across), in mature specimens. *Beaucarnea* has a single stem for many years but will finally branch. Stem ends display tufts of drooping, green, grasslike leaves. Older plants produce three-foot-long feathery plumes of clustered, tiny light yellow to white flowers that persist for a month or more; these plumes become reddish in fruit.

Beaucarnea recurvata has three- to six-foot-long, drooping leaves approximately three-quarters of an inch width, and smooth bark, whereas **B. stricta** has somewhat glaucous, bluish colored, erect leaves that are about two feet long and one-half inch wide and more corky, fissured bark. In its native habitat, *Beaucarnea* grows in full sun; however, it will tolerate partial shade. Mature plants are hardy to at least 18° F., but younger plants, especially those in containers, are only reliably hardy to the mid 20s.

All in all, beaucarneas are relatively trouble-free. Once established, plants need only occasional watering during dry seasons; one or two deep soakings a month between April and November are sufficient to sustain the plants in southern California's Mediterranean climate. If leaf tips brown, provide additional water. Beaucarneas require no shaping or pruning; the leaves are long-lived so even annual grooming to remove dead material is minimal. In addition, these plants are unaffected by typical garden insect pests.

B. recurvata is more readily available for sale than *B. stricta*. Both can be grown from seed quite easily. Fresh seed will germinate within a few days; older seed will come up reliably, albeit erratically, over six to twelve weeks. Seedlings should be large enough to pot up after about six months.

Nursery-grown seedlings in six-inch pots will be two to four years old. If the caudex is three inches in diameter or more, seedlings are ready to be planted directly in the ground. Initially, water generously and fertilize for fast establishment and growth. Try any *Beaucarnea* that is available; all will make a graceful, fountainlike addition to the landscape.

BORZICACTUS *Cactaceae*

With its vivid green, upright and basally branching stems reaching three feet, **Borzicactus samaipatanus** can develop into a striking specimen plant or an impressive mass planting. Indeed, it has been termed by some as the single best landscaping cactus. Short, dense, golden spines clothe the one- to two-inch-diameter stems which bear profuse, extremely showy deep orange-red to pastel coral pink flowers along the lengths of the upper stems. Flowers typically remain constantly open for about four days. Flowering begins while plants are still relatively small (twelve inches); light fertilizing will assure that plants remain in bloom throughout the growing period.

Borzicactus is a moderately fast grower, with branching beginning early in seedling development. Individual stems "age" after three or four years, becoming brown-spined and scarred. It may be desirable to remove these older branches; alternatively, one can take cuttings from newer material and start again.

Although this *Borzicactus* can withstand sub-freezing temperatures, such exposure may cause development of long-lasting discolorations on the stems.

Other *Borzicactus* species (sometimes included in the genus *Oreocereus*) are also popular. The very cold hardy **B. celsianus,** (Zones 8-10) called old-man-of-the-mountains, is a robust, columnar species with caramel-colored spines, prominent, abundant white hairs, and three-and-one-half-inch reddish flowers. Another cold hardy species, **B. hendriksenianus var. densilanatus,** makes a dramatic planting; three-inch yellow spines emerge from a stem completely covered with dense white hairs. Occasional magenta flowers add to its attractions.

Borzicactus samaipatanus.

BROMELIA *Bromeliacea*

Bromelia balansae, (Heart of Flame), a native of Argentina, is a thorny-leaved terrestrial bromeliad that forms dense thickets; it can become invasive if not controlled adequately. Its leaves are dark green, two to three feet long and about one inch wide, with menacing teeth on leaf margins; unexpected encounters with the leaves are painful. But *B. balansae* puts on a spectacular floral display: prior to the emergence of a dense panicle of whitish violet flowers, apical leaves turn brilliant red and remain that way during flowering. Leaf damage can occur at 28° F., but *B. balansae* performs well in Zones 9 and 10. It tolerates sun or shade. Moderate watering is recommended.

BULBINE *Liliaceae*

Bulbine alooides is a stemless perennial that is native to South Africa. The leaves are light green and very soft and fleshy; they are arranged in compact, aloelike rosettes about eighteen inches in diameter. Dense clusters of brilliant yellow flowers appear on three-foot stalks in spring and summer. Individual flowers are quite small but the collective visual impact can be dramatic.

B. alooides is typically propagated by removing offsets from parent plants. A single plant will in time produce a large clump of identical offspring even without physically digging and removing offsets. Although not often available in nurseries, this *Bulbine* is worth pursuing, especially as it is one of the few that grows well in shade.

More commonly available is the somewhat weedy **B. frutescens.** A succulent shrub to about two feet, it has brown stems with bright green, pencil-shaped leaves and dense racemes of bright yellow, orange, or white flowers borne on one- to two-foot inflorescences. Hardy to temperatures in the lower 20s, it is fast-growing and reseeds freely. It performs well at the Desert Botanical Garden in sun or shade if kept on the dry side in summer. For more unusual and showy flowers, try the self-sterile **B. frutescens 'Hallmark';** the bright orange flowers feature distinctive fuzzy yellow stamens.

Many bulbines for sale in succulent nurseries cannot tolerate frost, but they will survive temperatures right down to 32° F. Be sure to provide ade-

BROMELIA BALANSAE 'HEART OF FLAME' Viciously spined slender leaves in three-foot rosettes which blush brilliant red when in flower in late spring. Full sun to partial shade. Vigorous. Zones 9-10.

BULBINE FRUTESCENS 'HALLMARK' Shrub to two feet with bright green, pencil-shaped leaves and bright orange flowers with fuzzy yellow stamens. Hardy to the low 20s F. Zones 9-10.

CARNEGEIA GIGANTEA (SAGUARO) Plant to sixty feet in age with large columnar stems and wreaths of white flowers near branch tips in spring and early summer. Full sun; relatively cold tolerant. Slow-growing. Zones 9-10.

CEPHALOCEREUS SENILIS (OLD MAN CACTUS) Columnar plant, to forty-five feet in great age, covered when young with white hair-like growth; older plants bear nocturnal, rose pink flowers. Full sun; hardy to below 20° F. Fairly slow growing. Zones 9-10.

quate water during the growing season; even when dormant, plants should not be allowed to dry completely.

CARNEGIEA GIGANTEA *Cactaceae*

Better known as the saguaro, *Carnegiea gigantea* forms an unforgettable silhouette in the deserts of southern Arizona and Sonora, Mexico. Named in honor of the distinguished philanthropist and patron of science Andrew Carnegie, the large, columnar stems of this extremely long-lived species (up to 250 years) can reach sixty feet in height. Branching occurs only in older specimens, usually after six to eight feet of vertical growth.

Wreaths of white flowers form near branch tips in spring and early summer; the flowers are large, three inches long, opening slowly at night and remaining open until the following afternoon. The three-inch oblong red fruits are showy as well as edible.

Saguaros thrive in full sun in rocky or well-drained soil with good drainage. Although relatively cold tolerant, they may be damaged by prolonged freezes in the 20° F. range.

Acquiring a mature saguaro for home landscaping may be difficult (and costly), but it is worth the care and effort. Since *Carnegiea gigantea* is an endangered species, it is protected under state and federal laws. Check plants in the nursery where you shop to make sure they were collected legally; each saguaro should have a tag indicating the permit conditions under which it was taken. If you plant a saguaro without proper data indicating its legality, you can be prosecuted, an increasingly common occurrence in the Southwest as

Carnegiea gigantea.

Bulbine latifolia with *Kalanchoe fedtschenkoi* and *Veltheimia bracteata.*

ENDANGERED CACTI

Whether beloved giant panda or controversial spotted owl, animals threatened by extinction maintain a high public profile. In contrast, relatively few people comprehend the plight of an ever-increasing number of endangered plants, particularly many native U.S. cacti.

Cacti become endangered for a number of reasons, almost all of them involving humans. Human interference has damaged many cactus habitats through construction, overgrazing, ORV use, and mining. To be considered endangered, an organism must be on the verge of extinction over much or all of its range. The U.S. Fish and Wildlife Service has listed twenty-five native species of cacti as endangered or threatened, with nearly forty more under consideration. Many of these grow only on specific soil types, severely limiting their distribution. A few, such as Davis' green pitahaya, *Echino-cereus viridiflorus* var. *davisii,* are known only from one native population.

Adapted to a hostile environment, some rare cacti, especially some diminutive *Pediocactus* species, shrink and retract underground during the coldest and hottest times of year. Many have only recently been discovered, usually by chance, during their flowering period; a number undoubtedly still await discovery.

Endangered plants have also suffered from over-collection, especially before the passage of the Endangered Species Act in 1973. In Arizona, legal collection of the giant saguaro currently requires permits from both state and landowner. Plants thus acquired must be tagged documenting their legality.

authorities battle so-called cactus rustlers.

Once you have acquired your specimen, be sure to take special care in planting. Your field-collected plant will have very little root system. Do not bury it deeper than the original soil level, and be prepared to support it until it roots. (It will put on new growth at that time.) Water and fertilize generously to stimulate growth.

If field-collected saguaros are scarce, commercially propagated plants are an alternative; try to buy plants with established root systems. Twenty-year-old seedlings growing naturally in the desert typically are only one to two feet in height, though this can be achieved more quickly with generous watering and fertilizing. Nevertheless, if you want the drama of an eight-foot cactus column in your landscape, field-collected specimens are probably your best source. But why not plant a few seedlings for the future as well?

For a faster-growing look-alike, try *Echinopsis terscheckii* (synonym *Trichocereus terscheckii*).

CEPHALOCEREUS SENILIS *Cactaceae*

Cephalocereus senilis, the old man cactus, is a tall (to forty-five feet in great age), columnar native of the limestone hills of Hidalgo, Mexico. Its common name comes from the dense, white, hair-like growth that envelops young plants and imparts an unusual character. Flowers are nocturnal, rose pink, and about two inches long, but they will not be seen except on very large (over fifteen feet tall), old plants. This *Cephalocereus* is popular for landscaping because it has an attractive appearance from the seedling stage through to maturity and is cold hardy to temperatures in the teens.

Full sun and rocky or loose soil with good drainage are crucial to cultivation success. *Cephalocereus* is fairly slow growing from seed, reaching only one to two feet in twenty years in nature. However, with ample supplemental water and fertilizer, growth of plants in the garden can be much faster.

CEPHALOPHYLLUM 'RED SPIKE' *Aizoaceae*

Cephalophyllum 'Red Spike' (occasionally seen labelled in the nursery as *Cylindrophyllum* 'Red Spike') is a South African dwarf succulent possibly of hybrid origin. Nearly cylindrical green leaves are crowded in tufts on the main stem and at the ends of branches. Showy two-inch flowers are borne for a couple of months in spring. It should be noted that, in spite of its name, 'Red Spike' has magenta flowers. Ample moisture in the growing seasons of winter and spring will ensure maximum flowering; plants are typically kept drier in summer, although they will accept warm-season watering. At Desert Botanical Garden in Phoenix, the plant dies if not watered twice a week in summer, but good drainage is required as this genus is native to the sandy soils of coastal regions.

With its short or prostrate stems, *Cephalophyllum* is generally used as an accent plant or massed as a groundcover. Other more scrambling species of *Cephalophyllum*, like **C. stayneri**, can be used to cascade over a stone wall; both

CEPHALOPHYLLUM 'RED SPIKE' Groundcover succulent to six inches with tufts of nearly cylindrical leaves and magenta spring flowers. Full sun to partial shade. Vigorous. Hardy to mid-20s F. Zones 9-10.

CEREUS PERUVIANUS Basally branching columnar cactus to ten feet tall and fifteen feet wide with stems that age from light green to blue- and then gray-green; large white nocturnal flowers; red egg-shaped fruits. Full sun to partial shade. Vigorous. Zones 8-10.

CHEIRIDOPSIS DENTICULATA Clump-forming plant, to one foot across, with gray-white, red-tipped toothed leaves dotted with dark green, and large white or pink flowers borne in spring. Full sun to partial shade. Slow growing. Zones 9-10.

CLEISTOCACTUS STRAUSII (SILVER TORCH CACTUS) Cactus forming thick, branching columns to six feet high, with tubular burgundy flowers borne throughout the growing season and white, glassy spines. Full sun to partial shade. Hardy to the mid 20s F. Vigorous. Zones 9-10.

The bud was expanding in spasmodic jerks and beginning to send off the sweet elusive perfume. We could almost see those creamy petals unfold. The perfume became heady, intoxicating. Breathlessly, we watched. The night was still. It seemed to be watching too. At last a full-blown blossom, fully six inches across, gleamed in the white moonlight, its immaculate center filled with hundreds of waxy white stamens, yellow tipped, like so many altar candles.

OLGA WRIGHT SMITH, FROM *GOLD ON THE DESERT*, 1956.

are reliably hardy to the mid-20s.

'Red Spike' is easily propagated by cuttings taken in winter during its growing season, and flats of rooted cuttings are readily available in the nursery trade.

Less readily available but worth seeking out is **C. alstonii,** a slower growing plant with gray-green, dark-spotted leaves and three-inch vivid scarlet flowers with violet stamens.

CEREUS *Cactaceae*

Cereus peruvianus (also known as *C. uruguayensis*) is a tall, fast-growing, columnar, South American cactus that has been cultivated since 1576. Branching from the base, it can form bushes to ten feet tall and fifteen feet across. The stems are light green when young, turning blue-green and eventually gray-green with age. Short, prickly spines on the stems are not evident except under closer inspection. Large white flowers, six-and-one-half inches across, open at night; fruits are large, red, and egg-shaped, splitting open when fully ripe to expose white pulp peppered with black seed.

Among columnar cacti, *C. peruvianus* is one of the easiest to maintain and propagate. It grows best in full sun but will tolerate partial shade and can even be enjoyed grown indoors for extended periods. Though, like most cacti, *C. peruvianus* is inherently very drought tolerant, it will retain a more glaucous stem appearance and develop less basal corkiness if fertilized and watered generously during the hot, dry summer months. It is rarely grown from seed because it roots so easily from cuttings. Big cuttings (two to six feet long) can be taken at virtually any time of the year; thus, one can obtain a fine, larger specimen quite easily in the nursery trade. *C. peruvianus* is hardy to about 15° F.

Various monstrose forms of *C. peruvianus* are popular with collectors and landscapers alike. Unfortunately, many different cultivars are labelled 'Monstrosus', such that a plant sold under that name could sport morphology ranging from only slightly distorted to totally knobby in appearance. In any monstrose form, the plant's ribs are irregularly divided into tubercles, producing to varying degrees a tangled-appearing arrangement of bizarre, bumpy stem shapes. Monstrose stems, slower growing than normal forms, also typically retain their blue coloring, even in mature specimens.

Another attractive *Cereus* for landscaping is **C. forbesii** a native of northern Argentina. The erect stems, blue- to gray-green in color, will eventually reach about fifteen feet in height. Stems are more slender, less branched, and slower growing than those of *C. peruvianus*. Stout, black, needle-shaped spines are a dominant feature of the plant. The flowers are large, seven inches across, with white inner segments and pink-tipped middle segments. The fruits are attractive, plum-sized, and nearly spherical.

CHEIRIDOPSIS DENTICULATA *Aizoaceae*

Cheiridopsis denticulata, from the Cape Province of South Africa, is perhaps the hardiest member of its genus. *Cheiridopsis* forms a nice, compact clump, about one foot across, with gray-white, toothed leaves dotted with minute dark green spots, terminating in reddish tips. Flowers are very large, to four inches across, creamy white or pale pink suffused with orange, and borne on two- to three-inch stalks in spring.

Cheiridopsis is typically propagated by seed; cuttings are very slow and difficult to establish unless taken during the cool growing season. Young plants should be set out in the garden in winter or early spring, and seedlings or cuttings should be kept drier during the summer when they are not actively growing. For established plants, supplemental watering in early spring will produce the best growth; watering should be tapered off in summer.

CLEISTOCACTUS *Cactaceae*

Members of the large genus *Cleistocactus* can be generally separated into two basic types: the columnar and the sprawling. Both produce good landscaping candidates, depending upon the planting site and visual effect sought, and are widely available as either seedlings or rooted cuttings.

Of columnar cleistocacti, **C. strausii,** the silver torch cactus of Bolivia and Argentina, is perhaps the handsomest, as well as the hardiest (mid-20's). (*C. hyalacanthus* as sold in the nursery trade appears to be the same plant.) It forms thick straight columns to six feet high that branch from the base, composing an impressive clump over time. If old stems become unsightly due to corking or scarring, they can be excised to induce additional basal branching. Conspicuous spines are white, thin, and glassy, completely covering the stem. Flowering begins when the stems are about eighteen inches tall; the flowers are thick, tubular, and deep burgundy, usually about three-and-one-half inches long.

C. chacoanus is recommended as the best of the sprawling *Cleistocactus* forms, with the added benefit of being reliably hardy to the teens. Although the stems are a duller green and the spines not nearly as attractive as in *C. strausii,* the dense thicket of two-foot stems formed by *C. chacoanus* makes a dramatic landscape element. Clumps need renewal after five to ten years, done by removing old growth. Wrestling with the center of an aged, spiny, cactus thicket is obviously not a job for the faint-hearted, but the triumphant gardener will be rewarded with a rejuvenated and improved mature specimen.

Sprawling cleistocacti typically produce more flowers than their columnar kin, even as young cuttings, and *C. chacoanus* is no exception. Blooming on both new and old growth, it produces numerous striking, tubular, orange, two- to two-and-one-half-inch flowers. Flowers of some other species appear banded, usually orange with paler yellow tips, but sometimes with creamy pink or green bands as well.

Other sprawling cleistocacti to consider planting are **C. dependens,** with one-and-one-half-inch-thick stems sporting reddish gray spines and two-inch tri-colored flowers, or **C. ferrarii,** which also has attractive spination as well as tri-colored flowers.

Above: Cheiridopsis denticulata. Below: Cleistocactus chacoanus.

CORYPHANTHA MISSOURIENSIS VAR. CAESPITOSA Cluster-forming cactus, two to three inches tall, with beige to gray spines and fragrant yellow-green flowers borne in summer. Partial sun. Extremely hardy to -30° F. Fast growing. Zones 3-10.

COTYLEDON ORBICULATA Shrub two to three feet tall with branching stems and grayish white narrow to broad leaves. Bears inflorescences of red to orange pendent flowers in summer. Full sun to partial shade. Hardy to the mid 20s F. Fast-growing. Zones 9-10.

COTYLEDON TOMENTOSA SSP. LADYSMITHIENSIS Shrubby one-foot plant with fleshy, ovate, toothed leaves and pendent orange flowers borne in summer. Partial shade; protected site. Moderate growth rate. Zones 9-10.

CRASSULA ARBORESCENS (SILVER JADE PLANT) Branching shrub eventually to ten feet tall with waxy glaucous gray leaves and white or pale pink winter flowers. Full sun to partial shade, warm conditions. Slow to medium growth. Zones 9-10.

CORYPHANTHA MISSOURIENSIS *Cactaceae*

Native to Canada and the U. S. from North Dakota and Montana south to Texas and seen fairly commonly anywhere on the Great Plains, *Coryphantha missouriensis* is a truly hardy cactus, readily surviving temperatures as low as -30° F. It is probably the best globular-form cactus for northern gardens. For many gardeners, the principal charm of this species may be its hardiness; but an established plant can be quite attractive. It forms a two- to three-inch solitary globe (or larger cluster in var. *caespitosa*) with beige to gray spines and fragrant, yellow-green flowers, about one inch across, with delicate, eyelashlike hairs on the petal margins. Flowers are borne intermittently throughout the summer months. Colorful red, spherical fruits are often present simultaneously with the later season flowers.

To maintain the best appearance, *C. missouriensis* benefits from supplemental summer watering. During winter dormancy or under prolonged drought conditions, plants resemble flaccid, gray lumps on the ground; some retract completely underground. They promptly revive when watered in the spring.

C. missouriensis is not offered for sale commonly, but larger succulent nurseries still maintain and distribute selections.

C. vivipara is another widespread U.S. native ranging from Canada through the Great Plains to Mexico. There is an ecotype to fit practically any climate or hardiness zone. The common feature of nearly all the forms is bright magenta flowers with fringed petals similar to those of *C. missouriensis*.

C. recurvata, from Arizona and adjacent Sonora, Mexico, forms clumps of stout, oblong stems to six inches in diameter, densely clothed with golden spines. The flowers are inconspicuous greenish yellow. This species can take full desert sun, while the previous two generally prefer partial shade from grasses or other plants.

COTYLEDON *Crassulaceae*

The genus *Cotyledon* includes several desirable landscaping candidates; most are better-suited for southern California and do not perform well in the Arizona desert. From the Cape Province of South Africa comes **C. tomentosa ssp. ladysmithiensis** (often misspelled 'ladismithensis'), a shrubby one-foot perennial with thin, softly hairy branches that terminate in clusters of one- to two-inch leaves. *C. t.* ssp. *ladysmithiensis* is grown primarily for its unusual foliage. Individual leaves are egg-shaped, apple green, very thick and fleshy, and covered with minute white hairs. Leaf margins at the tip have small teeth and are tinged red. Flower stems are six inches tall, bearing eight to ten fuzzy, pendent, orange flowers.

C. t. ssp. *ladysmithiensis* grows best in partial shade and is most commonly grown as a container plant. However, in a protected site it should prove suitable in the landscape.

C. orbiculata, native to mountainous regions of Namibia and the Cape Province of South Africa, is a much larger shrub, two to three feet, and the most common member of the genus in cultivation today. Several forms are

Cotyledon macrantha.

CRASSULA CAPITELLA 'CAMPFIRE' Bright green leaves are suffused with red; compact clusters of white flowers bloom in spring. Grows to one foot tall. Full sun to partial shade. Fast growing. Zones 9-10.

CRASSULA PERFOLIATA VAR. FALCATA (AIRPLANE PLANT) Shrub to one to two feet with fleshy gray-green leaves and stalks of shiny bright red to orange flowers borne in summer. Full sun to partial shade; will not tolerate hard frost. Fast growing. Zones 9-10.

CRASSULA PUBESCENS SSP. RADICANS Small creeping ground cover with red leaves and clusters of pale yellow to white flowers. Full sun produces brightest foliage; hardy to the mid 20s F. Fast growing. Zones 9-10.

CYPHOSTEMMA JUTTAE Deciduous plant with three- to six-foot caudex, glaucous green toothed leaves, and insignificant yellow flowers followed by red grapelike fruits. Full sun. Hardy to the lowers 20s F. once established. Slow to moderate growth. Zones 9-10.

Left: Potted echeverias and *Cotyledon tomentosa* ssp. *ladysmithensis,* with a hanging *Sedum burrito.*

available in nurseries; most are hardy to at least the mid-20s. Stems are thick, erect, and freely branching. Leaves are variable in shape, from broad egg-shaped to spindle-shaped, from one-and-one-half to five inches long, grayish white, somewhat waxy or mealy, and often red-margined. Inflorescences reach two feet and bear about eight to ten pendent one-inch red to orange flowers in summer (late winter to early spring in the Arizona desert). Once established, this fast-growing species will thrive. In fact, it has naturalized in southern California near coastal Newport Beach.

Other *Cotyledon* species worthy of garden attention include **C. macrantha,** a low shrub with large, red-margined green leaves, about six inches long and three inches wide, and pendent orange flowers; and the freely reseeding **C. campanulata** (syn. *teretifolia*), with stout, terete, fuzzy green leaves with red tips and pendent yellow flowers borne in summer.

CRASSULA *Crassulaceae*

Crassula is a large, diverse genus with the majority of the species native to South Africa; though thriving in southern California, most species are intolerant of the summer heat in the Arizona desert. The most familiar to indoor gardeners is **C. ovata,** the common jade plant, a common sight with its shiny

Crassula pubescens ssp. *radicans* (small form) with *Aloe* and *Sedum*.

green, oval leaves. **'Ruby Jade'**, **'Crosby's Pink'**, and **'Hummel's Red'** are recommended selections with pleasant pink flowers; all have red-margined leaves when grown in full sun. **Crassula arborescens,** the silver jade plant, is a popular landscape subject. Although relatively slow-growing in pot culture, when planted in the ground it will flourish. The silver jade plant forms a shrub eventually to ten feet tall with stout trunks and branches. Leaves are one-and-one-half to two inches long, waxy, rounded, and glaucous gray; when grown in sun, leaves have red margins and fine dots on both surfaces. White or pale pink flowers are borne at branch tips in three- to four-inch bouquets in winter. Freezing temperatures injure *C. arborescens*, but plants will put forth new growth if damaged material is removed in late spring.

C. capitella, a complex species of variable form, is a smaller plant with short stems and basal rosettes of pointy two- to three-inch leaves. Flowers are white, borne in erect, elongate clusters. Plants are readily propagated by rooting the easily detached leaves, or by stem cuttings or division. *C. capitella* **'Campfire'** has bright apple green leaves suffused with red; *C. capitella* ssp. **thyrsiflora** (synonymous with *C. corymbulosa*) has dark red foliage when grown in intense sunlight and floppy inflorescences of musty, sweet-smelling flowers.

C. perfoliata var. **falcata,** the airplane plant, is a one- to two-foot shrub, usually branched. The gray-green, sickle-shaped leaves are thick and fleshy, four to six inches long, with blades standing nearly vertical to expose only the margins to severe midday sun. (Or are the plants maximizing photosynthetic surface area by allowing both sides of the leaf to receive sunlight? Research is under way to clarify this question.) Long-lasting inflorescences form in summer and are tall, fleshy stalks bearing hundreds of small, shiny bright red to orange, clove-scented flowers. *C. p.* var. *falcata* is propagated by seed, shoot cuttings, or leaf cuttings and is not tolerant of hard frost.

For growth in a shadier location, *C. lactea,* a fleshy perennial one foot tall, is a likely candidate. Stems are thick, with short branches that may be either erect or reclined. Leaves are one to two inches long, fleshy, flattened, and green with fine dots. Flowers are numerous, borne in scented white or pale pink clusters in winter. *C. multicava* also does well in shade where its nearly round, flat leaves become dark green. Flower stalks are delicate, branched, and pinkish, bearing white to pale pink blooms.

C. rupestris, often called the bead vine, is a highly variable, dwarfed, bushy species. It is typically grown in hanging baskets or trailing over a wall. Woody stems are slender and spreading; tightly packed leaves are small (less than one inch), blunt, and broadly triangular. The leaves sport varying shades of green and in sun are red-margined or entirely suffused with red or orange. In fact, the whole plant becomes bright red if grown in intense sunlight. Small pink or white flowers with a musty, sweet fragrance are borne in clusters. *C. rupestris* is easily propagated by cuttings taken in any season.

C. pubescens ssp. **radicans** is a small, creeping groundcover with intense red leaves in bright sun and capitate clusters of fragrant pale yellow to white flowers. It is hardy to the mid-20s.

CYPHOSTEMMA JUTTAE *Vitaceae*

This unusual caudiciform member of the grape family is native to Namibia and South Africa. Several short, thick branches emerge from the top of a massive caudex, three to six feet tall. The bark is yellow-green and peels off like paper in older specimens. Leaves are glaucous green, sometimes tinted red, to one foot long, with coarse teeth. Insignificant creamy yellow flowers are followed by red, grapelike fruits that are toxic if eaten.

Plants are leafless during winter, providing an interesting view of the stocky caudex. They are not resistant to severe frost, though established plants will tolerate temperatures in the lower 20s. Leaves do not reappear until May, even after the mildest of winters.

Cyphostemma juttae should receive adequate water and light fertilizing during the summer growing season for best growth. Propagated material available at the larger succulent nurseries is always seed grown, although even fresh seed germinate somewhat erratically. Plants with three- to four-inch caudexes (seedlings two or more years old) are ready to move from containers into the ground.

Ferocactus glaucescens with *Pelargonium echinatum, Calibanus hookeri,* and *Crassula muscosa.*

DELOSPERMA FOR COOL CLI-MATES

The live-forever family (Aizoaceae or Mesembryanthemacea) are usually associated with mild, Mediterranean climates, such as California, where they are used widely for landscaping. In recent years, however, over a dozen genera and dozens of species of ice plants collected at high elevations in South Africa have been shown to tolerate subzero cold at Denver Botanic Gardens. The genus *Delosperma* has proved to be particularly valuable as groundcover, particularly the species *D. nubigenum* and *D. cooperi*. *D. nubigenum* forms a very tight, rapidly spreading mat an inch or two high, covered with yellow flowers for several weeks in mid spring, that is a uniform green all summer and turns deep purple in winter. It can spread to a yard across in a year if properly sited. *D. cooperi* forms a larger mat with bluer foliage that stays rather uniform in color throughout the season; it forms a two-foot-wide mat, spangled with two-inch-wide purple-pink flowers from late spring to early summer. Due in large part to the efforts of Denver Botanic Garden's horticulturist Panayoti Kelaidis, these plants are being seen in more and more nurseries around the country.

DASYLIRION *Agavaceae*

Dasylirion is native to the southwestern U.S. and northern Mexico. The genus includes about fifteen species of rosette plants, mostly stemless, but a few more treelike. Numerous slender, arching leaves, often with spiny margins, spray forth from a central trunk to produce a graceful, rounded silhouette. In spring, a tall, paniculate inflorescence bearing bell-shaped, creamy white flowers emerges from the center of the plant.

Most *Dasylirion* species tolerate cold and drought very well. Moderate irrigation for the first two years after planting will assure that plants establish well. Once established, supplemental watering is not essential, though it will generate faster growth. Planting locations should be well-drained. Full-sun growth will be the most robust and symmetrical, but light shade will still allow striking specimens to flourish. *Dasylirion* also makes an excellent patio plant, though requiring a large container. **Dasylirion texanum,** also called sotol, comes from elevations over 2,200 feet in west Texas and adjacent northern Mexico. Leaves are glossy green and rather rigid, three feet long and about one inch wide, with recurved, rust-colored teeth along the margins. Mature plants are about four feet tall, with a spread of about the same. Greenish white flowers are borne in late spring and early summer on twelve-foot inflorescences.

D. longissimum is a striking species from interior Mexico with fountain-like rosettes of numerous, long, linear quarter-inch wide green leaves that arch gracefully. Rosettes are typically about five feet across, with russet-colored inflorescences reaching to ten feet.

D. wheeleri is from higher elevations (3,000-6,000 ft) of the extreme southwestern U.S. and northern Mexico. Its short woody trunk, occasionally branched, bears a basal, symmetrical, spherical rosette of three feet long, one inch wide, sword-shaped, blue-green, serrated leaves. Clumps are about three to five feet tall and four to five feet in diameter. Five- to fifteen-foot-tall plumes of very small, cream-colored flowers are borne in early summer. *D. wheeleri* is hardy to around 0° F. Plants are propagated easily from fresh seed planted in spring or young plants can be separated from the parent clump in late winter for transplanting if necessary.

DELOSPERMA *Aizoaceae*

Delosperma is a group of succulent shrubs or shrublets, densely branched and prostate to spreading. They need rich, well-drained soil that is not too damp and a sunny location; in winter, soil should be drier. Most vegetative growth occurs in summer, but the plant flowers almost all year. Propagation is easily accomplished through cuttings or seed. Species include **D. pruinosum,** which has solitary yellow or white flowers and **D. algoense,** with snow-white flowers. **D. nubigenum,** a fast-growing alpine with yellow flowers from Lesotho flowers is hardy from Zones 4 through 9 and **D. cooperi,** with bright purple-pink flowers from late spring to early winter, has proved hardy in the drier parts of Zone 5 through Zone 9; both need occasional water in the summer in dry areas.

DASYLIRION WHEELERI Forms a spherical three- to four-foot rosette of slender gray leaves with toothy margins. Full sun. Tolerates extreme drought or tropical moisture. Moderate growth rate. Zones 9-10.

DELOSPERMA COOPERI Forms a mat of bluish foliage up to two feet across, with two-inch bright purple-pink flowers in late spring to early winter. Full sun. Zones 5-9, may need watering in dry areas.

DIOSCOREA ELEPHANTIPES (ELEPHANT'S FOOT) Large tuber, to three feet in diameter, with corky protuberances; twining stem bears heart-shaped leaves and insignificant flowers. Full sun or partial shade. Slow to moderate growth. Hardy with winter protection to Zone 9.

DRACAENA DRACO Imposing dichotomously-branched tree with thick nearly horizontally spreading branches forming a topheavy-looking crown, yet not at all prone to breaking or toppling. Vigorous with ample water and fertilizer, slow otherwise. Full sun to partial shade. Zones 9-10.

We opened a leafe where the seede was and the leafe being opened there did appeare a Dragon, made with so much arte, that he did seem as though he had been alive, havying a long neck, the mouthe oppen, the bristles standying up like thornes, the Talye long and standying up on his feet, that surely there is no man whiche shall see hym that will not have marvell to see his Figure is made with so much arte, that it seemethe made of Ivorty and that no craftesman so perfit could make in better, in seeying what I sawe there did represent to mee so many aucient writers had, speaking a thousand desperate sauyings, because that thei would come to ye right knowledge to instruct us, wherefore it was called the bloud of Drago.
NICHOLAS MONDARDES, 1512-1588, FROM *JOYFULL NEVVES OF THINGS FOUNDE IN THE NEWE WORLDE.*

Below: Drosanthemum floribundum, a perennial groundcover often planted on slopes. Note that the portion in shade flowered just as profusely as the rest, but was delayed by about two weeks.

DIOSCOREA ELEPHANTIPES *Dioscoreaceae*

Dioscorea elephantipes, the elephant's foot, is another South African native. Somewhat bizarre in appearance, the plant consists of an eventually huge tuber, to three feet in diameter, with half or more above the ground. The tuber is edible, and was consumed by the Khoi-San people in its native South Africa in times of famine. The woody surface of the tuber is covered with faceted protuberances that exhibit annular growth rings. From the tuber emerges a twining stem, up to six feet long, that is somewhat woody and bears one-inch, heart-shaped, green leaves. The flowers are very small and insignificant and are produced on separate male and female plants.

The elephant's foot is hardy with winter protection in Zone 9. Though it is a winter grower, it can retain foliage year round where clement weather is the rule. Young seedlings not well established should not receive water when dormant.

D. macrostachya, a large Mexican, summer-growing vine, forms a flatter caudex with less prominent tubercles and larger, more elongate leaves. Trade in larger plants collected in the wild is no longer legal, and seedlings are uncommon in the nursery trade, though worth trying when available.

DRACAENA *Agavaceae*

Dracaena draco, the dragon tree, is native to the Canary Islands where it may reach enormous size, up to seventy feet in height. Stout, silvery-gray trunks remain unbranched for many years but eventually form a dense dome of thick, dichotomous branches. Two-foot rosettes of glaucous, blue-green leaves form at branch ends. Panicles of small, greenish flowers mature to form bright orange-red berries.

Dragon trees grow well in full sun or partial shade. Established specimens are hardy to about 20° F., although they may suffer some scarring from extended frost.

Damaging the plant results in the exudation of a dark red resin at the scar sites; this product, called "dragon's blood," has been collected commercially since ancient times, so extensively that *D. draco* has become an endangered species in the wild.

DROSANTHEMUM SPECIOSUM *Aizoaceae*

Drosanthemum speciosum, the dew flower or ice plant (only one of many "ice plants"), is a ground-hugging, fast-growing, branched shrub to about three feet. Branches are slender and gray with prominent internodes. Glistening green, nearly cylindrical leaves curve upward. Showy flowers are bright orange to crimson (sometimes with two-toned petals), about two inches across, somewhat cup-shaped, and borne singly. Spring-blooming in mild climates, *D. speciosum* is summer-blooming elsewhere. Flowers always close at night and open at midday.

D. speciosum is best grown in full sun with good drainage. It is hardy to Zone 9. The ice plant's main charm (besides its colorful flowers) is its extreme heat tolerance. Thus, it thrives in inland southern California and the low deserts. Although plants can survive long periods without watering, for best appearance they should receive occasional water in summer, as well as mini-mal fertilizing to support vigorous growth. Older plants may occasionally become rather sparse or rangy looking; pruning back to encourage new growth is recommended. Some gardeners may prefer to simply restart the plant from cuttings every four to five years. Cuttings are easily rooted if taken during the cool winter months. **D. bicolor** is similar to *D. speciosum* except for flower color, and is not quite as hardy.

D. floribundum, often mislabeled as *D. hispidum,* has hot pink flowers. It is grown extensively along the California coast between San Diego and Santa Barbara, turning whole hillsides bright pink in late spring.

When selecting a planting site for Drosanthemum, remember that it is easily damaged by trampling.

DUDLEYA *Crassulaceae*

Dudleya is a rosette-forming genus native to California and Mexico. They are generally coastal and grow in winter. Those mentioned here are more tolerant of summer water and a wider range of garden conditions.

D. brittonii, from coastal Baja California, is the most garden-worthy *Dudleya* in cultivation. It forms solitary, one-foot upright, bowl-shaped rosettes of numerous six- to ten-inch-long, one- to three-inch-wide, powdery white leaves (or green leaves, though the former is more desirable). Young plants have upright stems; in older plants, the stem elongates and becomes procum-bent, but the leaf rosettes always face upright. Flower stalks, usually pale pink

Stenocereus eruca and *Dudleya brittonii* at Huntington Botanical Garden.

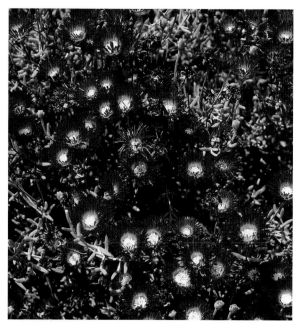

DROSANTHEMUM SPECIOSUM (DEW FLOWER, ICE PLANT) Prostrate shrub to three feet with slender gray branches, upward-curving leaves, and bright orange to crimson spring- or summer-blooming flowers. Full sun; heat tolerant. Vigorous. Zones 9-10.

DUDLEYA VIRENS Trailing stems, to twelve inches, bear rosettes of narrow, bright green to lavender gray or chalky white leaves and inflorescences of creamy yellow spring flowers. Full sun to partial shade; hardy to 25° F. Moderate growth rate. Zones 9-10.

DYCKIA 'EIGHT BALL' A hybrid of uncertain parentage, named here for the first time and presumably containing both *D. fosterana* and *D. platyphylla* in its lineage. Forms four- to six-foot hemispherical mounds of dark purple leaves with silvery undersides. Full sun. Moderate growth rate. Zones 9-10.

ECHEVERIA AGAVOIDES Fleshy rosettes of light green to gray-green leaves, often with red or darker markings as in cultivar 'Ebony'; slender stalks bear long-pedicelled pinkish flowers with yellow tips. Full sun, some afternoon shade in summer; hardy to the teens. Moderate growth rate. Zones 8-10.

to red in color, appear between April and June and are one to three feet tall, bearing small, pale yellow flowers. *D. brittonii* is considered hardy to about 30° F.

D. virens produces stems to twelve inches long that trail along the ground and branch to form many cup-shaped, three-inch rosettes. Leaves are fewer and much narrower than in *D. brittonii,* and range in color from bright green to lavender gray or chalky white. Inflorescences reach eighteen inches in height, bearing small, wide-open, creamy yellow flowers in spring. *D. virens* is hardy to at least 25° F.

Other dudleyas are worthy of note, including the native southern Californian-Arizonan species, **D. pulverulenta,** which resembles a flatter, sparser *D. brittonii* but is tricky to cultivate. For a more heat tolerant plant capable of survival even in the low desert, **D. arizonica** and **D. saxosa** are recommended. For the rockery, **D. greenii 'White Sprite'** is a chalky white, very compact cluster of two-inch rosettes. **D. cymosa** presents more floral interest, with its showy yellow or orange flowers. Often from higher elevations, it also displays greater cold hardiness, but is somewhat difficult to grow.

A combination of cool nights (40° F.) and rainfall trigger winter to spring growth in dudleyas. They should be grown in partial shade anywhere away from the coast (*D. brittonii* can take full sun) and not overwatered during their summer dormancy period. Some gardeners find that dudleyas are very difficult to grow unless water is drained out of the rosette; planting them sideways helps. Many cannot tolerate the summer heat in the Arizona desert.

Dudleyas are propagated from seed sown in winter; count on at least one year passing before seedlings are large enough to be planted directly in the ground. Offsets are desirable if available. Cuttings from older plants that have become leggy can be taken and rerooted successfully only during the winter months. One other note on *Dudleya* cultivation: when watering dudleyas, care must be taken as high-pressure watering can remove the white chalky covering from the leaves.

Hechtia argentea.

DYCKIA *Bromeliaceae*

Dyckia fosterana, a terrestrial, Brazilian native in the pineapple family, forms a small, solitary, silvery purple rosette to about six inches, with recurved leaves bearing silvery spines along the margins. Long-lasting inflorescences are unbranched, with brilliant orange flowers from spring to summer. *D. fosterana* branches or offsets to form clumps more slowly than other species. Foliage color is most striking when plants are grown in full sun, but they will easily tolerate partial shade. *D. fosterana* is both frost and drought tolerant.

A number of cultivars and clonal selections of *D. fosterana* are available. For example, **'Foster's Original'** is a white clone. Hybrids of *D. fosterana* and *D. platyphylla* having different foliage colors exist in the nursery trade as well, such as **'Hummel's Olympiad'** with dark purplish leaves and **'Eight Ball'** with very dark purple leaves with silvery undersides in six- to ten-inch rosettes which clump to form dense hemispherical rounds four to six feet across; the flowers are the typical orange, borne on arched spikes.

Above: Echeveria gibbiflora selection with E. pulvinata (white). Below: E. agavoides, Echinocactus grusonii, Dyckia 'Eight Ball', Sedum nussbaumerianum.

Hechtia, a related genus, also has some attractive species for landscaping purposes. In general, hechtias make pleasant foliage plants, but their flowers are less noteworthy than those of *Dyckia*. However, they have the advantage in hardiness. Hechtias are more difficult to obtain in the nursery trade. Most are very spiny, and thus somewhat difficult to handle. *H. argentea* is one of the best, if you can find it.

ECHEVERIA *Crassulaceae*

Echeveria, another rosette-forming Mexican genus, features several outstanding garden plants. Several species are sometimes called hen-and-chicks, a reference to their offsetting habit.

E. agavoides forms firm, fleshy, dense rosettes with epidermal cells that seem to glisten in the sunlight. Leaves are four to eight inches long, usually light green to gray-green, often with red margins near the stiff, spinelike leaf tips. Stems are thick and short, usually offsetting to form clumps. Flowering stalks are slender, about eight to twenty inches long, with a few one-half-inch flowers; they have pinkish corollas with yellow tips. But this species is grown for its foliage, not its inconspicuous flowers. *E. agavoides* is the hardiest of the

Echeveria 'Pulv-Oliver'.

echeverias listed here, enduring temperatures in the teens.

Several *E. agavoides* cultivars have been selected for garden use, including **'Ebony'**, which has dark purplish brown leaf margins, and **'Red Edge'** and **'Lipstick'**, both with strongly red-margined leaves. Entire leaves of **E. agavoides 'Rubra'** blush red in full sun. **E. agavoides var. corderoyi** is a more floriferous version of the species that also has more leaves per rosette. Light frost brings out leaf color. Overwatering and overfeeding can diminish leaf color.

E. colorata rivals *E. agavoides* in hardiness, weathering temperatures in the low 20s. Several hybrids of these two species exist; they share the cold tolerance of their parents and are often suffused red like *E. agavoides*. *E. colorata brandtii* resembles some of these hybrids, forming formidable rosettes up to twelve inches across with numerous erect leaves six inches long and one-half inch wide. *E. colorata* var. *colorata* has eight-inch rosettes with fewer, broader leaves four inches long, to two inches wide, chalky white with red-margined tips. In cold weather, they take on a lovely pinkish-crimson look.

E. elegans is a smaller species that grows best in partial shade, with leaves densely crowded in a tight rosette about four inches across. Because of its compact, clumping form, it is ideal for planting in tight spaces or pocket rockeries. The thick, swollen leaves are pale olive green to white with faintly translucent margins. Inflorescences are about ten inches tall, with one-half-

Echeveria x *imbricata,* grown in full sun, forms dense mats of many-leaved rosettes. Shade-grown rosettes, such as that seen in the picture on the opposite page, have a more open and symmetrical appearance.

inch light pink flowers. Very similar species are **E. albicans** and **E. potosina,** which differ only slightly in floral form.

E. pulvinata, sometimes called rosy hen-and-chicks, is an almost shrubby species with stems up to ten inches tall. Leaves are about two inches long by one inch wide; though green, their dense covering of soft white hairs lends the plant a silvery appearance. Inflorescences, up to a foot tall, branch horizontally and bear yellow to orange flowers half an inch long from winter to spring. Hybrids, such as the familiar **'Pulv-Oliver'**, are popular with collectors and form durable garden plants. 'Pulv-Oliver' has fuzzy green leaves with red margins and stays compact in full sun; it is hardier than species echeverias, being reliable to the low20s. Long-lasting inflorescences of orange flowers are pleasant, though not dramatic.

E. x imbricata, a hybrid between *E. glauca* and *E. gibbiflora* var. *metallica,* is one of the choicest for container or landscape use. It is tolerant of full sun or partial shade, forming rosettes about six inches wide, with gray-green to blue-green leaves. Water droplets from overhead irrigation look like spheres of mercury on the surface of the waxy rosettes. Flower stalks, appearing in spring, are about ten inches tall, bearing half-inch flowers with deep pink, yellow-tipped corollas.

Other *E. gibbiflora* hybrids and selections are also popular; most have bigger leaves, often with crinkly edges and warty surfaces. A favorite hybrid is **'Perle von Nurnberg'**, a cross of *E. gibbiflora* 'Metallica' and *E. potosina,* which has rich pinkish purple leaves and four-inch rosettes. **'Lace'** and **'Blue Curls'** have wavy pink edges. **'Paul Bunyan'** is covered with caruncles, and **'Arlie Wright'**, rich burgundy red throughout, is named for the daughter of Dick Wright of Fallbrook, California who has created most of the *E. gibbiflora* hybrids available. All of these benefit from annual beheading and rerooting to achieve maximum size.

Echeverias are inherently very drought resistant but will do best in the garden with periodic fertilizing and deep watering. Division of offsets is the easiest means of propagation, but seed, stem cuttings, and leaf cuttings are also used. *E. gibbiflora* selections are propagated from stem cuttings only; leaves may root but seldom if ever form new shoots. Nurseries sell vegetatively propagated material; shop around to select an attractive clone.

Transmission of plant-weakening viruses during propagation has lately become a problem in both dudleyas and echeverias. To avoid the spread of this slowly debilitating problem, precautions should be taken. See the chapter on techniques for details.

ECHINOCACTUS Cactaceae

Echinocactus grusonii, the Mexican golden barrel cactus, is certainly one of the quintessential landscape cacti. Globular, light green stems grow very large, up to four feet tall and two feet in diameter. Individual specimens are very long-lived and often offset in age to form massive clumps four feet tall and six feet across. Thick, golden yellow spines lend the plant its common name. Flowers

ECHEVERIA 'MORNING LIGHT' Four to five-inch rosettes of flat chalky lavender leaves with pink markings; ten-inch inflorescences bear half-inch pinkish flowers with yellow tips. Full sun to partial shade. Hardy to the upper 20s. Moderate growth rate. Zones 9-10.

ECHEVERIA ALBICANS Compact, clumping plant with thick, pale olive to white leaves in tight rosettes, four inches across. Ten-inch inflorescences bear half-inch pink flowers. Partial shade. Hardy to the upper 20s. Moderate growth rate. Zone 9-10. Shown with *E.* 'Perle von Nurnberg'.

ECHEVERIA X IMBRICATA Plant forming rosettes to six inches wide with gray-green to blue-green leaves and deep pink, yellow-tipped spring flowers. Full sun to partial shade. Hardy to the mid 20s. Vigorous. Zones 9-10.

ECHINOCACTUS GRUSONII (GOLDEN BARREL CACTUS) Globular, light green stems, eventually to four feet tall and clumping, bear thick, golden yellow spines and satiny yellow summer flowers. Full sun; hardy to the teens. Slow-growing in drought conditions. Zones 9-10, marginal in Zone 8.

Echinocereus scheerii var. *kobresianus.*

are satiny yellow, about two inches across, and borne in summer, usually several at once. **E. platyacanthus,** the spineless barrel cactus, also has nearly globular stems at first, but these are bright green and can reach nine feet in height in old age, often with wooly tops, and with diameters up to three feet. *E. platyacanthus* has prominent ribs like *E. grusonii,* but smoother and more symmetrical. *E. platyacanthus* stems typically do not form offsets. Flowers are yellow and about two inches across. **E. grandis,** a more uncommon species, is grown for its attractive red banding between ribs.

Most echinocacti are easily grown from seed. Liberally watered and fertilized, seedlings will grow rapidly. They are ready to be planted in the ground when stems reach about four inches in diameter, but protect new transplants from bright sun until they are established. Under drought conditions, they will survive but grow painfully slowly. Most echinocacti are reliably hardy to the teens.

Mature specimens are prone to unsightly scarring at the base as they age; this problem can be averted to a great extent by providing generous applications of fertilizer and ample water.

ECHINOCEREUS *Cactaceae*

Echinocereus triglochidiatus, one of the so-called hedgehog cacti of the Southwest, forms clumps of individual stems, each two to three inches in diameter and up to one foot tall. Clumps reach about three feet in diameter in great age. Numerous one-inch, pale gray spines cover the plant, making a large clump worthy of its hedgehog name. The goblet-shaped, one-and-one-half- to two-inch flowers are brilliant scarlet or crimson (pink and orange forms are also available) and remain open at night. The one-inch, oblong, bright red, fruits are also showy. The plant is hardy to at least 0° F. and does best in Zones 7-8.

E. engelmannii, native to the southwestern U.S. and northern Mexico, forms one- to two-foot-tall clumps, with individual stems three to four inches thick. It is hardy to the teens and has attractive two-and-one-half- to three-inch magenta flowers. It does best in Zone 9 and is marginal in Zone 8.

E. cinerascens, native to central Mexico, also has the clumping habit. Two-inch-thick stems, to one foot long, bear glassy white spines. Flowers are rose to magenta with paler throats, about three inches long, and borne in spring.

E. viridiflorus is a smaller species with stems to about six inches tall (but often only two inches and clustering) with attractive red and white spines. Flowers are small (one inch) and green and generate a pleasant lemony fragrance. Since *E. viridiflorus* is native to the American Great Plains, it can easily overwinter temperatures down to 0° F.

E. reichenbachii var. albispina from Oklahoma, another cold-hardy species, has six-inch-tall clumps of two-inch-wide stems bearing short, white spines and pink flowers with pale throats. Zones 7-10.

The larger-flowered Mexican *Echinocereus* species are popular with container succulent growers. A few species can prove effective for outdoor planting as well. **E. pentalophus** (from south Texas and Mexico) forms tangled, floppy

ECHINOCACTUS PLATYACANTHUS (SPINELESS BARREL CACTUS)
Nearly globular bright green stems, about two feet in diameter, bearing yellow summer-blooming flowers, grow to nine feet tall in old age. Full sun to partial shade. Slow growing. Zones 8-10.

ECHINOCEREUS TRIGLOCHIDIATUS (HEDGEHOG CACTUS) Plant forming stem clumps to three feet across with pale gray spines, goblet-shaped scarlet or crimson flowers, and bright red fruits. Full sun. Moderate growth rate. Zones 5-10, best in 7-8.

ECHINOCEREUS SCHEERI Tangled, floppy nine-inch stems form clumps; pink to magenta tubular flowers are nocturnal. Full sun to partial shade. Fast growing. Zones 9-10.

ECHINOCEREUS PENTALOPHUS Clump-forming plant with tangled six-inch stems and magenta flowers. Full sun to partial shade. Fast growing. Zones 9-10.

Echinocactus grusonii, Echinopsis terscheckii.

clumps of one-inch stems that topple over when they reach six inches in height; five-inch flowers are magenta with pale throats and prominent green stigmas. **E. scheeri** is vegetatively similar to *E. pentalophus,* but with longer stems (nine inches) and pink, red, or magenta tubular flowers in April. Both species are hardy to Zone 9, at least to the mid-20s.

The larger and spinier *Echinocereus* species grow best in full sun with superb drainage. Thinner-stemmed, less spiny species may prefer a bit of shade. Thin-stemmed species are propagated from cuttings; thicker-stemmed plants are easily grown from seed. Check larger succulent specialty nurseries for the species suggested here; smaller nurseries tend to supply *Echinocereus* plants more suitable to pot culture.

ECHINOPSIS *Cactaceae*

Echinopsis, the sea urchin or Easter lily cacti, includes a large group of South American plants whose generic status is especially muddled these days, with the genus recently having been expanded to include a number of other genera that were formerly segregated (*Lobivia, Trichocereus,* etc.). *Echinopsis* is most often represented in the landscape by one of its many hybrid forms. Globular, clumping forms of *Echinopsis* were popularized by Harry Johnson's Paramount hybrids, which entered the nursery trade after World War Two. **'Paramount Sunset', 'Peach Monarch',** and **'Stars And Stripes'** are three famous representatives of that series. Many other hybridizers have worked with the globular *Echinopsis* group since.

Taller, columnar forms of *Echinopsis* are represented in the nursery trade today by Mark Dimmitt's incredible hybrids that have been selected for their large, colorful, showstopping flowers. Cultivars include **'Apricot Glow',** with flower segments that are dark apricot orange at the tips grading to light yellow orange at the base, **'First Light',** with pastel pink petals with pale yellow bases, **'June Noon',** with yellow- and white-striped petals, and **'Volcanic Sunset'** with huge, flat, five-inch flowers of solid red-orange.

E. terscheckii (synonym *Trichocereus terscheckii*) is perhaps the largest member of the genus. Native to Argentina, it is reliably hardy to the teens and can withstand extreme heat as well. It makes an excellent substitute for the slower growing saguaro; it has the same habit and size but with ample water and fertilizer can grow eighteen inches a year and bear eight-inch-wide flowers.

Echinopsis grows best in full sun in moderate climates but may perform better in partial shade in hotter, inland zones. Growth is moderate to fast given supplemental watering and fertilizing. Plants are tolerant of most soil types, but will be most reliable with good drainage.

EPIPHYLLUM *Cactaceae*

Epiphyllum, the so-called orchid cacti, is native to tropical and subtropical America and the West Indies. *Epiphyllums* are predominantly epiphytic, making them ideal subjects for hanging baskets. At maturity, the spineless stems are flat and leaflike. Flowers are usually large, nocturnal, and fragrant. Colors

ECHINOCEREUS CINERASCENS Clumping plant with one-foot stems covered with glassy white spines; rose to magenta flowers are borne in spring. Full sun to partial shade. Moderate growth rate. Zones 9-10.

ECHINOPSIS 'CASSANDRA' One of a series of fairly globular Northridge hybrids created by Bob Schick, selected for its floriferousness and magnificent flowers which last only one day but are produced several times during the growing season. Full sun to partial shade. Fast growing. Zones 9-10.

ECHINOPSIS 'PEACH MONARCH' One of the many globular-stemmed hybrids grown for their large colorful flowers (six inches long, three inches across); forms clumps to one foot across. Full sun to partial shade. Fast growing. Zones 9-10.

ECHINOPSIS 'VOLCANIC SUNSET' Columnar stems to two feet long offset from the base to form clumps. Red-orange flowers to five inches across are produced off and on throughout the growing season. Full sun to partial shade. Moderate growth rate. Zones 8-10.

EPIPHYLLUM X MYSTIC MOOD (ORCHID CACTUS) Epiphytic plant with small flexible spines on three-angled stems. Diurnal four-inch flowers have magenta petals surrounding pale pink to white ones near the center. Partial to full shade. Fast growing. Zones 9-10.

EUPHORBIA XANTII Shrubby plant to six feet tall producing a tangled network of slender, barely succulent stems and bright pink cyathophylls, which fade to white, borne in late winter through spring and summer. Hardy to the 20s F. Fast growing. Zones 9-10. Shown with *Yucca valida*.

EUPHORBIA MILII (CROWN OF THORNS) Spiny shrub one to six feet depending on variety. Bright red bracts beneath flowers provide longlasting color through spring and summer. Full sun to partial shade. Moderate growth rate. Zones 9-10.

EUPHORBIA LAMBII Plant to six feet with slender blue-gray leaves in tufts at stem ends and chartreuse spring flowers. Full sun to partial shade; hardy to the mid 20s F. Fast growing. Zones 9-10.

range from white in most species through yellow, orange, and all shades of pink, red, and purple in hybrids which are diurnal and not as fragrant. Epiphyllums flower freely throughout southern California, but in the Phoenix area it is almost impossible to get them to flower outside the greenhouse. Parentage of hybrids for sale in nurseries might include *Aporocactus, Nopalxochia, Disocactus,* or *Heliocereus,* as well as *Epiphyllum.*

Among the species, **E. phyllanthus,** distinguished by its long floral tubes, is probably the hardiest, surviving temperatures down to 30° F. in protected sites. Stems can reach ten feet in length, with numerous two-foot branches. Oblong fruits are bright pink or reddish magenta and from two to three-and-one-half inches long. **E. crenatum** **'Chichicastenango'** is attractive even when not in bloom due to the unusual asymmetric lobing of the stems.

All epiphyllums are propagated by stem cuttings. Select a rooted cutting in bloom to be certain of obtaining the floral color you want and also to avoid purchasing a shy-flowering hybrid that rarely produces any bloom. As with echeverias and many other plants, precautions should be taken to avoid virus transmission in case your plant in a carrier. See Chapter 4 for details.

EUPHORBIA *Euphorbiaceae*

Euphorbia is a huge genus, primarily from Africa, whose members show a wide range of diversity in habitat and morphology. Care should be taken in handling all members of the genus, as all produce a characteristic white latex upon wounding. This latex ranges in toxicity from very poisonous to extremely irritating.

E. caput-medusae, the Medusa's head, is composed of numerous spineless stems, either lying on the ground or arched upward, covered with tiny, deciduous green leaves. The main stem (or "head") is stout and usually partially buried. Branches are one inch thick and up to thirty inches long. *E. caput-medusae* is grown for its bizarre shape and attractive large white or pink-edged nectar glands, which are borne in great numbers at the ends of the branches. This South African native is hardy to the low 20s. Moderate watering during the growing season is recommended. *E. caput-medusae* is propagated only from seed; cuttings of side branches will seldom form a central head.

E. milii, the crown-of-thorns, is a leafy, spiny shrub native to Madagascar. Depending on the variety, it can be between one and four feet in height, occasionally taller if allowed to climb on its neighbors, with branches proportionate to size, from one-quarter to one inch in diameter. *E. milii* eventually becomes woody. Stems are covered with sharp, thin, stipular thorns. Leaves are fleshy, ovals (or thinner and elongate) seen usually on young growth. Long-stalked inflorescenses bearing numerous red or yellow cyathophylls make this species showier in bloom than most euphorbias. If given sufficient water, particularly during the dry period, it will retain more leaves than if allowed to dry out completely. Some *E. milii* varieties hardy to the mid-20s include **E. milii var. splendens** and **E. milii var. hislopii,** both of which have bright red cyathia and reach about one and six feet in height, respectively. *E. milii* is recommended by the Desert

Epiphytes are unique plants which use other plants or rocks for support instead of soil. They are often found high in the canopy of the rain forest where there is light. They obtain water and nutrients from the humid air of the canopy and from debris that has settled and decayed in crevices where the plants are attached. They cling to their support with aerial roots and are not parasitic. This special group includes most orchids and bromeliads, as well as some cactus and ferns, among others. Roots of epiphytes need good air circulation or the plant suffers noticeably. *Above: Epiphyllum* growing on trees.

Yucca whipplei, Echinopsis huascha, Euphorbia resinifera.

Botanical Garden for the Phoenix area; most varieties thrive in Zone 10 and in Zone 9 with some protection.

E. grandicornis is a succulent, spiny, much-branched shrub that reaches about six feet. Lateral branches, which are clearly divided into segments of seasonal growth, are ascending, with three-angled stems that have horny, dark gray margins. Stems are solid green or lightly striped and three to six inches in diameter. Thorns borne in pairs on the stems are the dominant feature of the species; these are very hard, up to three inches long, and dark gray at maturity. *E. grandicornis* is usually propagated from cuttings, but it can be grown from seed. Seedlings are attractive, with green and white variegated stems. Old plantings become impenetrable thickets.

E. horrida is another shrubby form, but one that resembles a basally branching columnar cactus. The upright stems, six inches across, are beautifully ribbed, with many (up to fourteen), angled, winglike ridges to one inch high. Clusters of rough thornlike dried inflorescences, some up to two inches long, are borne along the ridges. Stems reach up to four feet tall and six inches in diameter and are hardy to the low 20's.

E. canariensis, the Canary Island spurge, forms a huge, spiny, much-branched shrub or tree to twenty feet tall and fifteen to twenty feet in diameter. (Typically, it is seen as a six- to ten-foot shrub.) Stems usually have five edges; they are punctuated by pairs of persistent, short brown spines that indicate where the minute, deciduous leaves were once borne. *E. canariensis* is very poisonous. It is reportedly hardy to the mid-20s, but one was damaged at Arizona-Sonora Desert Museum under a blanket at 26° F. It is best in Zones 9 and 10.

E. ingens (synonymous with *E. candelabrum*), from South Africa's Transvaal, is another spiny tree reaching up to fifty feet in height. With growth rates of several feet a year, it has been used as a timber tree in some parts of its native range. Stems are initially four-angled, eventually maturing into round trunks. Branches are erect, medium green, and leafless. Flowering branches have winglike ridges and small, inconspicuous spines that become very conspicuous if you handle the plant. Seedlings are dark green with paler green variegation. *E. ingens* grows best in full sun and tolerates a wide range of soil and moisture conditions. It can freeze to the gound in Zone 9, and thrives in Zone 10. It is among the more toxic euphorbias.

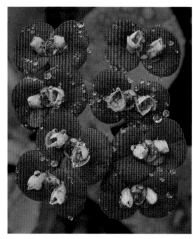

Above: Euphorbia milii flower. *Below: Cephalocereus polylophus* and a monstrose form of *Euphorbia ingens* at Ganna Walska Lotusland in Santa Barbara.

E. lambii is an attractive, leafy Canary Island species with slender gray stems bearing tufts of thin leaves at their tips and chartreuse flowers in spring. Individual plants live for five to ten years; under favorable conditions, they reseed freely. *E. lambii* is tolerant of a wide range of soils and is hardy to the mid-20s. It is typically grown from seed; cuttings are very difficult to establish. It thrives in Zone 10, where it can reseed itself.

E. mauritanica, the pencil euphorbia, is a spineless shrub that branches profusely to form a clump of cylindrical, pencil-thick stems about three to four feet tall and three to five feet across. One-inch green leaves, seen only on new growth, soon fall, leaving just the dense, erect branches. Attractive yellow cyathia are present during the early spring blooming season. *E. mauritanica* is hardy to the low 20s. Plant this species where young children or curious pets will not discover it; *E. mauritanica* is said to produce one of the more poisonous latexes found in the genus.

E. xantii, native to Baja California, produces a tangled network of slender, barely succulent, one-eighth-inch stems that form a shrub six to eight feet tall and can spread by underground runners. Long-lasting, bright pink cyathophylls appear in late winter and persist through spring, gradually fading to white. Cool night temperatures apparently produce a richer pink coloration. *E. xantii* is hardy to the 20s.

E. myrsinites is a smaller, more prostrate shrub to about six inches tall. Glaucous, one-inch-long gray-green leaves densely cover the stems and remain throughout the year. Cyathia are yellow. It is perhaps the hardiest species discussed here, surviving outdoors in Denver.

E. biglandulosa, an herbaceous perennial to two feet, grows from a rhizome, producing spreading to prostrate branches that form a clump three to five feet across. Leaves are glaucous, to two inches in length, and more widely spaced than in *E. myrsinites*. *E. biglandulosa* reseeds itself in southern California. Mature plants benefit from occasional pruning. Old, floppy stems should be removed after flowering to promote new, erect growth.

E. tirucalli, the milkbush, originally from tropical eastern Africa, is actually a succulent, spineless green tree, reaching up to thirty feet. Branches are usually clustered somewhat irregularly at the crown. Leaves are tiny and not persistent. *E. tirucalli* is hardy to about 25° F. The species is said to be very poisonous. It is used as a tall hedge in drier areas of South Africa and in other parts of the world. The cultivar **'Sticks On Fire'** is popular for its yellow-orange new growth.

FEROCACTUS   *Cactaceae*

Ferocactus is a North American genus composed mostly of desert species. All perform best with excellent drainage. Native to northern Mexico and the southwestern U.S., **F. wislizenii,** the fish-hook cactus, is a solitary globe when young, stretching into a column to six feet tall at maturity. Stems are about two feet thick, with many (twenty to thirty) ribs, and numerous needle-shaped, two-inch-long spines surrounding hooked and flattened three- to

All *Euphorbia* should be handled with care; use gloves and eye protection whenever handling them; make sure skin is not exposed. Although some species are innocuous, others are extremely caustic; some cause blisters and some squirt toxic latex several feet when cut. *Above: Aeonium lindleyi,* which is reputed to be an antidote for *Euphorbia* sap.

Opposite: Euphorbia xantii with deep pink flowers following a period of cool nights (40s); shown growing with *E. ingens, E. lambii, E. mauritanica,* an *Aloe striata* hybrid, and *Quercus agrifolia* (Coast Live Oak).

The ocotillo, like other out-standing individuals of the forest, has its following. Hummingbirds drink from the deep red tubes of its flowers borne at the tips of its long thorny stems in April and May. The desert mule deer relish the flowers and manage somehow to stamp the long stems down until they can reach their sweet-meat. The Indians make a sort of barbed-wire palisade out of the branched. I happened on a small burial plot tightly barri-caded by such a fence. Many of the stems had rooted and were green with leaves.
MAY THEILGAARD WATTS, FROM *READING THE LANDSCAPE OF AMERICA*

four-inch-long, central spines, that range in color from red to gray. The central spines have noticeable ribbing on their flattened surfaces. *F. wislizenii* is mid- to late-summer blooming, with flowers two-and-one-half inches long and usually orange but sometimes red to yellow, borne in a crown near the stem apex. Warty, lemon yellow, two-inch-long fruits soon follow.

F. wislizenii needs no supplemental watering where annual rainfall is at least ten to twelve inches. It is hardy to at least 5° F. *Ferocactus* is typically propagated by seed; plants with stems four inches in diameter are ready to plant directly in the ground. Larger plants, to two feet tall, that have been legally collected in habitat are sometimes available. Make sure such a specimen has a collection tag indicating its legal status.

F. herrerae, hardy to the teens, is a popular variety because of its ease of culture and attractive spination: central spines are heavy and red, while radial spines are white and bristly.

Other *Ferocactus* species can make worthy garden specimens. *F. acanthodes* (probably more correctly called *F. cylindraceus*), also native to the American Southwest and northern Mexico, looks quite similar to *F. wislizenii* but has denser spines. Since it is native to the Desert Botanical Garden area, it is easily found and often used there. *F. latispinus* var. *latispinus* is a very compact species, with globular stems appearing compressed in height, though up to sixteen inches across. Spines are prominent, flattened, hooked, and yellow to red in color. Flowers are usually purple, about two to three inches across, and borne in summer. This variety of *F. latispinus* is native to Mexico and is hardy to only the mid-20s.

F. emoryi var. *emoryi* (synonym *F. covillei*) from Arizona and northern Mexico is a choice slow-growing, heat-loving variety with bold clusters of few, stout hooked spines borne on widely spaced conical tubercles. The globular stem eventually becomes columnar with the tubercles merging to form ribs. Northern forms have bright red flowers, southern forms are gigantic plants with yellow flowers. This species is said to be depleted by commercial collecting and land development; purchase of seedlings is suggested.

F. emoryi var. *rectispinus* is a slow-growing variety from Baja California. It is characterized by long central spines, to ten inches, colored pinkish to gray. Stems are glaucous gray-green globes, eventually becoming cylindrical to six feet tall. Yellow flowers, two inches across, are produced in spring.

F. glaucescens is prized for its glaucous gray, globular stems and yellow spines. A beautiful clump-forming species; old plants are very decorative.

F. robustus, hardy to the low 20s, is a clumping species, unusual in a genus known for producing solitary stems. As an anomaly, it may be rather difficult to find. Mature specimens consist of bristly mounds three or more feet across, composed of individual four-inch stems. Flowers are yellow, one to two inches across.

FOUQUIERIA   *Fouquieriaceae*

Several species of *Fouquieria* make desirable landscape plants. *F. splendens,* the

EUPHORBIA INGENS Spiny tree to fifty feet tall with leafless, flowering branches bearing small spines. Full sun. Fast growing; a slower-growing monstrose form with weeping branches is shown here. Zones 9-10.

EUPHORBIA MAURITANICA (PENCIL EUPHORBIA) Spineless, profusely branching shrub with pencil-thick stems to three to four feet tall, bearing yellow cyathia in early spring; leaves are not persistent. Full sun to partial shade. Does not tolerate overwatering. Fast growing. Zones 9-10.

EUPHORBIA TIRUCALLI 'STICKS ON FIRE' (MILKBUSH) Succulent, spineless tree to thirty feet with yellow-orange stems in this cultivar; tiny leaves are not persistent. Highly poisonous. Full sun. Fast growing with little care except water. Zones 9-10; smaller plants freeze in Zone 9.

FEROCACTUS EMORYII Globular stems with bold spines borne on conical tubercles that merge into ribs as the plant becomes columnar. Red to gray spines and yellow summer flowers. Full sun. Slow growing. Zones 8-10.

Some succulent plants (not cacti) are filled with water—so full and tender that they are easily injured by physical contact. An innocent act such as bumping into a plant may result in broken stems or leaves or even a bruise that turns into a scar weeks after the incident is forgotten. Injuries usually heal and the plant survives, but is forever changed visually. Depending on the growth habit, scars may eventually be covered by new growth. Plants like *Gasteria armstrongii* (above) or *Dudleya virens* however, will have obvious scars forever. These plants grows slowly and in such a way that the broken tips and calloused creases in the leaves will always be visible. When a plant becomes unsightly, it should probably be replaced.

ocotillo, is one of the most distinctive and ornamental plants in the Sonoran desert. Ocotillo forms a shrub from five to twenty feet tall, with a spread of five to ten feet. Stems are slender and rigid, branching from the base, and turning from reddish brown in youth to gray with age; they are covered with thorns. Clusters of bright green, one-inch leaves clothe the stems after rains, but most of the year, the stems are barren. Spectacular brilliant lipstick-red flowers, each about one to two inches long, are borne in ten-inch clusters from March until June.

Ocotillo grows best in full sun or very light shade in well-drained soil. It is hardy to at least 10° F. and extremely heat tolerant. Although slow growing in its natural environment, ocotillo will grow vigorously if fertilized and provided with supplemental watering. Added water also causes the plant to retain its leaves for much longer periods.

Ocotillo is usually propagated from stem cuttings or from seed, but the latter is a slow process even in cultivation. It is sometimes seen growing as a living fence where individual branch cuttings have been lined out close together and rooted. A note of caution about wild-collected ocotillos: they are often collected just as they come into leaf, and though they may appear to be established, they aren't. Be certain to check the the plant's root system for rupture or shredding to avoid transplant shock and/or the need to reestablish. The best bet is to purchase an established ocotillo, not a newly harvested one.

F. columnaris, Baja California's Boojum tree, is a bizarre specimen hardy to the teens. Its columnar trunk may reach up to fifty feet (but usually twenty to thirty feet), tapering to the apex, often hollow, and bearing spreading, spiny branches. Bright green leaves are deciduous. Bell-shaped, creamy white flowers are borne in fifteen-inch panicles.

F. macdougalii and *F. diguetii* are shrubbier species with good basal branching, both about ten to twenty feet tall, hardy to the 20s, and bearing tubular red flowers. The former grows quickly and flowers in two to three years, over a long season; the latter takes twenty years to flower from seed.

Fouquieria seedlings are large enough to plant in the ground when the caudexes reach about one inch in diameter.

GASTERIA   Liliaceae

Gasteria, a South African genus, is characterized by swollen flowerbases. Most gasterias grow best in partial shade (they are typically grown under shrubs for protection from sun) and are hardy to the upper 20s in well-drained situations. They are propagated from offsets or rooted leaf cuttings. Leaves can be broken into as many as ten pieces, and each leaf section will root.

Gasteria acinacifolia, one of the largest species of the genus, forms two-foot rosettes of sword-shaped, very dark green leaves with transverse bands of small greenish white flecks. Leaf keels are off-center, giving the leaves an interesting asymmetry. Leaves are rounded at the tip, about fourteen inches long and two inches wide. Red flowers, about two inches long, are borne on four-foot-tall panicles. *G. acinacifolia* grows well in sun or shade, although shade is better for darker leaf color. Established plants withstand either mois-

FEROCACTUS ROBUSTUS Globular to columnar plant to six feet with thick, ribbed stems, red to gray spines, and orange or red to yellow summer flowers. Unusual for its clumping habit, forming mounds to three feet or more across. Full sun. Slow growing. Zones 9-10.

FOUQUERIA SPLENDENS (OCOTILLO) Shrub to twenty feet with reddish-brown thorned stems aging to gray and red flower clusters in spring. Full to very light shade; heat tolerant. Slow growing. Zones 8-10.

GASTERIA 'GREEN ICE' Plant to four inches with thick, warty, tongue-shaped leaves. Partial shade; hardy to the upper 20s. Slow growing. Zones 9-10.

GRAPTOPETALUM PARAGUAYENSE (GHOST PLANT) Plant with spatulate, glaucous-lavender to gray leaves and spotted white inflorescences in late winter and early spring. Full sun or partial shade; hardy to the mid 20s F. Moderately fast-growing. Zones 9-10.

ture or drought and are very resistant to common garden pests.

G. batesiana is a smaller species forming rosettes to eight inches with horizontally spread (even recurved), warty, rough leaves with irregular white bands. Leaves are broadly triangular to tongue-shaped and pointy. In intense light, they turn golden bronze to dark olive in color; in shade, they are dark green. Some *G. batesiana* hybrids are also available, most notably:

'Green Ice', a slow-growing selection with thick leaves of creamy green.

'Little Warty', a fast-growing, variegated clone with warty, striped gray and green leaves. 'Little Warty' offsets vigorously, soon forming clumps.

G. nitida var. **armstrongii**, often seen for sale as *G. armstrongii,* is a smaller (four-inch), slowly offsetting species with only two to five distichous, tongue-shaped leaves. Leaves are solid dark green, prostrate, and very thick and warty with pointed tips. A massed planting of a dozen or so plants is probably best to showcase this variety.

G. ellaphieae, G. glomerata, and **G. baylissiana** are all attractive dwarf species with bright orange flowers and distinctive foliage. They are the most recommended species for small pots and planters.

GRAPTOPETALUM *Crassulaceae*

Graptopetalum, closely allied to *Echeveria,* is another attractive rosette-forming genus native to Mexico. Most graptopetalums are better suited for container or rock gardening. However, **G. paraguayense,** the ghost plant, is an excellent landscape plant for either full sun or partial shade. *G. paraguayense* forms loose rosettes from one-foot stems that are initially erect but become prostrate. About fifteen to twenty-five fleshy, spatulate leaves, one-and-one-half to three inches long, thick, and pointy compose each rosette. Leaves are glaucous lavender, turning gray in age. Red-spotted white flowers, about half and inch across, are borne on branched six-inch inflorescences in late winter and early spring.

G. paraguayense is moderately fast growing and easily propagated by rooting detached leaves. It is hardy to the mid-20s and is also a good container plant.

x*Graptoveria* 'Opalina' is one of the many choice *Echeveria* hybrids produced by Robert Grim of San Jose, California and selected for their beautiful foliage. 'Opalina' is a hybrid of *Echeveria colorata* var. *colorata* and *Graptopetalum amethystinum*. It has plump rosettes of pink-flushed milky green leaves, reminiscent of the shifting colors of opal. It has proven hardy to the low 20s, a characteristic derived from *E. colorata,* which is also a very fine garden plant.

GYMNOCALYCIUM *Cactaceae*

Gymnocalycium is a widely distributed South American cactus genus that is quite easily propagated. One of the larger and more landscape-worthy species is **G. saglione.** Stems are solitary and globular, to about one foot in diameter, with thirteen to thirty-two low, rounded ribs that are somewhat tubercled. Stems of mature specimens eventually become columnar to about three feet,

Aeonium 'Zwartkop' and *Graptopetalum paraguayense* receive the afternoon shade of a cedar tree at Huntington Botanical Garden.

but they are very slow growing. Heavy, recurved brown to yellow-brown one-and-one-half inch spines cover the plant. Flowers, borne repeatedly throughout the growing season, are urn-shaped, white or flushed pale pink, and about one-and-one-half inches long. Fruits are red. *G. saglione* is hardy to the lower 20s.

G. denudatum is a squat species, about two to four inches tall and three to six inches across. Stems are globular and slowly offset to form clumps. The species is popular for its spidery spine clusters that are pressed against the surface of the stem and its large white to pale pink flowers, two to three inches in diameter. **'Pink Beauty'** is a choice selection with stronger pink flowers; several appear on the cover of this book.

G. stellatum is another compact species that makes for a distinctive mass planting. Stems are only one inch tall but four inches in diameter with a brownish color enhancing their resemblance to sea urchins. Flowers are off-white with reddish throats.

HAWORTHIA *Liliaceae*

A number of different South African *Haworthia* species are appropriate garden plants, especially appreciated as beautiful and unusual groundcovers. All perform best in part shade with supplemental watering. Most are easily propagated from offsets or cuttings.

H. attenuata forms a matlike growth of graceful rosettes, each about three inches in diameter. Lower leaf surfaces are glossy dark green with white bumps that sometimes merge into bands. About twenty varieties and forms of this species have been recognized. The best selections are prominently banded.

H. cymbiformis, the window plant, is another mat-former. Numerous squat

xGRAPTOVERIA 'OPALINA' Rosettes to six inches of plump pink-flushed milky green leaves. Full sun to partial shade. Moderate growth rate. Zones 9-10.

GYMNOCALYCIUM SAGLIONE Solitary globular stems to one foot across with tubercled ribs usually with heavy recurved spines. (This specimen is unusual for its lack of spines.) Flowers urn-shaped, white, one-and-one-half inch. Full sun to partial shade. Moderate growth rate. Zones 9-10.

HAWORTHIA ATTENUATA Mat-like plant comprised of triangular-leaved rosettes; lower leaf surfaces are glossy dark green with white bands. Partial shade. Moderate growth rate. Zones 9-10.

HAWORTHIA CYMBIFORMIS among a bed of *H.* 'Cuspidata'. Both make excellent groundcovers in partial to full shade. Fast growing. Zones 9-10.

Echeveria 'Violet Queen', *Sedum pachyphyllum, Haworthia coarctata.*

three-inch rosettes sucker to form a dense carpet. Leaves are broadly oval, about one-and-one-half inches long, smooth, and somewhat translucent at the apex. Leaves are usually light green but can become orangish in sunnier positions. A selection with variegated leaves is also very popular. Flowers, like those of most haworthias, are pale and insignificant. The wiry racemes are easily plucked to maintain a neater appearance.

H. 'Cuspidata' is a robust, dark green hybrid of *H. cymbiformis,* probably with *H. retusa,* with four-inch rosettes. It, too, makes a good groundcover in shade.

H. turgida looks similar to *H. cymbiformis* and is a typical shade-preferring species with smaller lance-shaped leaves, only three-quarters of an inch long, that are pale green in two- to three-inch rosettes.

H. coarctata is unusual in the genus for being a sun-loving species. Suckering stems to eight inches long and triangular to lance-shaped, dark green, two-inch leaves are usual, but in bright light, leaves turn deep red. The under surfaces of the leaves have bars of greenish white bumps.

HESPERALOE PARVIFLORA *Agavaceae*

Hesperaloe parviflora, the red yucca, is native from Texas to Mexico. It is a dense, clumping plant, very slow-growing, reaching a height of two to four feet with a spread of about the same. Leaves are narrow, grooved, gray-green, to three feet long; all together, they curve up from the base to form a stiff rounded clump. Distinctive fibrous threads decorate leaf margins. The fleshy flowers are showy dull red with yellow insides, nodding, just over an inch long and borne in clusters on four- to six-foot spikes in late spring and early summer. A less common creamy yellow-flowered form also exists.

   Hesperaloe grows best in full sun. Though inherently drought tolerant, it will perform best with about one inch of supplemental watering per month during the summer. It will also tolerate diverse soil conditions. New or established plants will benefit from light fertilizing in early spring. *Hesperaloe* is hardy to about 0° F. It is typically propagated by seed or by dividing mature clumps.

HYLOCEREUS *Cactaceae*

Aloe, Kalanchoe fedtschenkoi, Aeonium 'Sunburst'.

Hylocereus undatus is one of several cacti known as night-blooming cereus or queen-of-the-night. Its three-angled vining stems can climb about thirty feet

HESPERALOE PARVIFLORA (RED YUCCA) Clumping plant to four feet with narrow, grooved, gray-green leaves and dark red to cherry pink flower clusters in late spring-early summer. Full sun; hardy to 0° F. Slow growing. Zones 7-10.

HYLOCEREUS UNDATUS Three-angled vining stems climbing to about thirty feet with fragrant, night-blooming flowers up to twelve inches across. Edible red fruits are sometimes produced. Full sun or partial shade. Hardy to the mid twenties. Fast growing. Zones 9-10.

KALANCHOE BLOSSFELDIANA Plant to one foot tall with glossy dark green, red-margined leaves and bright red flower clusters borne in winter. Full sun or partial shade; hardy to the upper 20s F. Fast growing. Zones 9-10.

KALANCHOE MARNIERANA Plant to two feet with smooth-margined overlapping oval leaves and loose cymes of coral pink flowers with purple calyces. Shade tolerant; hardy to the upper 20s with protection. Fast growing. Zones 9-10.

KALANCHOE BEHARANSIS 'FANG' (FELTBUSH) Felt-covered branches bear triangular leaves with white fang-like proliferations on their undersides; fuzzy grayish flowers appear in spring. To twelve feet tall. Full sun to partial shade; tender. Fast growing. Zones 9-10.

KALANCHOE TOMENTOSA (PANDA PLANT) Felt-covered gray leaves with brown margins one two-inch long leaves. Fast growing. To two feet tall outdoor; often grown as a one-foot tall windowsill container plant. Full sun to partial shade. Fast growing. Zones 9-10, with protection.

KALANCHOE 'PINK ZINFANDEL' Foliage turns burgundy in winter; spring-blooming flowers are hot pink fading to pale pink. Full sun to partial shade; hardy to the mid 20s F. Fast growing. Zones 9-10. Shown with *K. grandifolia* in background.

LAMPRANTHUS SPECTABILIS 'PINK BETTY' Semiwoody perennial used as a mat-forming groundcover with glaucous, incurving leaves; pink daisy-like flowers begin blooming in April. Full sun, good drainage. Replant tip cuttings in winter to renew every few years as needed. Fast growing. Zones 9-10.

up the trunks of a palm tree. This vigor makes *H. undatus* one of the most common grafting stocks. In the landscape, *Hylocereus* can add interest to a tree trunk or create a large mounded shrub in the open. On summer nights, the dinner-plate-sized flowers emerge but wilt in the middle of the next day. This ephemeral beauty is sometimes followed by fist-sized, scaley red fruit with a delicious sweet flavor. The plant is hardy to the mid twenties.

KALANCHOE *Crassulaceae*

Kalanchoe is a large, diverse genus originating predominantly in South Africa and Madagascar with varied foliage types, usually fleshy, and simple to compound, often with scalloped or toothed margins. Colors cover a full spectrum of greens and pastels. They are generally tender, but several make excellent landscape plants with protection in Zone 9. In addition to their colorful foliage, many bear attractive flowers which are typically four-petaled and often pendent.

Some kalanchoes produces tiny plantlets along the leaf margins. When mature enough to grow on their own, they drop from the mother plant and take root wherever they fall. *Above: Kalanchoe daigremontiana* (devil's backbone).

K. blossfeldiana is a compact, bushy perennial up to one foot tall with erect stems and branches. Leaves are smooth, glossy dark green with crenate, red margins. Flowers are bright red, borne in clustered inflorescences that normally appear in January and last for many weeks. Flowering is controlled by photoperiod, so inflorescences can be induced at other times of the year by varying the light regime experienced by the plants. Most of the common kalanchoes in commerce are selected clones or hybrids involving this species, and many color variants are available now in a wide range from yellow through apricot to orange and even magenta flowers. All are hardy to the upper 20s.

K. fedtschenkoi, sometimes called rainbow scallops, is a scallop-leafed, erect plant to about two feet tall. Adventitious roots are frequently formed and dangle down from aerial regions to take hold where they brush the ground. Numerous leaves, one to two inches long, are crowded along the stems; these are typically gray-green but blush pink in full sun. Margins are reddish and strongly scalloped near the leaf tips. Flowers are borne in loose cymes. Corollas are coral colored, with each about one-and-one-half inches long. *K. fedtschenkoi* is propagated almost exclusively by stem cuttings. In full sun bedding, the pastel rainbow visual affect is quite pronounced.

K. marnierana is a two-foot-tall perennial with one-inch-long, smooth-margined oval leaves that are closely packed along the stems in an attractive, overlapping arrangement. Long-lasting inflorescences are loose cymes bearing one-and-one-quarter-inch flowers with coral pink corollas and bell-shaped purple calyces. *K. marnierana* tolerates shade better than most kalanchoes. It is hardy to the upper 20s when grown in a protected spot.

K. synsepala forms offsets at the end of long stolons like spider plants (*Chlorphytum*), lending itself to hanging-basket culture. It can also be used for mass plantings in protected shady areas. Its attractive large pointy leaves (to eight inches long and three inches wide) are glabrous green with red margins and

ICE PLANTS

Members of the *Aizoaceae* family are often called mesembs, a contraction of their former family name *Memsembry-anthemaceae.* This family is also commonly known as ice plants, a reference to species with glisten-ing water-storing cells on their surfaces that make them icy or crystalline in appearance. The word *mesemb* means midday, and many members of this fami-ly open in the midday sun. Some common ice plants are *Drosanthemum, Lampranthus,* and the ubiquitous *Carpobrotus* often seen planted along California's highways.

arranged in a few opposite pairs per stem. Hardy to Zone 9 with protection.

K. tubiflora, the chandelier plant, is a tall-growing species with slender, erect stems that rarely branch. Stems are gray-green to pale red, up to three feet tall, suckering at the base. Gray-green leaves are narrow and cylindrical, one to six inches long, and about one-quarter inch thick, with dark violet-brown flecks and several small teeth on both sides of the tip. Small plantlets are abundantly produced at the leaf tips. In the fall, the main stems ends growth with the formation of a one-foot-tall inflorescence with numerous one-and-one-half-inch, pendent, bell-shaped, salmon flowers. Because of the large number of plantlets produced, *K. tubiflora* can become a spreading nuisance. If you do not wish your colony to grow, cultivate the surrounding area to pre-vent establishment of the readily detached leaf sprouts. Alternatively, use this species as an under-planting element and enjoy the effect when inflorescences emerge through other foliage and bloom. *K. tubiflora* is widely naturalized in the tropics, as is the even more ubiquitous tropical weed *K. pinnata* (mother of thousands) with simple oval leaves with scalloped red margins. Individual leaves are sometimes sold for their remarkable ability to proliferate with adventitious marginal sprouts nourished entirely by the parent leaf.

K. beharensis, the feltbush of Madagascar, is a tender species widely valued for its sculptural merits. Four-sided, felt-covered branches bear distinct, angu-lar leaf scars. Leaves are triangular, four to fifteen inches long and three to fourteen inches wide, and usually crowded toward branch tips. *K. beharensis* performs well in full sun or partial shade, reaching heights up to twelve feet. It can also make an excellent, medium-sized container plant. Several different clones and hybrids are available in the nursery trade; these differ in leaves pri-marily, with some selections having rust-colored fuzz on the leaves and others being yellowish gray or naked. All have fuzzy dull gray or yellowish flowers. One cultivar, **'Fang',** has unusual cell proliferations on the undersides of leaves, causing the plant to look as if it is dripping with gray wax (or is abundantly provided with fangs.)

K. tomentosa, the panda plant, is a popular windowsill container plant but can also make an attractive mass planting outdoors in sheltered situations. It is hardy to the upper 20s. The typical form has two-inch-long one-half-inch-wide leaves covered with gray felt and ornamented with marginal brown blotches. Several color variants are also available: 'Chocolate Soldier', with brown fuzz covering the leaves and flowers and 'Ginger' with yellowish fuzz.

K. grandiflora, from India and East Africa, is an erect species, about two feet tall, with bluish gray green, oval leaves, two to three inches long, which have rounded teeth along the margins. Flowers are medium yellow, about one-half inch across, and pleasantly lemon-scented.

Kalanchoe 'Pink Zinfandel', a hybrid of unknown parentage, described here for the first time, is a handsome foliage variant, having burgundy-colored foliage in winter. In spring, long-lasting hot pink flowers are produced that fade over time to pale pink. 'Pink Zinfandel' is hardy to the mid-20s.

Opposite: *Lampranthus, Drosanthe-mum, Gazania.*

LAMPRANTHUS *Aizoaceae*

Lampranthus, another "ice plant," is tops for color intensity. All are fast-growing, mounding, or mat-forming groundcovers. They tend to become somewhat woody and leggy but are easily renewed by planting whole handfuls of cuttings directly in the ground in winter. They will root within a week or two.

Native to the Cape Province of South Africa, **L. spectabilis** is a somewhat woody perennial, about two to four feet across, with prostrate branches. The leaves, crowded on short shoots, are glaucous, about one to three inches long, incurving, and terminating in a red bristle. Solitary flowers, which open only on sunny days, are one-and-one-half to two inches across, on two- to four-inch pedicels, borne starting in April. Petals of the daisy-like flowers are purple or red-violet, and filaments are white. *L. spectabilis* is grown easily from cuttings taken in winter. There are many selected clones of note, including **'Pink Ice'**, with pale pink flowers, **'Pink Betty'**, with darker pink blooms, and **'Red Shift'**, which has smaller flowers that open red and turn magenta.

L. aurantiacus is initially an erect shrub; when it reaches about one foot in height, branches droop over and become prostrate, lending itself to use as a groundcover. Flowers of the species are yellow to orange and borne from February to March. Leaves are heavier-textured than those of *L. spectabilis.* Noteworthy cultivars include **'Glaucus'**, with pure, bright yellow flowers, **'Sunman'**, with yellow-orange blooms, and **'Gold Nugget'**, with day-glow orange flowers. 'Gold Nugget' is the most vigorous of the cultivars.

L. piquetbergensis, a more unusual species and hence more difficult to locate for sale, is a mounding groundcover grown as an attractive foliage plant, with dark red stems and gray, tugboat-shaped leaves (keel and all) with smooth margins. Flowers are small (less than one inch), medium pink, and borne in March.

L. deltoides (synonym *Oscularia deltoides*) is very similar to *L. piquetbergensis,* but bears a few red-tipped teeth on the leaf margins. It is also more readily available. Both are hardy to the low 20s.

LOPHOCEREUS *Cactaceae*

Lophocereus is native to northern Mexico and southern Arizona. **L. schottii,** called senita or whisker cactus, is a slow-growing but worthwhile landscape species for full sun locations. Senita branches from the base, with numerous stems rising from a central trunk at ground level. These gray-green stems, four to eight inches across, reach up to twelve feet tall. A single, well-branched senita specimen can be ten to twelve feet in diameter at maturity. Spines are gray and bristly, about two inches long at stem tips but shorter and stouter lower on the stems. Nocturnal flowers, borne in spring and summer, are medium pink and about one-and-one-half inches in diameter. Senita is hardy to the mid 20s, though scarring may occur after prolonged exposure to such temperatures.

Another popular landscape subject is the form of *L. schottii* called **'Monstrosus'**, the totem pole cactus. 'Monstrosus' is found only in Baja,

LAMPRANTHUS AURANTIACUS 'SUNMAN' Spreading shrub or groundcover to one foot tall; yellow-orange flowers bloom February to March. Full sun. Fast growing. Zones 9-10.

LOPHOCEREUS SCHOTTII 'MONSTROSUS' (TOTEM POLE CACTUS) Polelike, knobby spineless stems. Thrives in desert heat. Slow growing. Zones 9-10.

MAMMILLARIA GEMINISPINA Mound-forming plant to six feet across covered with numerous chalk-white spines; carmine-red flowers are slightly cup-shaped and bloom in spring. Full sun to partial shade with excellent drainage; heat tolerant. Moderate growth rate. Zones 9-10.

MAMMILLARIA COMPRESSA Clump-forming plant to six feet whose deeply tubercled stems are ringed with small red-purple flowers in spring; beige or white spines are recurved. Full sun to partial shade with excellent drainage; heat tolerant. Moderate growth rate. Zones 9-10.

California. Light green, somewhat glaucous stems have irregular ribs, giving the plant an unusual appearance: picture smooth lumps of wax that were stacked, compressed, and then slightly rotated. Spines are typically few or absent. 'Monstrosus' has been collected to near extinction; it is, however, well established in the nursery trade.

Both forms do best in full sun in intense desert heat, and are hardy to the teens.

MAMMILLARIA *Cactaceae*

Mammillaria has long been popular with container succulent collectors, but many species are also handsome in the landscape, and many are reliably hardy to the mid-20s or lower.

M. geminispina, from central Mexico, forms magnificent mounds up to six feet across in age (more commonly two to three feet), composed of stems up to eighteen inches tall, each about three inches across. Stems produce a milky sap when wounded. Spines are the dominant attraction in this species, being numerous and chalk white. Spine tips may be dark brown or black, but this

Mammillaria compressa, Sedum **x***rubrot inctum, Aloe striata* hybrid, *Senecio mandraliscae.*

feature is typically unnoticeable when plants are viewed from a distance. Flowers are carmine red, about one-half inch long, and somewhat cup-shaped.

M. compressa, also from central Mexico, forms six-foot clumps, with individual, deeply tubercled stems to twelve inches tall and four inches in diameter. Spines are recurved, less numerous than in *M. geminispina,* and beige or white, often with brown tips. Flowers are small (less than one-half inch) but make a colorful show of deep red-purple when produced in rings around each stem in spring.

M. muehlenpfordtii forms single green stems eight to twelve inches across and tall covered with numerous golden spines. *M. muehlenpfordtii* is noteworthy for its unusual (in cacti) dichotomous branching that often results in stems that resemble heads with eyes.

M. parkinsonii, commonly called "owl-eyes," is a smaller, white-spined species that also branches dichotomously. In both species, small purplish red flowers are borne in rings near the stem apex in spring and summer.

M. magnimamma is a large complex of clumping mammillarias. The choice forms have three- to four-inch green stems sporting strongly recurved, black-tipped spines and one-half-inch red flowers.

M. mystax belongs to a complex of large, solitary stemmed plants whose members are probably best for use as landscape accents. One form of *M. mystax* (synonym *M. huajuapensis*) has short, black spines and six-inch stems, blushing purplish red in intense sunlight. Other *M. mystax* forms have longer, tan spines to two inches that all but conceal the stems. Flowers are rose-purple and about one-quarter inch in diameter.

Mammillaria mystax.

MYRTILLOCACTUS *Cactaceae*

Myrtillocactus geometrizans, the blue candle, is native to Mexico and Guatemala. It is a candelabralike tree to about fifteen feet tall, with columnar branching stems and joints from one to three feet long and three to four inches thick. Stems are blue green when young with short spines and small greenish white, fragrant flowers to about one inch in diameter. In age, the spines are strong, thick, and brownish black and the stems have dark gray bark. Pea-sized fruits are wine red to purple, edible, and very sweet; they resemble raisins when dried. Plants typically will begin to flower when they are about two feet tall. *M. geometrizans* is somewhat tender (30° F.) and requires ample moisture year round.

M. cochal, native to Baja California, is another branching species with bluish green stems, though more gray-green than *M. geometrizans.* Some authorities in fact lump *M. cochal* together with *M. geometrizans.* However, *M. cochal* has more prominent, two-inch-long, flattened central spines and tends to lack a central trunk. It is also hardier, though neither is reliably hardy in any frost. Creamy white flowers open in daylight, often several together. This species is more difficult to locate in nurseries.

Both of these *Myrtillocactus* species have strong root systems and thus are sometimes used for grafting stock. *M. geometrizans* stems start to branch when

MYRTILLOCACTUS COCHAL Branching plant more than ten feet high and across with bluish-green stems and flattened central spines. Full sun to partial shade; hardy to the mid 20s. Fast growing. Zones 9-10.

NOLINA LONGIFOLIA Broad-trunked shrub to ten feet tall, topped by a fountain of long, thin, toothed leaves; creamy white flowers appear from May through June. Full sun; hardy to the low 20s. Moderately slow growing. Zones 9-10.

NOTOCACTUS LENINGHAUSII (GOLDEN BALL CACTUS) Plant forming clusters to three feet tall with saucer-shaped yellow summer-blooming flowers and ribbed stems covered with golden yellow spines. Full sun to partial shade; hardy to the mid 20s F. Moderate growth rate. Zones 9-10.

NOTOCACTUS MAGNIFICUS Plant to one foot tall and clustering with blue-green, ribbed stems bearing numerous thin, flexible spines; yellow flowers bloom in summer. Tolerates some shade; hardy to the low 30s F. Moderate growth rate. Zones 9-10.

about two feet tall, and *M. cochal* stems even sooner: plants soon develop an improbably top-heavy appearance. However, the tenacious roots perform admirably, and even massive specimens seldom if ever topple.

NOLINA *Agavaceae*

Nolina, often called bear grass, is native to the deserts of Arizona, New Mexico, Texas, and Mexico. The genus includes about twenty-five species, most of which are three to five feet tall, with a spread of three to six feet. Typically, they are slow to moderate in growth rate.

There are two basic growth forms; both have long leaves, about one-third inch wide. One form looks like a large, coarse clump of grass. **N. palmeri** and **N. bigelovii** show this morphology. Leaves emerge in a tight rosette, three or six feet in diameter, respectively. A broad-trunked, shrubby form to ten feet tall, as typified by **N. longifolia,** is topped by green leaves about three feet long spilling in a fountainlike display. Leaf edges have tiny teeth. Flowers are small, creamy white, and borne on a four- to six-foot stalk from May through June. It is very slow growing, and trunks develop only in age.

N. brittoniana and **N. atopocarpa,** Florida natives, are excellent for sandy areas in the southern U.S.

N. longifolia is hardy to at least the 20s; other species are hardy to 10° F. It grows best in full sun in very well-drained soil and has a minimal water requirement. However, *Nolina* looks best with monthly irrigation in the summer. It also responds well to fertilizing in early spring, but this is not strictly necessary. In fall, dead stalks and old, dried leaves should be removed.

Nolina longifolia, aloes.

NOTOCACTUS *Cactaceae*

Notocactus leninghausii, the golden ball cactus, is native to southern Brazil. It has a columnar habit at maturity, branching from the base to form large clusters to three feet tall. The "multi-tiered" or "city skyline" appearance of the clusters, with stems of widely varying heights within a clump (a result of basal branching) makes *N. leninghausii* a landscape standout. Individual stems are bright green, about four inches in diameter, with numerous ribs. Stems are densely covered with fine, bristly, golden yellow spines. Flowers are saucer-shaped with all parts pure yellow, about two inches across, and borne near the stems tips, usually several at a time. Flowering typically begins after the stem has reached about four inches in height. *N. leninghausii* is hardy to at least the mid-20's.

N. magnificus, also from Brazil, is equally hardy, with blue-green globular stems that eventually resemble stretched ovals. Ribs are straw yellow in color due to large numbers of densely placed, thin, flexible spines emerging from areoles along the ribs. Yellow flowers are generously produced and about two inches in diameter. To prevent scarring of the stem, grow in a protected, partly shaded site and water and fertilize generously during the season.

N. submammulosus, an Argentinean species, is one of the most common notocacti and hence easiest to find; it is hardy at least to the low 20s. Green stems are globose and tubercled, about four inches in diameter. Of the two central spines in each spine cluster, one points up and one points down. Flowers are three to four inches in diamter, satiny yellow with bright red stigmas. Mature plants offset sparingly but will happily reseed in a rockery.

Another hardy species is **N. sellowi** (or you could substitute the very similar **N. tephracantha**) which has a wide South American distribution. Stems are solitary, flattened disks about two to three inches tall and four to six inches across with narrow, sharp ribs. Flowers are similar to those of *N. submammulosus* in color but are somewhat smaller. *N. sellowi* thrives in full sun with good drainage; under these conditions, plants will reliably persist for many years.

OPUNTIA *Cactaceae*

Opuntia includes some of the most "cactus-looking" of cacti–what many people think of when they hear the word "cactus." One large section of the genus bears the common name cholla. There are many different chollas that are useful in landscaping, including some that are very cold-hardy. **O. bigelovii,** the teddy bear cholla, is native to rocky, mountainous areas of the American Southwest and northern Mexico. It performs well only in hot, arid areas. The teddy bear cholla is treelike, up to eight feet tall. Stem segments, two to ten inches long, are cylindrical, about two inches thick, and light green. Terminal joints are very easily detached, so don't plant *O. bigelovii* near a path or other high-traffic area. All segments are densely clothed in straw yellow spines. Flowers, produced from February through May, are greenish yellow, sometimes with pale lavender streaks, up to one-and-one-half inches across and borne mostly at shoot tips.

O. compressa (syn. *O. humifusa* var. *austrina*) is native to the eastern U.S. It typically has low, spreading growth but sometimes produces erect stems, to three feet tall. Stems are dark green, with sparsely distributed, twisted spines that are first white then later turn gray. Flowers are bright yellow. *O. compressa* is hardy as far north as coastal New York State.

O. ficus-indica, the Indian fig or spineless cactus, comes from tropical America; its exact origins are unknown. Indian fig forms a bush or tree from six to eighteen feet tall with oval-shaped green or gray-green stem segments, each twelve to twenty inches long and four to eight inches wide. Spines are usually present but sparse and insignificant. Flowers are canary yellow or orange-red, about three inches long and four inches in diameter. The fruits are edible, usually red but also purple, white, or yellow and two to three-and-one-half inches long. *O. ficus-indica* is widely grown for fruit and forage in the tropics and subtropics and has naturalized in many regions. It is hardy at least to the mid-20s. 'Burbank's Spineless Cactus' is a popular variety of the species for home landscaping.

O. violacea (syn. *O. gosseliniana* var. *santarita,* also sold as *O. santa-rita*; common name Santa Rita prickly pear) is a hardy species from Texas to Arizona

OPUNTIA VIOLACEAE VAR. MACROCENTRA Pods that are reddish in winter or during drought bear long black spines near the margins and yellow flowers with red centers appear in late spring. Full sun; hardy to the teens. Moderate growth rate. Zones 9-10.

OPUNTIA ERINACEA VAR. URSINA (GRIZZLY BEAR CACTUS) To one foot tall, several feet across, densely covered with white, flexible spines, bearing pale yellow flowers in summer. Full sun. Hardy to 10° F. Slow growing. Zones 8-10.

O. MACRORHIZA (PLAINS PRICKLY PEAR) Forms low clumps of bluish green pads with yellow flowers often with red centers. Full sun. Moderate growth rate. Zone 5-10.

OPUNTIA MACRODASYS Shrub to three feet tall with yellow glochids (varieties with white and cinnamon glochids also occur). Full sun. Moderate growth rate. Zones 9-10.

Opuntia, Echinopsis.

and northern Mexico that easily survives temperatures in the teens. Four-foot-tall plants, six feet across, have six- to eight-inch-long joints, almost circular, with widely spaced areoles bearing a few spines. *O. violacea*'s main attraction is its reddish pads; stem segments turn reddish purple under extreme conditions, either during winter or under prolonged drought. Flowers are pale yellow, two to three inches across, and borne in late spring, followed by one-inch oval, fleshy purple fruits.

O. macrocentra, the purple prickly pear, is another southwestern U.S./northern Mexico species with some of *O. violacea*'s character—reddish pads in winter or during drought, but it has the added attraction of bearing long black spines near the margins of the pads. The purple prickly pear is smaller overall, being only about eighteen inches tall and two to three feet across. Flowers are yellow with red centers, borne in late spring.

O. robusta, famous for its dramatic silhouette, grows up to ten feet tall and broad, with silvery blue gray stem segments, eight to fourteen inches in diameter, almost circular in outline. *O. robusta* can be an excellent container plant; an entire branch can be lopped off and planted in a pot where it will survive for years even in partial shade.

O. polyacantha, a low and creeping species, is the most widespread high desert and Great Plains *Opuntia*, hardy to 0° F. It is characterized by numerous thin, flexible, beige to gray or brownish spines. Flowers are usually yellow, but some forms have pink, red, or even purple flowers.

O. erinacea var. ursina, the grizzly bear cactus, is densely clothed in long, white, flexible spines. Flowers are of the typical pale yellow, not-too-showy opuntia variety. The grizzly bear cactus is hardy to at least 10° F. but also can withstand intense desert heat (though it does not do well in the Tucson area, usually shriveling and dying in summer).

PACHYCEREUS *Cactaceae*

Pachycereus marginatus, also sold as *Lemaireocereus marginatus*, is better known as the organ pipe cactus of central Mexico. The large, tree-like plants with stems either unbranched or basally branched can reach nine to twenty-five feet in height. Stems are glossy dark green, usually with five broad, rounded ribs and short spines emerging from nearly continuous felty, brown areoles. Flowers, often in pairs, are up to two inches long, tubular, and off-white with reddish or brown outer segments. Fruits are globose, about one-and-one-half inch across, with yellow-red flesh.

P. marginatus is valuable in the landscape for its exceptionally straight, polelike aspect. It is hardy to at least the low 20s, though unprotected tips freeze in the 20s. Plants sold in nurseries are usually rooted stem cuttings and large, landscape-size specimens are often available.

PACHYCORMUS *Anacardiaceae*

Pachycormus discolor, the elephant tree, is a bizarrely contorted, slow-growing endemic caudiciform of Baja California. Swollen, gnarled trunks covered

PACHYCEREUS MARGINATUS (ORGAN PIPE CACTUS) Treelike plant to twenty-five feet tall with glossy dark green, ribbed stems, short spines, and tubular off-white flowers borne in summer. Full sun; hardy to the low 20s F. Slow growing. Zones 9-10.

PACHYCORMUS DISCOLOR (ELEPHANT TREE) Swollen, gnarled trunks covered with papery bark, up to twenty feet in height. Tiny, green, pinnate leaves and clusters of small deep rose flowers, fading to off-white. Full sun. Hardy to temperatures in the 20s. Zones 9-10.

PACHYPODIUM GEAYI Columnar, thich-trunked tree, to ten feet or more in height. Thorny stems bear dark green leaves in terminal rosettes. Creamy yellow flowers appear on mature plants. Full sun; withstands light frost. Fairly vigorous. Zones 9-10.

PELARGONIUM ECHINATUM (CACTUS GERANIUM) Long-petioled leaves appear in spring along with umbels of purple-spotted white to blushing pink flowers. Grows to two feet tall, spreads four to five feet. Full sun or partial shade; hardy to the mid 20s F. Slow to moderate growth rate. Zones 9-10.

Pachypodium geayi

with greyish white to yellowish white papery bark can reach up to twenty feet in height, producing several stout, horizontal main branches and numerous, somewhat stubby secondary branches. In cultivation, plants sometimes tend to be more columnar rather than the contorted forms produced in the wild. The trunk is composed of spongy wood rich in latex ducts; the white, milky sap will ooze from bark wounds for hours. Tiny, green, pinnate leaves are drought deciduous. Small flowers are borne in clusters; at first, they are deep rose in color, but they gradually fade through pale pink to off-white.

Pachycormus is best grown in full sun. Plants should be watered regularly when in leaf; even during summer dormancy, they should not be allowed to dry completely. *Pachycormus* is hardy to temperatures in the 20s.

PACHYPODIUM *Apocynaceae*

Pachypodiums, from South Africa and Madagascar, provide exotic accents for the landscape. Most are frost-tender, but those mentioned here can withstand a light frost with only minor damage to newly emerging growth.

P. geayi has a columnar, slightly barrel-shaped stem that can reach thirty feet in height and three feet in diameter at the base, but is more commonly six to ten feet tall with a twelve-inch trunk. Branches form a loose crown atop tall old trunks. Young stems, densely covered with three-quarter-inch thorns, are attractive, about two inches thick, with silvery gray bark. Leaves are narrow and linear, about eight to twelve inches long, and born in rosettes near branch tips. They are dark green with reddish bases. *P. geayi* is deciduous during Madagascar's dry season, which corresponds with winter in southern California. Cues that cause leaf loss seem to be related to both ambient temperature and water availability. Flowers are large and creamy yellow, appearing on short-stemmed inflorescences, but only seen in mature plants (six feet tall or larger).

P. lamerei, the Madagascar palm, is similar in appearance to *P. geayi,* with a spiny, bottle-shaped trunk. However, leaves are bright, shiny green and much wider (one inch) and the flowers are white with yellow centers and longer tubes.

P. succulentum, the hardiest of the pachypodiums, withstands temperatures in the upper 20s once established. It has a thick, short, caudiciform stem base with a long, tapering, tuberous root. Numerous erect branches, up to about two feet long but only one-quarter inch in diameter, are covered with pairs of dense thorns. Lance-shaped leaves, deciduous during the winter, have hairs on both sides. Flowers are small and hairy, with narrow, tubular corollas appearing either pink or white from a distance but actually having red central stripes against a white or pink background.

Pachypodiums grow best in a humus-rich but loose soil. All require ample water when leafed out but very little after leaves fall. However, plants should never be allowed to dry out completely. Plants for sale in nurseries will be seedlings, usually quite small, but these will grow and establish quickly in the ground. Larger plants of *P. geayi* and *P. lamerei* may be available also. Where climate precludes planting in the ground, pachypodiums make excellent container plants to be set out in the garden during the warm seasons.

PELARGONIUM *Geraniaceae*

Pelargonium echinatum, the cactus geranium, is a South African native grown for its delicate flowers. It forms a small, low shrub with a few erect, succulent stems that are covered at maturity by hardened, thorny stipules. Long-petioled, basically heart-shaped but sometimes much-divided or lobed leaves appear in spring. These have silvery, pubescent blades. Flowers are white, blushing pink with reddish purple spots and are borne in umbels of three to six flowers. Dark magenta flower forms are also available. Flowers are borne mainly in spring, but occasional rebloom occurs throughout the growing season.

Pelargoniums and aloes.

P. echinatum performs best in full sun in loose, sandy soil, growing actively only during the cool seasons of the year. It usually becomes somewhat dormant during the dry season–generally losing its leaves, and not growing. *P. echinatum* is hardy to the mid-20s. It is typically propagated from cuttings, but these can be extremely slow to root.

Numerous other winter-growing, geophytic species like *P. incrassatum,* with a tuft of parsleylike foliage and bright magenta flowers, and *P. triste*, with pubescent carrotlike foliage and yellow flowers, do well in southern California.

PERESKIA *Cactaceae*

Pereskia grandifolia, the rose cactus, is the best known and most widespread species of *Pereskia* in cultivation. The genus *Pereskia* is also one of the first cactus genera ever to be described by botanists (in 1703). Native to Brazil, *P. grandifolia* forms a shrub or small tree to fifteen feet tall with a very spiny trunk. It grows rampantly if watered and fertilized. Juvenile branches are solid green with two-inch-long, black spines, but these stems eventually develop a beautifully patterned, snakeskinlike bark. The mature trunk is woody and not jointed. Rose-colored flowers, each about one-and-one-half inch across, are borne in clusters and continue to be produced over a prolonged period from late spring through early summer.

Though commonly grown as a house plant, *P. aculeata,* a lax shrub or vine, is a good landscape plant in frost-free climates. It needs support for optimum growth (up to thirty feet), so it can be espaliered against a wall or used to disguise a chain-link fence. *P. aculeata* is handsomely covered by creamy yellow or pinkish blossoms in late spring or early summer, followed by spiny, yellow, edible fruits.

Pereskias grow best in full sun but will withstand partial or even quite dense shade, though perhaps not flowering under such conditions. They are very drought-resistant, although leaves will shrivel and fall off when water is in short supply. They tolerate a wide range of soils, provided nutrients are available and drainage is reasonable. They are easily grown from big cuttings taken during the warm seasons or from seeds. Optimal growth occurs at tem-

PERESKIA GRANDIFOLIA (ROSE CACTUS) Shrubby plant to fifteen feet tall with spiny trunk and clusters of rose-colored spring-to-early-summer flowers; mature stems display patterned bark. Sun or shade; tender. Vigorous. Zones 9-10.

PILOSOCEREUS LEUCOCEPHALUS Blue-green stems display woolly ribs with needle-shaped spines and develop a thick, white pseudocephalium; waxy, white, tubular flowers are borne in summer. Full sun to partial shade. Moderate growth rate. Zones 9-10.

PLEIOSPILOS NELII (SPLIT ROCK, CLEFT STONE) Compact succulent with two to four leaves in opposite pairs, two to four inches across, dark gray-green to reddish spotted; salmon pink-yellow flowers produced in January. Full sun to partial shade. Slow to moderate growth rate. Zones 9-10.

PORTULACARIA AFRA 'VARIEGATA' (ELEPHANT BUSH) Mounding to two-and-one-half feet or cascading with red stems and small green and creamy yellow leaves. Full sun to partial shade. Moderate growth rate. Zones 9-10.

peratures in the 80s F. Temperatures near freezing will cause leaves to turn yellow and fall off while still fleshy and hard frost will kill most species. *P. grandiflora* will recover from damage suffered in the mid 20s.

PILOSOCEREUS *Cactaceae*

Pilosocereus, sometimes included in *Cephalocereus,* has a wide distribution, from the West Indies, through Mexico, Central, and South America. Most species are treelike or bushy columnar-stemmed cacti that develop pseudocephaliums (wooly, flowering regions along one side of the stem near the apex) and have nocturnal flowers.

P. leucocephalus (syn. *P. maxonii; P. palmeri*) from eastern Mexico and central America is a particularly handsome species with blue-green stems and white wooly ribs with brown spines, hardy to the lower 30s. Bat-pollinated flowers are waxy, short-tubed, and white. These are borne sparingly in summer. *P. leucocephalus* develops a particularly noteworthy and beautiful pseudocephalium of thick, white wool. It also has attractive globular magenta fruits that split open to reveal bright magenta, spaghettilike pulp and black seeds.

Plants can be purchased as rooted stem cuttings or seedlings.

PLEIOSPILOS *Aizoaceae*

Pleiospilos is a small genus of "living stones" from the Cape Province of South Africa. **Pleiospilos nelii,** the split rock or cleft stone, is the most compact species, a perennial succulent with dark gray-green to reddish leaves that have many small, dark dots. Leaves are thicker at the tips. Flowers, produced in January, are about two inches across, with salmon pink-yellow petals. Typically, little or no water is provided outside the winter growing season for this species.

P. bolusii, hardy to the low 20s, is a compact plant that is indistinguishable from the surrounding stones in its native environment. It is better-suited for landscaping because it is not as water-sensitive as *P. nelii*. Leaves, usually a single fat pair but sometimes two pairs, are rough-textured with flattened upper surfaces and keeled undersides. Growth occurs from late spring to summer, with flowering at the end of the growth period. Two or three flowers per leaf pair are produced in early fall; these are large (three inches) and yellow to orange. They open in the late afternoon and have an enticing coconut fragrance.

A closely related genus, **Rabiea,** may be preferred where greater cold hardiness is desired. *Rabiea* has narrower leaves but equally showy yellow flowers.

Plants available for sale in nurseries are seedlings. When planting out in the landscape, *Pleiospilos* species will be best located in rockeries with superb drainage. Since plants are easily grown from seed, bringing on a large batch of seedlings for use in an unusual mass planting may be desirable. Other species besides those mentioned above are worth trying if available.

PORTULACARIA *Portulacaceae*

Portulacaria afra, the elephant bush, is a much-branched succulent South African shrub or small tree to twelve feet with soft wood. Branches emerge nearly horizontally. Leaves are small (one-half inch long) and evergreen or

Portulacaria afra 'Variegata' with *Crassula falcata.*

deciduous under extreme drought. Flowers are born in pale pink clusters but are rarely seen in cultivation. *Portulacaria* can be grown outside in Zone 10; it is not frost tolerant.

The variety **'Variegata'** has green and yellow variegated leaves and a more lax, mounding growth form. It is useful for planting along walls to cascade over or as a tall groundcover (two-and-one-half feet).

PUYA *Bromeliaceae*

Puyas, pineapple relatives from Chile, make wonderful accent plants in a spacious garden, forming dense, impenetrable clumps. They are easily grown outside without protection in Zone 9.

P. venusta has slender, silvery recurved leaves forming three-foot rosettes. Flower stalks emerge in late spring bearing heads of striking deep violet, tubular flowers.

P. coerulea froms three-foot rosettes of two-foot-long, narrow, green to silver leaves. Inflorescences to six or seven feet tall are branched and carry dark purple, two-inch-long, tubular flowers. *P. spathacea* is similar but the flower stalks are showy in and of themselves by virtue of their red color. *P. alpestris* is another lookalike when not in flower. It forms three-foot rosettes of arching, two-foot leaves whose undersides are densely covered in white scales. Two-inch bell-shaped flowers are a remarkable and distinctive metallic blue-green.

P. berteroniana has three-foot-long, light green leaves, one-half inch wide and tapering, forming rosettes to five feet across. Plants can reach ten to twelve feet in height with glossy green bell-shaped flowers, to two inches

Puya alpestris

PUYA SPATHACEA Densely clumping plant to six feet or more across with showy red flower stalks carrying deep blue tubular flowers. Full sun; hardy to the low 20s F. Moderate growth rate. Zone 10.

PUYA COERULEA Long, narrow, green to silver leaves are borne on clumping plants, to six feet or more across, with branched inflorescences of deep blue tubular flowers. Full sun, hardy to the low 20s F. Moderate growth rate. Zones 9-10.

RUSCHIA SPINESCENS Branching shrub to two feet tall and two to four feet across with terminal clusters of reddish cruciform thorns maturing to gray; abundant pink flowers are borne in spring. Full sun. Moderate to fast growth rate. Zones 9-10.

SANSEVIERIA SUBSPICATA (RED-EDGED SANSEVIERIA) Thin, flat, lanceolate leaves; white racemes appear in summer. Partial shade in arid climates; hardy to the upper 20s F. Moderate growth rate. Zones 9-10.

across, borne in panicles.

P. chilensis is a similar species forming imposing thickets of branched or unbranched stems to fifteen feet tall and eight inches in diameter bearing five-foot rosettes of leaves about three feet long and two inches wide. Yellow-green bell-shaped flowers are two inches across and borne in panicles.

RUSCHIA *Aizoaceae*

Ruschia spinescens, from South Africa, is a shrub to two feet in height and two to four feet in diameter. Branches terminate in clusters of sharp, cruciform thorns that are reddish when new and mature to gray. Abundant, one-half-inch pink flowers are borne at branch tips as well. Foliage is grayish and fleshy. Mass plantings of *R. spinescens* make a good, thick mounding groundcover to three feet tall, but single plants can be appealing as accent plants.

R. granitica, also from South Africa, is used as a slow-growing but eventually quite dense, very low (two-inch) groundcover; it has slender, creeping stems with erect flowering shoots bearing two to four leaves. Leaves are oval, pointed, and blue-green with reddish keels. Flowers are solitary, about one-half inch in diameter, and magenta pink. *R. granitica* is hardy to the mid-20s. It has the advantage of growing well in partly shaded conditions as well as in full sun.

Ruschias are winter-spring growers that flower after growth, usually in mid- to late spring. Propagation is by stem cuttings taken during the growing season.

SANSEVIERIA *Liliaceae*

Sansevieria is a diverse genus of ornamental foliage plants native to tropical Africa and southern India. Most species are not hardy (except *S. subspicata,* see text below) at temperatures below 32° F., and all are subject to spotting and scarring if cultural conditions are less than ideal. In their native habitats, populations of sansevierias tend to look somewhat sparse and bedraggled.

S. cylindrica is very distinct, with three to four sharp, elongated, cylindrical leaves emerging from a rhizome. The dark green leaves, usually furrowed, may be up to five feet long and often have silvery stripes and cross bands, especially when young. Flowers are white to pale pink, about one-and-one-half inches long, borne on three-foot racemes. *S. cylindrica* tolerates heavy soils very well. Like most sansevierias, it is propagated by rhizome divisions or by leaf cuttings.

S. trifasciata, often called the snake plant or mother-in-law's-tongue, comes originally from Zaire. Leaves are swordlike, stiff and erect, and up to four feet long and three inches wide. Leaves are typically olive to dark green with whitish green transverse stripes. Flowers are small (one-half inch) and greenish white, either solitary or in small clusters, atop two-and-one-half-foot racemes. Flowers drop copious nectar, leading to generally untidy mold growth underneath; but inflorescences are easily removed if desired. *S. t.* **'Laurentii'** has leaves with golden-yellow marginal stripes. There are numerous other selections

Sansevieria trifasciata 'Futura', a compact, short growing broad type that mimics *S. t.* 'Laurentii'.

varying in shades of green, degrees of variegations, and leaf size, with some as small as four inches long. Many of these are unstable sports and must be maintained by rhizome divisions. Leaf cuttings will revert to nonvariegated forms.

S. subspicata, the red-edged sansevieria, produces thin, flat, lanceolate leaves, two feet long, borne on slender petioles. Young leaves are pale green, but mature to dark green, without variegation. The foliage has a metallic quality to which color and substance both contribute. White flowers are solitary or in pairs on one-and-one-half-foot racemes. *S. subspicata* is among the hardiest of the sansevierias, withstanding temperatures in the upper 20s.

Sansevierias benefit greatly from generous watering and fertilizing and frequent division. In arid, inland climates, even with these added supplements, sansevierias perform best when grown in partial shade. In regions with high summer humidity, sansevierias can excel as summer bedding plants.

SCHLUMBERGERA *Cactaceae*

Schlumbergera, including those plants formerly included with *Zygocactus,* is a Brazillian species of epiphytic cacti with green, flat-jointed stems either spineless or bearing short bristles. Abundant, tubular, bilaterally symmetrical flowers are produced at stem tips in winter. Flower color ranges from white through pink, red, and purple to orange and yellow. Several species are popular with succulent growers, but the hundreds of hybrid cultivars are more commonly represented in collections. A hybrid of **S. opuntioides** and **S. russelliana** called 'Exotica' is prized for its vigorous growth habit as well as its abundant magenta flowers. It is also hardier than most, tolerating temperatures in the mid 20s.

Schlumbergera perform best when grown on acidic soil in shady areas with high humidity. They are sensitive to photoperiod, meaning that flowering can be increased or synchronized by manipulating the amount of light the plants receive. Decreasing day length will force *Schlumbergera* into bloom.

Many schlumbergeras in cultivation show the presence of virus infections when specially tested in a laboratory. Generally, there are no morphological symptoms of infection in this genus, but good sterile technique should be used for propagation to prevent the infection of other plants via shears or other tools. Also, aphids should be carefully controlled as they can transmit viruses from plant to plant.

SEDUM *Crassulaceae*

With a wide variety of growth forms and requirements, sedums have long been popular garden plants. Most are of easy culture and are readily propagated by division or cuttings which may be planted, without callusing, most of the year.

The readily available **S. dasyphyllum,** native to north Africa and mediterranean Europe, is a low perennial with small, rounded, crowded leaves that are fleshy, bluish green, and covered with short hairs. It makes a fine-textured

Some species of *Sedum* are hardy throughout North America. Below: *Sedum spectabile* 'Autumn Joy' in the autumn perennial border at The New York Botanical Garden.

Sedum nussbaumeranum with *Echeveria* 'Perle von Nurnberg'

groundcover especially charming for surrounding rosette plants like echeverias and sempervivums. *S. dasyphyllum* grows best in partial shade inland. It is hardy to the upper 20s. Flowers are small and white.

The more uncommon **S. dendroideum,** from central Mexico, is a much-branched shrub that can reach seven feet in height or trail to eighteen feet along the ground. The main trunk can be four inches in diameter. Glossy green, two-inch-long leaves are densely crowded (resembling rosettes) near stem tips. Leaf margins usually have red or dark green glandular dots. Many-flowered panicles of yellow blooms, each about one-half inch across, are borne on stout, erect, one-foot-tall inflorescences in late winter and early spring. In the garden, a mass planting of *S. dendroideum* can even be shaped and treated as a hedge, although individual specimen plants always are more architecturally attractive. Similar to *S. dendroideum* but easier to locate is **S. dendroideum ssp. praealtum.** *S. d. praealtum* stays low, about two feet tall, with a four- to five-foot diameter, and produces showy yellow flowers in late winter.

S. nussbaumeranum (syn. *S. adolphii*), another Mexican species, makes a small, succulent perennial of eight to twelve inches with a loose leaf arrangement.

Sedum **x***rubrotinctum 'Aurora', Adromischus kitchingii, Echeveria gibbiflora, Epiphyllum crenatum 'Chicicastenango'*

SCHLUMBERGERA TRUNCATA V. DELICATA Ephiphytic cactus with flat jointed stems with a few large teeth on the margins. White flowers with delicate magenta tracing at the throat are produced in spring. Rich acidic soil and partial shade are best. Moderate growth rate. Zones 9-10.

SEDUM NUSSBAUMERANUM Succulent groundcover eight to twelves inches high with pointed yellowish-green or copper-colored leaves borne in rosette from near stem tips. Full sun to partial shade. Moderate to fast growth rate. Zones 9-10.

SEDUM BURRITO A smaller version of burro's tail, *Sedum morganianum*, with smaller, rounded, easily detached leaves on stems cascading to three feet or more. Partial to full shade. Slow to moderate growth rate. Zones 9-10.

SEDUM PALMERI Another hanging basket or groundcover plant with glaucous gray-green leaves in two-inch rosettes. Brilliant yellow flowers in winter even in full shade. Partial to full shade. Moderate growth rate. Zones 9-10.

The yellowish green leaves are pointed, about two inches long, and arranged in a rosettelike manner near shoot tips. Leaves usually have a slight keel on the underside and tend to turn brown with red edges in bright sunlight. White flowers are produced in spring. Among the most desirable forms of *S. nussbaumeranum* are those with copper-colored foliage. Typically, *S. nussbaumeranum* is used in the garden as a tallish groundcover.

Sedum x rubrotinctum, called Christmas cheer, is a four- to six-inch perennial that branches from near the base and makes an excellent groundcover. Leaves are club-shaped, less than one inch long, and lustrous green, often suffused with red in bright light, especially in winter–hence, the Christmas motif. Inflorescences appear in winter bearing cymes of delicate one-half-inch yellow flowers. **'Aurora'** is a choice cultivar with pink new growth that turns orange in winter. 'Aurora' tolerates full sun if sufficiently watered or considerable shade and drought. It must be propagated from stem cuttings to preserve the characteristic variegation; leaf-propagated material will revert to the typical green leaf form.

S. pachyphyllum, the jelly bean plant, is a southern Mexican species that resembles in form a taller and more open *S. x rubrotinctum*. Club-shaped leaves are cylindrical and curved and are gray-green with red or purplish tips. Stems

Sedum reptans, Echeveria elegans, Echeveria pallida.

SEDUM xRUBROTINCTUM (CHRISTMAS CHEER) Basally branching perennial four to six inches tall with club-shaped, lustrous green leaves often tinged with red; cymes of small yellow flowers appear in winter. Full sun to partial shade. Fast growing. Zones 9-10.

SEDUM SPURIUM Temperate perennial groundcover with lax stems bearing dark green leaves and pink to purple summer flowers; some forms turn red before dormancy. Full sun to partial shade. All zones.

SEDUM SPECTABILE 'AUTUMN JOY' Erect one-and-one-half to two-foot stems bear three-inch-long leaves and flat clusters of tiny autumn-blooming pink flowers. Full sun to partial shade. All zones.

SEDUM X RUBROTINCTUM 'AURORA' A choice cultivar with pinkish new growth that turns orange in winter. Full sun to partial shade. Zones 9-10.

reach about one foot in height. Half-inch yellow flowers are borne on four- to five-inch stems in showy profusion in late winter or early spring.

S. spectabile, native to China and Korea, *S. spurium,* from southern Europe, and *S. sieboldii,* from Japan, are all temperate species that make good summer bedding subjects. However, these species are not drought tolerant (though they are considered xeriscapic in the East) and hence require generous watering for good performance; they typically die back to the ground in winter in cool climates. The *S. spectabile* selection **'Autumn Joy'** is most frequently seen. It has erect stems, one-and-one-half to two feet tall, with three-inch-long leaves and flat clusters of tiny (less than one-half-inch) pink flowers that appear in autumn. *S. sieboldii* is another autumn-bloomer. It has arching, six- to nine-inch stems and glaucous, round, scalloped-edged blue leaves one-half inch long. Pink flowers are borne in dense, rounded clusters in autumn; in winter, the plant dies back to the ground to reemerge the following spring. *S. spurium* has lax stems and dark green, one-half- to one-inch leaves. Flowers are pink to purple and borne in summer. Selected forms turn brilliant red in cold weather before going dormant.

SEMPERVIVUM *Crassulaceae*
Sempervivums, referred to as hens-and-chicks or houseleeks, are popular rock garden plants in temperate climates.

Sempervivum arachnoideum, growing in a New Jersey rock garden.

SEMPERVIVUM ARACHNOIDEUM (COBWEB HOUSELEEK) White webbing stretches from tips of densely pubescent leaves held on small rosettes; summer flowers are pink or white. Spreading groundcover or crevice-filler. Full sun to partial shade. Fast growing. Zones 4-9.

SEMPERVIVUM TECTORUM (shown with cultivar). Flattened two- to five-inch rosettes of oval, gray-green leaves with red or purplish tips. Purplish red flowers, about one inch across, are borne in summer. Full sun to partial shade. Fast growing. Zones 4-9.

SEMPERVIVUM X FAUCONNETTI ISimilar to *S. tectorum,* but with smaller, denser rosettes and slightly hairy leaves. Full sun to partial shade. Fast growing. All zones.

SEMPERVIVUM TECTORUM 'COMMANDER HAY' Cultivar of *S. tectorum,* with pointed dark red and green leaves. Full sun to partial shade. Fast growing. All zones.

S. tectorum, the most widely grown species, is native to the mountainous regions of south and central Europe where it has a long history of practical use. Extracts of the plant exuded from cut leaves are said to give immediate relief to burns. The Emperor Charlemagne (AD 768-814) decreed mandatory planting of "houseleeks" on the roofs of all dwellings to protect them from fire. *S. tectorum* has flattened two- to five-inch rosettes of fifty to sixty oval, gray-green leaves (three-quarter-inch wide and three inches long) with red or purplish tips. Numerous more diminutive selections and hybrids are widely cultivated as well. Purplish red flowers, about one inch across, are borne in summer on eight- to eighteen-inch-tall stalks that appear shaggy due to the presence of abundant white hairs. *S. tectorum* is extremely hardy.

S. arachnoideum, the cobweb houseleek from southern Europe, has small (two-inch) wide rosettes of densely pubescent leaves; a webbing of white, cottony strands stretches from leaf tip to leaf tip. Flowers, borne in summer, are usually pink, but some choice clones have white flowers.

Another hairy sempervivum is **S. ciliosum,** a hardy native of Bulgaria. Partially closed one-inch rosettes of one-inch leaves have a silvery appearance due to long, hyaline hairs on leaves. Flowers are greenish yellow, about one-inch wide. Several selected clones are available; these are typically sold under their locality names.

Most sempervivums are propagated by offsets. Seedlings grow well when available; however, some species may fail to flower even after mature size is attained.

SENECIO *Asteraceae*

Senecio is a genus with worldwide distribution, but most of the 110 succulent species originate in southern Africa, Arabia, the Canary Islands, or Mexico.

S. mandraliscae, hardy to the 20s, is a succulent perennial to about twelve inches in height. Glaucous leaves are semi-cylindrical, flattened on the upper surface, and about four inches long, terminating in a sharp point. Flowers are

Senecio mandraliscae, Cassia odorata.

SENECIO MANDRALISCAE Succulent perennial to one foot with semi-cylindrical, pointed, glaucous leaves and inconspicuous white flowers. Full sun to full shade; hardy to the 20s F. Moderate to fast growing. Zones 9-10.

SENECIO MEDLEY-WOODII Shrub two-and-one-half feet tall with fleshy, white-haired obovate leaves turning purple in sun; yellow daisy-like, fragrant flowers appear in spring. Full sun to partial shade. Moderate growth rate. Zones 9-10.

SENECIO SERPENS Plant to one foot, similar to *S. mandraliscae,* tall with glaucous blue semi-cylindrical leaves and inconspicuous white flowers. Full sun to partial shade; hardy to the 20s F. Moderate growth rate. Zones 9-10.

SENECIO RADICANS Trailing plant similar to string-of-beads but with more elongate, pointed leaves. Inconspicuous heads of white flowers followed by dandelionlike puffballs. Partial to full shade. Fast growing. Zones 9-10.

white and inconspicuous, borne on long peduncles. *S. mandraliscae* grows well in full sun to partial shade; it is extremely drought tolerant in shade. It is vegetatively propagated from untreated cuttings taken in winter and early spring. **S. serpens** is similar to *S. mandraliscae* but has blunter two-and-one-half-inch leaves, grooved on the upper surface.

S. kleiniiformis, called spearhead, also resembles *S. mandraliscae* but has arrow-shaped leaves that are a different shade of blue borne on more prostrate stems. It is also more floriferous though the flowers are insignificant and are somewhat untidy unless groomed. *S. kleiniiformis* is hardy to the mid-20s.

S. medley-woodii is a two-and-one-half-foot-tall shrub distinguished by the dense, white, wooly hairs on the obovate, fleshy green leaves. Leaves will turn purplish when grown in full sun. Two-inch flower heads are large, daisy-like, yellow, and fragrant. *S. medley-woodii* will tolerate frost for only brief periods.

S. haworthii, the cocoon plant, has cylindrical leaves, one to two inches long, that are shrouded in pure white hairs. It is hardy to the mid-20s. *S. haworthii* makes a good bedding plant, about one foot tall. It is propagated from cuttings taken in September or October.

S. rowleyanus is a succulent, mat-forming perennial that makes a good hanging basket subject. It is not drought tolerant and so is best grown in shade. Stems are slender and prostrate, rooting at nodes. Leaves are green and beadlike, about one-quarter inch in diameter, with a narrow translucent band. A white-variegated form is also available. Flower heads are small and solitary; ray flowers are absent, and disk flowers are white, followed by typical dandelionlike puffballs.

S. bulbinifolius looks similar to *S. rowleyanus* in its creeping habit, but it is slightly more upright (to six inches) with elongated leaves about an inch long. It bears ray and disk flowers in heads that resemble small yellow daisies and are delightfully fragrant.

All the senecios listed are widely available at succulent nurseries.

STENOCEREUS (syn. Machaerocereus) *Cactaceae*

S. eruca, the creeping devil of Baja California, is unusual within its family for boldly spined, prostrate stems that root as they grow along the ground, with the original parts eventually withering away, leaving behind a skeleton of sun-blackened spines. Growing points reach upward. Long, crawling branches are thick (four inches in diameter) and covered with flattened, translucent pink or yellow (aging gray) spines and can reach up to twenty feet in length. Flowers are white and five inches long, opening only after dark to attract moths. Fruits are one-and-one-half inches long and bright scarlet. *S. eruca* is best in a climate with some maritime influence where it grows vigorously. It is weak and slow in the desert heat; in desert situations, try the similar *Echinopsis thelagonus* (syn. *Trichocereus thelogonus*).

S. eruca is an exciting choice for mass-planting. Single specimens should be avoided—a lone, creeping stem looks too much like a columnar cactus that fell over.

STENOCEREUS ERUCA (CREEPING DEVIL) Prostrate stems to ten or more feet armed with bold flattened spines. Nocturnal white five-inch flowers are produced in summer. Full sun. Moderate growth rate. Zones 9-10.

STETSONIA CORYNE (TOOTHPICK CACTUS) Fiercely spined succulent to thirty feet with columnar, ribbed stems, dark green aging to gray-green; white, funnel-shaped nocturnal flowers bloom in summer. Full sun. Hardy to the teens. Moderate growth rate. Zones 8-10.

CYANOTIS SOMALIENSIS (PUSSY EARS) Succulent, trailing perennial with hairy leaves. Flowers are small, less than one-half inch, deep magenta with densely hairy stamens. Partial to full sun. Moderate growth rate. Zones 9-10.

TRADESCANTIA SILLAMONTANA (WHITE VELVET) Plant forming cushions of white, hairy stems with velvety leaves and magenta-rose summer flowers. Partial to full shade. Moderate to fast growth rate. Zones 9-10.

Uncarina flower.

S. thurberi, the organ pipe cactus, is native to southern Arizona and northern Mexico and is a popular species for cultivation. Stout stems four inches in diameter branch freely from near the base, reaching heights up to twenty-five feet tall (fifteen feet is more common). Young stems are dark green tinged with purple, but older stems turn blue-green. Areoles are prominent, surrounded by rust-colored hairs, and sporting short, glossy dark brown to black spines. Nocturnal flowers borne in spring and summer are apical, pink with white margins, and about three inches long. These are not usually produced until the stems reach four to five feet in height. Red, globose, three-inch fruits are edible.

S. eruca is reliably hardy to the low 20s, but *S. thurberi* loses its growing tips in the low 20s.

STETSONIA *Cactaceae*

The monotypic genus *Stetsonia*, the toothpick cactus, is a large, imposing, and fiercely spined native of the low, salty deserts of Argentina and Bolivia.

S. coryne towers to heights up to thirty feet, branching from a thick basal trunk, up to two feet across, to form numerous (one hundred or more) columnar, dark green aging to gray-green, strongly ribbed four-inch diameter stems. Three-inch-long sharp, awl-shaped brown or black spines, aging gray, emerge from prominent white areoles. Nocturnal, white, funnel-shaped flowers can reach six-and-one-half inches in length. *S. coryne* is hardy to the teens. It grows best if given ample water in the summer.

Stetsonia makes a superb landscape plant but is greatly under-utilized by garden designers. Large, seed-grown specimens are sometimes available at succulent nurseries.

TRADESCANTIA SILLAMONTANA *Commelinaceae*

T. sillamontana, white velvet, is a slow-growing perennial from northeastern Mexico that forms small cushions of white, hairy stems, about two-and-one-half inches long, with velvety leaves. The somewhat succulent green leaves are less than one inch long near the base of the stems but up to two inches long and one inch wide above. Flowers are magenta-rose, about one-half inch across, and borne in summer. Plants are persistent, surviving well in dry partial shade. *T. sillamontana* is often sold as a houseplant. It is not considered frost-hardy when grown in the open; however, growing under trees in a protected site, it will survive light frost.

A related genus in the family is **Cyanotis.** *C. somaliensis,* pussy-ears, is a succulent perennial from tropical Africa that is hardy to about 30° F. It has green, one-and-one-half-inch-long, sickle-shaped leaves with long white hairs that are borne along creeping stems. Flowers are produced only sporadically, are small (less than one-half inch), magenta, and characterized by densely pubescent stamen filaments. *C. somaliensis* is another excellent candidate for planting in dry shade.

TRICHODIADEMA BULBOSUM Tuberous-rooted plant with wiry, spreading stems and spinelike white bristles at leaf tips; magenta flowers bloom in spring. Full sun to partial shade. Hardy to the mid 20s F. Fast-growing in fertile soil. Zones 9-10.

UNCARINA GRANDIDIERI Small tree or shrub to twenty-five feet with trunk to one foot across, lobed green leaves, and very showy yellow flowers with a dark spot in the throat, produced throughout growing season. Full sun to partial shade. Tender. Moderate to fast growing. Zones 9-10.

VELTHEIMIA BRACTEATA Bright green glossy strap-shaped leaves with wavy margins. Showy flowers in late winter and spring. Partial to full shade. Winter growing but tolerates summer water if provided good drainage. Vigorous. Zones 9-10. Shown with *Kalanchoe fedtschenkoi*.

YUCCA WHIPPLEI (OUR LORD'S CANDLE) Clumping shrub with leaves borne in dense, three- to five-foot rosettes. Following several years of growth, five-foot clusters of nodding, creamy white, fragrant flowers are borne on tall stalks. Full sun. Hardy to 10° F. Slow growing. Zones 8-10.

TRICHODIADEMA BULBOSUM *Aizoaceae*

Trichodiadema bulbosum, a roadside weed of South Africa, is a tuberous-rooted plant bearing spinelike groups of white bristles at the leaf tips. When planted in coarse but fertile soil, it will produce sizeable clusters of carrotlike roots within a few years. Above ground, wiry stems spread out into a thick net. Flowers are magenta, about three-quarters of an inch in diameter. *T. bulbosum* is hardy to the mid-20s, especially when kept rather dry during the cool season. It is typically propagated from stem cuttings, but seeds are easy if available. When planting, one can leave the roots partially exposed above the ground for a bizarre and interesting appearance.

Other species of *Trichodiadema* with white or yellow-orange flowers may be available, but none are as good as *T. bulbosum*.

UNCARINA *Pedaliaceae*

Native to dry regions of Madagascar, uncarinas are deciduous shrubs or small trees characterized by the small, hooked harpoons that decorate the seed capsules.

U. grandidieri is a fast-growing tree that can reach up to twenty-five feet in height, with a trunk up to a foot across. The five- to six-inch leaves are lobed, and covered with viscid, glandular hairs. Showy two-and-one-half-inch yellow flowers with purplish red spots in the throat are borne in loose clusters on young shoots. *U. decaryi*, a less common species, has more divided leaves and shorter harpoons on the fruits.

Uncarinas are propagated from seed or by cuttings under mist. Occasional applications of dilute fertilizer will hasten growth, especially in young plants. Both species are very frost tender and should be grown outdoors only in protected sites. They can come back from the roots after temperatures in the mid 20s.

VELTHEIMIA *Liliaceae*

Veltheimia is a bulbous, perennial herb from South Africa that blooms in spring and dies back in summer. Veltheimias are grown for their showy flowers, tubular and pendulous, borne in dense terminal racemes in spring.

V. capensis has lance-shaped, one-foot-long glaucous green leaves, each about one-and-one-half inches wide and somewhat fleshy with wavy margins. Flower scapes are about one foot tall and quite stout, usually mottled with purple; flowers are one inch long and pale pink with greenish tips.

V. bracteata (synonym *V. viridifolia*) has longer, strap-shaped leaves that are much wider (four inches). These are bright green and glossy on both sides. Scapes are taller, to two feet, dark purple with yellow spots. Flowers are one-and-one-half inch long and pinkish with yellow spots. Though winter-growing, *V. bracteata* will tolerate summer water if provided good drainage. It is especially useful for mass bedding in shady situations.

Veltheimia capensis flower.

YUCCA *Agavaceae*

Yucca brevifolia, the famous Joshua tree, is native to the Mojave desert from California to Utah. Slow-growing stems are simple at first, eventually branching dichotomously and attaining heights of ten to forty feet, with branches spreading to twenty feet or more. Trees have angular, picturesque profiles with fissured gray bark. Young leaves are dull green and stiletto-like, to sixteen inches long and one inch wide, with minutely toothed margins, borne at the top of the tall, wide trunk or at the ends of irregularly-shaped branches. Older leaves turn brown, persisting for a while before eventually falling. Twenty-inch panicles of greenish or creamy white, lilylike three-inch flowers appear at the ends of branches in late spring.

    Y. brevifolia grows best in full sun with good drainage. It is extremely heat tolerant but also hardy to 10° F. For faster growth and optimal appearance, provide supplemental watering during the warmest months, although plants can do without it once established. Joshua trees are propagated by offsets handled as cuttings or from seed. Occasional opportunities arise for legal collection in the wild, and some nurseries may have larger specimens for sale.

Bulbine latifolia, Kalanchoe fedtschenkoi, Veltheimia bracteata, Aeonium castella-paivae.

Tall, stately *Yucca filamentosa* is a dramatic accent plant for perennial borders; it is hardy in most of North America.

More mature plants are sometimes difficult to establish; they must be staked until they have rerooted. Small plants are slow to form a trunk but good growing conditions will speed the process.

Y. filamentosa, the hardy Adam's needle of the southeastern U.S., is clump-forming and nearly stemless. Erect, flexible, spreading leaves, two-and-one-half feet long, one inch wide, and spatulate narrowing abruptly to a stout terminal spine, form two-foot rosettes. Leaf margins have long, curly threads. Inflorescences, up to fifteen feet tall, are panicles of two-inch white to cream flowers. It is not as drought tolerant as other species. Several cultivars are available with yellow leaf edges ('Bright Eye', 'Bright Edge'). All hardy to Zone 4.

Y. filifera is a shrub or tree to thirty feet in height with three-foot rosettes of blue-green leaves that are shorter and stiffer than those of *Y. filamentosa*. Inflorescences are about five feet long, arching, with creamy white flowers. *Y. filifera* is hardy to Zone 7.

Y. rigida, the blue yucca, is a slow- to moderate-growing native of the Chihuahuan desert of Mexico. It is typically branched and always evergreen, with stems reaching up to fifteen feet in height with a spread of five to six feet. Three- to five-foot rosettes of rigid, spreading leaves are narrow and blue-green, up to three feet long and one-and-one-half inch wide, with yellow margins bearing tiny teeth. Dead leaves persist in clinging to the stem. Small flowers are borne on panicles in spring. *Y. rigida* is hardy to 10° F. .and requires no supplemental water once established. It is propagated from seeds and offsets and require little maintenance other than occasional removal of old, dried leaves and flower stalks.

Y. whipplei, our Lord's candle, native from southern California to northern Mexico, is also hardy to 10° F. It is a slow-growing, clumping shrub. Leaves borne in dense, three- to five-foot rosettes are rigid, grey-green, about two feet long and three-quarters of an inch wide, with terminal spines and finely toothed margins. Following several years of growth, five-foot clusters of nodding, creamy white, fragrant flowers, two-and-one-half inches long, are borne on tall (eight-foot) stalks. After flowering, the central plant dies, but others from the clump will fill in if allowed. *Y. whippiei* grows best in full sun and is tolerant of a wide variety of soil types as long as drainage is good. No supplemental water is required once the plants are established if annual rainfall is a least eight inches, but occasional watering will speed growth. Removing dying plants after flowering and occasionally clipping off old, dried leaves are all the grooming practices required by this low-maintenance plant.

Plants are easily propagated from seed. Germination is rapid at temperatures near 80° F. with nearly one hundred percent germination within ten days of sowing.

YUCCA CARNEROSANA (SPANISH DAGGER) Arborescent, solitary or clumping plant to fifteen feet with terminal three-foot rosettes of stout leaves. Three- to four-inch white flowers are borne on branched inflorescences in late spring. Full sun. Moderate growth rate. Zones 8-10.

YUCCA FILAMENTOSA (ADAM'S NEEDLE) Forms clumps of one- to two-foot rosettes of flexible leaves with marginal white threads and terminal spines. Two-inch white to cream flowers are borne on inflorescences to fifteen feet tall in summer. Full sun to partial shade. Moderate growth rate. Zones 4-10.

YUCCA ALOIFOLIA 'MARGINATA' (SPANISH BAYONET) Arborescent, solitary or branched to twenty-five feet. Two-and-one-half foot leaves are blue-green with yellow margins. Large white or purple-tinged flowers borne in two-foot panicles in summer. Full sun to partial shade. Zones 8-10.

YUCCA SCHIDIGERA (MOJAVE YUCCA) Shubby or clump-forming, to eight feet with three-foot rosettes of rigid, gray-green leaves margined with curled fibers. Flowers white or cream, often tinged purple are borne on three-foot panicles in late spring. Full sun. Hardy to 0° F. Zones 6-10.

Adromischus maculata.

OTHER SUCCULENTS

There are more than five thousand species of succulent plants. We have tried to describe the ones we think are most useful in the landscape. However, it was difficult to limit our selection; some beautiful and valuable plants were left out. On the following pages are provided brief descriptions of some of the many other succulents that merit a place in the landscape. Most are hardy to Zones 9 and 10 unless otherwise mentioned.

Adromischus Small plants with fleshy, often spotted leaves. Need part shade.

Aloinopsis Small mesembs with spatulate leaves and half-inch flowers with many red-striped yellowish petals.

Beschorneria *Agave* relative with a basal rosette of slender flexible leaves and graceful red-stalked inflorescences with pendent green flowers.

Bowiea volubilis is known as the climbing onion for the resemblance of its green onionlike above-ground bulbs. Delicate twining leafless stems form a fernlike mass on the ground or climbing up neighboring plants.

Bursera Much-branched trees or shrubs with thick trunks, peeling bark, and delicate leaves similar to *Pachycormus* but with strongly aromatic, resinous foliage.

Calibanus hookeri A caudiciform succulent with tufts of blue-green, fibrous grasslike leaves and corky bark. Caudex can grow to the size of a Volkswagen!

Carpobrotus edulis Fast-growing ice plant with pastel yellow to pink flowers often planted as a groundcover along southern California freeways.

Ceropegia woodii (heart vine, rosary vine) Small heart-shaped leaves in pairs on slender trailing stems; a wonderful plant for hanging baskets.

Espostoa Columnar cacti with straight erect stems covered with dense cottony fibers.

Fascicularia bicolor *Puya*-like bromeliad with showy heads of pink flowers nestled in rosette centers.

Faucaria (tiger jaws) Clumping mesembs with intriguing toothy leaves and large yellow flowers. Good rockery accents or unusual lumpy mass planting.

Ficus Several species, most notably *F. palmeri* from Mexico, make excellent caudiciform container specimens or, in mild climates, landscape shrubs or small trees.

Furcraea *Agave*-like plants but with large, narrower-leaved rosettes, either stemless or atop stout trunks to ten feet or more. Tall, branched inflorescences often form prodigious numbers of bulbils. Some are frost tender and most prefer light shade.

Glottiphyllum linguiforme Another clumping mesemb with many petaled yellow flowers similar to *Faucaria* but with toothless, green, fleshy tonguelike leaves.

Gerrardanthus macrorhizus A vining cucumber relative with graceful thin ivylike foliage but with a massive biscuit-shaped caudex, sometimes grotesquely gnarled.

Harrisia Slender stemmed low thicket forming cacti with large nocturnal flowers often followed by long lasting yellow to red tennis ball sized fruits. *H. martinii* from Argentina is among the hardiest species (Zone 8).

Jatropha Mostly tropical shrubs with orange to red flowers and succulent or caudiciform stems. *J. podagrica* of tropical America is useful outdoors in frost-free climates. *J. cordata* is a hardier shrub or small tree from the southern U.S. and northern Mexico.

Kensitia pillansii One of numerous shrubby mesembs, this species is unusual for it many slender white and magenta spoon shaped petals.

Leuchtenbergia principis (agave cactus) A *Ferocactus* relative with large yellow flowers and unusual long tubercles resembling agave leaves but each bearing an apical areole with a cluster of dried grass-like spines.

Lithops (living stones) Ice plant relatives generally grown as container specimens. They have proven to be surprisingly cold hardy grown in dry rockeries, especially when protected beneath a blanket of snow.

Machairophyllum Another genus of clump forming mesembs with smooth fleshy leaves and attractive yellow flowers that open in mass on spring evenings.

Maihuenia poeppigii A cold hardy Argentine cactus with small cylindrical leaves on mat forming spiny stems.

Melocactus Globular cacti forming a bristly orange flowering cap or cephalium at maturity. Most are quite tender and water sensitive. A few of the Brazilian species can tolerate temperatures in the low 30s and some winter water if provided excellent drainage.

Neoporteria Recently combined with the genus *Eriosyce,* this Chilean genus of cacti has spiny, often dark bodied stems that produce delicate magenta flowers in winter. Requires excellent drainage.

Nyctocereus Columnar or sprawling cacti with large nocturnal white fragrant flowers. *N. serpentinus* is the hardiest with erect or sprawling thicket-forming stems. Nocturnal blooms make this a queen of the night or night blooming cereus. Another night blooming cereus genera is **Selenicereus,** with dinner- plate-sized nocturnal white flowers is another queen of the night.

Orbea variegata Perhaps the hardiest (25°) of the succulent milkweeds of the subfamily *Stapeliae,* commonly referred to as stapeliads. In summer its fleshy jointed stems produce two inch starfish like flowers, yellowish with liver colored spots, and a slightly unpleasant aroma to attract fly pollinators.

Orostachys A genus of small rosette forming *Sempervivum* relatives mostly from central Asia and therefore extremely hardy. Rosettes bolt to form spikes of flowers after which they die but offsets usually persist. *O. fimbriatus* is one of the easiest to grow in milder climates, being more heat tolerant than most, and has attractive white flowers with red anthers.

Othonna Mostly winter growing allies of *Senecio* with small yellow daisy flowers. Most are slow growing caudiciforms ideal for containers or a summer dry rockery. *O. capensis,* without a caudex, is a vigorous yearround grower with small club-shaped leaves on trailing stems that create a dense groundcover.

Phytolacca dioica Do you have a lot of room? Then try this fast-growing pokeweed relative. Its massive caudiciform base can spread to ten feet across or more. Its soft branches form a tree like crown to fifty feet high and across though it is really just an overgrown herb!

Piaranthus Another genus of stapeliads (succulent milkweeds) with small creeping potato shaped, jointed stems. Half inch star shaped flowers are attractively spotted or banded and have a curious musty fragrance. Some are surprisingly hardy (Zone 9) nestled between stones of a rockery.

Rebutia Small clumping cacti with abundant flowers produced near the base of the stems over several weeks in spring. Flower colors range from white through yellow orange, red, pink, and magenta.

Rhipsalidopsis Epiphytic cacti related to *Schlumbergera* with pink or red flowers.

Rhipsalis (mistletoe cacti) Tropical epiphytes with often spineless spaghettilike stems. Good hanging basket plant in Zone 10 or with protection in Zone 9.

Rhombophyllum Small cushion forming mesembs with yellow flowers and antler-shaped leaves. Hardy to Zones 8-10.

Stapelia Prized for their large unusual flowers. *S. gigantea* is among the most impressive of the stapeliads for it pod like buds which open into star-shaped flowers six inches across. *S. leendertziae* is among the hardiest (25°) with four-inch-long dark purple bell-shaped flowers.

Stenocactus (brain cactus, wave cactus) Solitary or clustering, with stems resembling small ferocacti but with wavy ribs. Excellent rockery plants.

Stomatium agninum Slowly spreading mesemb resembling *Pleiospilos* with thick fleshy paired leaves and yellow flowers. A persistent rockery accent or small area groundcover.

Synadenium grantii (African milkbush) A frost tender *Euphorbia* relative with fleshy green obovate leaves, purple in cultivar 'Rubra'.

Sulcorebutia Clump-forming cacti similar to *Rebutia* with pectinate spines and a range of vivid flower colors from yellow to orange, red, and magenta.

Thelocactus Solitary or offsetting squat globular to short columnar cacti with large white, pink, or bicolored flowers. *T. bicolor* has attractive red and white spines. *T. hexaedrophorus* bears clusters of clawlike reddish spines on bold rounded tubercles with grayish skin.

Tillandsia Epiphytic bromeliads with rosettes of leaves covered with silvery scales and a wide range of small beautifully-colored flowers. Need partial shade.

Titanopsis Dwarf stonelike mesembs with rosettes of warty leaves and small flowers similar to Aloinopsis

Ficus palmeri.

Rhipsalidopsis.

plant selector

Opposite: Echinopsis, Cercidium, Encelia.

COMPANION PLANTS

The traditional way of growing cacti and other succulents is in gardens that are completely devoted to that group of plants. And there are good reasons for doing so; the dramatic structure, texture, and colors of succulents combine with spectacular results. Since cultural requirements are similar for the group, planting them together–and excluding other plants that require different care and will not necessarily look right in combinations–makes good sense.

However, there is a vast range of non-succulent plants that can greatly enhance a succulent landscape. In many contemporary gardens, these plants are used to provide contrast, counterpoint, and accents–to integrate a new layer of shapes, scents, and colors. They allow the gardener to experiment with a much wider selection of plant material, and, if used correctly, bring out the best in both the succulents and the companion plants.

Most categories of garden plants can be incorporated into succulent gardens. Herbaceous annuals and perennials add interest while bridging gaps in succulent bloom. Desert shrubs and small trees, native to climates similar to cacti and often found growing with them in the wild, are unbeatable companions; their forms, though dissimilar, are often complementary. Grasses can provide groundcover as well as softening an overall effect when that is desired.

One primary factor must be considered when choosing companion plants: cultural requirements. Most succulents require a specific set of conditions: bright light, little water, good air circulation, and balanced fertilizer, especially during the growing season. Companion plants should share these requirements.

However, similar cultural requirements alone will not assure that companions harmonize with or enhance their succulent neighbors. Thus, aesthetics are introduced into plant selection, whereby a perspicacious gardener needs to consider the appearance of likely companions. In some cases, plants that are extremely drought tolerant–truly xeriphilous–are aesthetically incompatible. With the enormous range of shapes, textures, and forms available on the market, it is fairly easy to find other plants that work in the succulent landscape. But that doesn't mean you will be happy with every xeriphilous plant labeled "drought tolerant" at your local nursery. Using companion non-succulents in the succulent landscape requires thought and planning–often as enjoyable as the results.

In the opinion of the gardeners at The Huntington, some plants just don't work well with succulents. We avoid lush tropical plants for two reasons. First, their cultural requirements are radically different, typically requiring considerably more water and shade than the rest of the garden would need. Secondly, we think their totally different textures and color palettes don't play well off the muted foliage of succulents. Contrast is often the best part of a landscape–but sometimes it's simply jarring. To us, a canna or camellia mixed in with cacti is intellectually and aesthetically wrong–they look like they don't belong together because they truly don't. Their differences can be read in their leaves. The abundant, often large foliage of tropicals is evidence of their

climatic and geographic origin; mixed with succulents, they create an unbelievable landscape, shouting out the fact that they would never occur together in nature. Planted together, they create at best a scene of whimsy and fantasy rather than of natural harmony.

In considering companion plants for inclusion in any style of garden, three broad categories emerge: the not-recommended, the culturally appropriate but aesthetically questionable, and the highly recommended. The first category, the not-recommended, are plants that for some reason are not appropriate for the planned garden. For succulent landscapers, this category includes water and fertilizer guzzlers–shrubs like camellias, peonies, roses, hebes, and azaleas, and trees like maples, dogwoods, and redbuds. Herbaceous plants like hostas, astilbes, and alchemillas that demand damp shade and copious water year round in warm climates occupy a similar forbidden niche. Such plants should be erased from your gardening palette, before temptation sets in and insidious stray pansies ("for color") nudge into the front of your mellow-toned blue-gray-green succulent patch.

The great range of plants that can be grown with additional water tempts many a southwestern gardener to mix in whatever strikes his fancy. If he loves roses as well as succulents, you'll see hybrid teas proudly juxtaposed between striking agaves and contorted opuntias in his garden. If you like that sort of eclectic mixture, and are willing to take the extra time and effort to make them grow together, it is certainly your prerogative. But with the vast and enticing array of other plants available, it is unnecessary to do so.

XERISCAPE PLANTS The second category of plants to ponder are those that form appropriate companions for succulents according to cultural requirements but are disturbing from most aesthetic viewpoints. For succulent gardeners, these are herbaceous plants that will survive with low water (although not necessarily looking their best) like daylilies, composites of various kinds, (*Achillea, Echinacea, Rudbeckia,* marigolds, most zinnias, etc.), cannas and *Verbena.* Shrubs like *Juniperus sabina* and *Mahonia* and trees like *Pinus halepensis* and *Prunus lyonii,* though popular xeriscaping elements, do not mesh well in general with succulents. In addition, many favored xeriscaping plants of other climatic regions prove unsuitable in the Southwest. For example, plants classified as xeriscape candidates in the Northeast or Midwest may tolerate drought well enough in Pennsylvania or Iowa, but will expire when receiving only monthly watering while the thermometer lingers at 112° F. for weeks on end.

Although there are many large trees that can be recommended for the Southwest, most should be kept far from the succulent beds. Leaves or branches that drop onto prickly plants are difficult to remove, and most succulents don't flourish in the dense shade that many of these plants create. Some trees that work well in the southwest in other parts of the garden are Brazilian pepper, which has graceful lacey foliage and good drought-tolerance but drops resinous leaves; avocado, which provides delicious fruit and is drought-tolerant after it is established, but whose large leaves produce dense shade and whose surface roots compete with succulents; some *Eucalyptus*

Top left: *Echinacea* and *Rudbeckia*. Top right: *Tagetes lemonii*. Above: *Nerium* (Oleander). All of these are good xeriscape plants, but don't mix well with succulents.

The subtropical garden at Huntington Botanical Gardens uses a great many xeriscapic plants. Succulents would not be effective in this garden, just as these plants would not be appreciated in a succulent garden.

species that are very drought tolerant and whose straplike leaves, often complementary in color to succulents, do not create too much shade, unfortunately would create a resinous mess of dense leaf litter made worse by broken branches; and Chinese elm, which is valuable in dry climates because it is virtually unkillable, but whose dense shade and leaf drop take it out of consideration as a companion to succulents.

Though many shrubs are extremely good partners to succulents, some that are great desert plants should only be used elsewhere. Oleander, often used as a hedge, is extremely heat and drought tolerant—some people think it is overused, but that's partly because it is so well-suited to hot, dry climates. But its bright, lush colors overpower most succulents. *Plumbago*, a lovely spreading shrub with light blue or white flowers and vivid green foliage, is too large and invasive for the succulent garden but is great for a larger landscape. *Fremontodendron* is valuable for its extreme drought-tolerance—but it won't tolerate the watering that most succulents need during their growing period. Ombu is too big; castor bean is too invasive and out of scale (in addition to having seeds that are lethal if ingested)—but all are great xeriscape plants.

GOOD COMPANIONS One reason that it is easy to exclude impractical plants from the succulent garden is that there are so many plants that make perfect companions—plants with similar cultural requirements as well as forms and colors that blend or complement those of the succulents. What follows is a list of some successful companions for succulents. This list is far from comprehensive, but does give a hint of the range of possibilities.

TREES AND SHRUBS Desert shrubs and trees are the most obvious and often the best choices for companion plants. Because they are native to the same general climate zone, they require virtually the same conditions and care as desert cacti and other succulents. Because they've also had to adapt to these conditions, they have some of the same physical characteristics, such as blue-gray color. But they are also different, and it is the differences that make them desirable. Their foliage is often feathery, a lovely counterpoint to the almost-monolithic columnar cactus. The infrastructure of these shrubs placed among the dense solidity of the succulents provides a sense of depth to the garden. The qualities that make them useful here–their loose, airy, open habit–make them less apt candidates for traditional perennial borders, where some of the previously-mentioned xeriscape shrubs are perfect. If every plant has its place, the succulent garden is certainly a great place for desert shrubs.

Desert trees and shrubs are not quite as forgiving of neglect as succulents; you can't leave them in their bare-root form for a couple of months and then forget to water them for a few more and still expect them to bounce back. They also take some time to establish.

Acacia cavens, from Argentina, is an extremely drought-tolerant small tree (to twenty feet) that produces an abundance of fragrant, yellow pompom flowers in early spring. Although it casts a fair amount of shade and sometimes causes

Acacia cavens **provides light shade for succulents.**

problems with leaf drop, its feathery foliage is a welcome addition to the succulent landscape. Numerous other dryland acacias occur, such as *A. cymbispina,* the bullhorn acacia from Mexico with inflated paired spines, and *A. karoo,* from South Africa, with long white spines. *A smallii* (sweet acacia) and *A. erioloba* (camelthorn) are popular in the Phoenix area. There is a suitable form for any situation among the dozens of xeric species.

Arctostaphylos Compact shrubs with dark red bark and small urn-shaped white flowers; to eight feet tall. Best in areas of coastal influence or high elevation.

Atriplex lentiformis (quailbush), a California native, has silvery oval or arrow-shaped leaves and insignificant flowers. A spreading shrub, it grows to ten feet or more and is one of many silver-leaved plants that combine nicely with other plants.

Brachychiton rupestris (bottle tree), of Queensland, Australia, has a swollen, bottle-shaped trunk that looks succulent, and divided palmate leaves. It is not recommended for the Phoenix area.

Caesalpinia is both heat and drought tolerant and a delicate, feathery counterpoint to cacti. *C. gilliesii* (bird of paradise shrub) from South America and *C. pulcherrima* (Barbados pride), from the Caribbean, are open, drought-tolerant species well-suited for the succulent garden, but *C. cacalaco* must be mentioned for its unusual branches covered with bold thorns showing unusual growth rings. All the species bear beautiful red or yellow flowers in spring. Propagate by seeds, which sprout more readily if soaked in warm water overnight; transplant seedlings as soon as first true leaves appear.

Below: *Calliandra californica* with *Agave, Salvia, Cereus,* and *Encelia* at The Desert Botanical Garden in Phoenix.

ARCTOSTAPHYLOS DENSIFLORA 'HOWARD MCMINN' Forms a low, mounded mass of one-inch leaves green leaves with pale pink flowers in winter; becomes open to expose dark red bark trunks. Grows up to six feet tall. Zones 7-10.

CAESALPINIA CACALACO To ten feet tall. Branches covered with bold thorns showing unusual growth rings. Clusters of yellow flowers with red stamens from spring through summer. Zones 8-10.

CAESALPINIA GILLIESII (BIRD OF PARADISE SHRUB) Open habit, to ten feet tall. Clusters of yellow flowers with long bright red stamens from spring through summer. Heat and drought tolerant. Zones 8-10.

CALLIANDRA CALIFORNICA (RED FAIRYDUSTER) Evergreen shrub with compound leaves and brilliant red blooms from spring through summer and into fall. Best in hot climates, full sun. Zones 8-10.

Cassia artemesioides.

Calliandra californica (red fairyduster) is an evergreen native to Baja California that is hardy to temperatures in the teens as well as to desert conditions; it needs heat to thrive. It has tiny, dark green compound leaves that are a fine background to its long-lasting brilliant red blooms. At Desert Botanical Garden, it blooms from March to December. Plant in spring or fall, never in the heat of summer. *C. eriophylla* has pink blooms and lighter foliage than *C. californica.* It blooms in the spring and then becomes deciduous and does not rebloom that year.

Cassia (senna, shower tree) is a large genus of trees and shrubs, among the showiest of the tropicals and subtropicals. *C. artemesioides* (wormwood) from Australia produces feathery gray-green foliage and attractive yellow flowers. Although it reseeds itself, it is not invasive and is extremely drought tolerant.

Ceanothus is a genus of shrubs mostly from western North America prized for their fragrant clusters of white to blue flowers. Most of the Pacific coast species and their derivatives are hardy to Zone 8 but do not do well in desert conditions. One of the choicest is the hybrid *C.* 'Concha' which forms a mounding shrub to six feet covered with cobalt blue flowers.

Cercidium floridum, of the southwest U. S. and northern Mexico, forms a small tree to thirty feet with an attractive structure of blue-green-barked branches, hence the common name of palo verde, meaning green stick in Spanish. *C. microphyllum* and *C. praecox* are other useful paloverdes. *C. farinacea* is a more billowy (though still small) shrub. The small leaves are drought deciduous, photosynthetic functions being performed by the bark.

Chilopsis linearis, (desert willow), another Southwest native, often grows along desert washes where its deep roots tap ground water reserves allowing it to grow year round. Its light feathery texture is different from that of many other shrubs, and its leaf drop is not as significant. It flowers even in extreme heat, producing blooms of pink, lilac, or purple, and grows to twenty feet or more.

Chorisia speciosa, the floss-silk tree from South America can grow to fifty feet, has a swollen trunk that looks almost succulent, and a thorny light green bark. Although leaf drop is a problem, it creates a bright shade. It's flowers are magnificent—delicate pink and white.

Cistus (rockrose) is a low mounding or prostrate shrub native to the Mediterranean region. Rockroses have exceptionally pretty and abundant flowers, white to pink, of simple design and often with a spot of color at the base.

Cordia parviflora of the Sonora desert reaches about eight feet in height and makes an excellent border shrub. It is a very drought-tolerant ornamental with tiny, deeply veined gray-green leaves. In summer, it blooms profusely with papery-looking white flowers about one inch in diameter; bloom will continue in a rainy summer or with deep irrigation. Its relative, *C. boissieri* (Texas olive) gets much larger over time and has big, olive-colored leaves. Its blooms are over two inches wide, pure white with a yellow throat, in clusters.

Cotoneaster congestus is a low mounding shrub with dark green foliage and white flowers followed by longlasting red berries.

Dalea pulchra is a beautiful late winter/early spring blooming shrub, usually six to eight feet tall. It is characterized by tiny gray-green leaves. In late winter,

CASSIA ARTEMESIOIDES (WORMWOOD) Three to five feet tall. Feathery gray-green foliage and attractive yellow flowers in late winter and early spring. Extremely drought-tolerant. Zones 8-10.

CEANOTHUS 'CONCHA' Mounding shrub to six feet tall covered with cobalt blue flowers. Does not tolerate extreme heat or cold. Zones 8-10. Shown with *Furcraea gigantea* and *F. selloa* 'Marginata'.

CHORISIA SPECIOSA (FLOSS-SILK TREE) Tree to fifty feet with swollen trunk and thorny light green bark, huge pink and white flowers. Zones 8-10.

CISTUS (ROCKROSE) Low mounding shrubs with abundant white simple flowers. Tolerate heat, wind, and drought. Zones 9-10.

DALEA GREGGII (TRAILING INDIGO BUSH) Prostrate evergreen groundcover with clusters of purple flowers. Extremely heat and drought tolerant. Zones 8-10.

DALEA FRUTESCENS Prostrate evergreen groundcover with clusters of purple flowers. Extremely heat and drought tolerant. Zones 8-10.

DODONEA VICOSA (HOPBUSH) Evergreen shrub with narrow green or purple foliage. Tolerant of heat, drought, poor soil, and wind. Zones 8-10.

ERYTHRINA ACANTHOCARPA Stiff open six-foot shrub with dense heads of showy green-tipped red flowers. Heat and drought tolerant. Zones 9-10.

the plant blooms with a profusion of lavender blossoms. The overall effect is of a light purple powderpuff. The plant blooms for almost four months, from February until May. Its long bloom season and great drought and heat tolerance make this an ideal plant for the desert; its color and form make it a perfect companion to succulents. Other species in the genus to consider are *D. frutescens* and *D. greggii*.

Dodonaea viscosa (hopbush) of the New World tropics and subtropics is tough as nails. The commonly grown *D. viscosa* 'Purpurea' has dark foliage, and can be pruned into a small open tree or shrub with attractive peeling bark. It is often used as a backdrop or screen. *D. microzyga*, from Australia, is a smaller, mounding shrub with longlasting terracotta-colored fruits.

Encelia farinosa (brittlebush) is the quintessential desert shrub, native to the southwest U.S. and northern Mexico. Its gray foliage forms a compact ball and is covered with long-stemmed yellow daisies in spring. It becomes large and leggy if overwatered.

Erythrina, the coral tree genus, includes many shrubby forms. *E. acanthocarpa* of South Africa; forms a stiff open six-foot shrub with dense heads of showy green-tipped red flowers. *E. flabelliformis* is another shrubby species native to the Southwest.

Geijera parviflora (Australian willow) is a drought-tolerant small tree with an open habit and a wispy, willowy look.

Agave colorata, Gomphrena globosa 'Strawberry Fields', Artemisia 'Powys Castle', Cheiridopsis denticulata, Cotoneaster congestus.

Erythrina acanthocarpa in The Huntington Desert Garden.

plant selector

*Encelia farinosa, Justicia californica,
Penstemon parryi, Carnegiea gigantea*

Guaiacum coulteri, a purplish-blue-flowered relative of the common desert creosote bush is native to Mexico. It usually grows eight feet tall and is hardy to 25° F.

Justicia californica (chuparosa) of the deserts of the Southwest and northern Mexico has gray sticklike stems with small gray-green leaves on a shrub to six feet tall. Its tubular red flowers attract hummingbirds. There is also a yellow-flowered form.

Larrea tridentata (creosote) is considered by some to be the world's oldest plant, with some clones believed to have persisted for over 10,000 years. A handsome shrub, its main attraction is its heady aroma that brings with it the essence of the desert. It is a very common in Arizona and throughout the southwest. There is probably no more drought-adapted plant on earth; its ability to wrench water from dry soil is legendary. It does, however, produce a compound that impedes the growth of neighboring plants. The plants are lovely, open and airy, and offer a wonderful light shade for smaller plants. In spring, they are coated with small yellow flowers that are followed by hairy white fruits. Dark green in spring, creosote acquires a yellow cast in summer; it looks beautiful when backlit by the summer sun.

Leucophyllum frutescens (Texas ranger) is native to Texas and Mexico and often used as an informal hedge. It produces an abundance of rosy purple bell-shaped flowers in summer and holds on to its silvery foliage throughout the year. It is less successful in areas of the country where humidity and night temperatures are high. It needs very well-drained soil, but can tolerate alkalinity. Best planted in fall. 'White Cloud', ' Green Cloud' and 'Compacta' are cultivars developed at Texas A&M University. 'Green Cloud is the largest, growing over ten feet tall; it is often called "barometer bush" because it blooms after the rain. *L. laevigatum*, known as cenizo, is less formal in shape, with small green leaves and masses of dark blue blooms. Other exciting new species and cultivars are appearing on the market.

Mahonia nevinii, native to southern California, grows eight to ten feet tall. It has narrow gray spiny leaves and attractive red berries. It is very drought tolerant and makes an effective barrier or backdrop.

Myoporum parviflorum, from hot, dry, interior Australia, is a low (six-inch) bright-green groundcover with small leaves and white flowers. It looks good planted as a groundcover near agaves.

Parkinsonia aculeata, similar to *Cercidium,* is a leguminous desert tree (to thirty feet) with blue-green bark, yellow flowers and wispy foliage that casts light shade. A good "nurse" tree in desert climates for plants that need a little protection.

Phylica plumosa (featherhead) is a South African shrub to four feet tall with soft fuzzy linear leaves densely covering the stems. Backlighting makes it appear to glow.

Pithecellobium flexicaule (Texas ebony) has interesting gnarled fruit pods; when left to grow naturally, it makes a terrific evergreen hedge and can reach a height of fifteen feet or more, enough to hide almost anything.

JUSTICIA CALIFORNICA (CHUPAROSA) Shrub to four feet or more with gray sticklike stems with small gray-green leaves and tubular red flowers. Zones 8-10.

LEUCOPHYLLUM FRUTESCENS (TEXAS RANGER) Four- to eight-foot tall evergreen shrub with rosey-purple bell-shaped flowers and silvery foliage. Drought and heat tolerant. Zones 8-10.

PARKINSONIA ACULEATA (MEXICAN PALO VERDE, JERUSALEM THORN) Desert tree to thirty feet with blue-green bark, yellow flowers and wispy foliage that casts light shade. Very heat and drought tolerant. Zones 7-10.

PHYLICA PUBESCENS (FEATHERHEAD) Shrub to four feet with soft fuzzy leaves. Especially attractive when backlit. Zones 9-10.

Salvia greggii, Bulbine latifolia.

Rosmarinus officinale has succulent-looking leaves; the prostrate form looks particularly good as a groundcover or cascading over a wall. Upright forms are also available with flowers in varying shades of blue.

Rhus lancea, African sumac, is an extremely heat- and drought-tolerant tree, to twenty or thirty feet high and across. Its leaves are dark green with three narrow leaflets. Its bark has a dark rust color. *Rhus ovata,* sugarbush, is a Southwest native shrub, eventually to twenty feet high and across. It is grown for its glossy green ovate leaves and ornamental flower clusters on a dense rounded shrub which is amenable to pruning to reveal interesting bark and trunk character.

Salvia greggii is the one of the best salvias for the deserts. It is small in stature–making it appropriate for interplanting among succulents–and extremely drought and heat tolerant. Its leaves are small, obovate, and clustered at their tips, along with flowers that are typically red; there are also selected forms with white, yellow, salmon, plum, and burgundy flowers. Other useful salvias are *S. leucantha,* which forms a spreading shrub densely covered with fuzzy purple flowers most of the year, and *S. apiana,* a tough California native with a more open habit.

Simmondsia chinensis (jojoba) is a Southwest native that has become known as a source of fine oil yielded from its nuts. It is less well known as a superb shrub for the desert as well as coastal xeriscaping. It forms a dense, rounded shrub of simple leathery gray leaves and is useful as a background or screen.

Sophora secundiflora (Texas mountain laurel) has flowers that look like wisteria and smell like grape Koolaid™. A dense, dark green evergreen shrub that can reach ten feet in height, it puts out large hanging panicles of violet purple blooms followed by dark pods filled with bright red seeds. Although somewhat slow-growing, it blooms young. It is a favorite food plant of pipevine swallowtail butterflies.

Sphaeralcea ambigua, (desert mallow) native to the southwest U.S. and Mexico, has showy (though small) hibiscus-shaped orange flowers, grayish foliage, and an open, vase-shaped habit. It is very drought tolerant.

Tecoma stans var. angustata, (Arizona yellowbells) from the southwest U.S. and northern Mexico, is a tall shrub (up to eighteen feet) with long, serrated green leaves on tall wands of stems and loose heads of large, intensely yellow tubular flowers in spring. This plant thrives on heat; it is best in a western exposure.

VINES

Often, a vine can provide a great backdrop to a succulent landscape. Because they can be a little further away, rather than being mixed in, they do not need to be as similar in either culture or aesthetics. In fact, if a hint of lushness is desired in a desert garden, a tropical vine like bougainvillea is the best way to achieve it. Beware of vines that spread too rapidly, like passionflower.

Antigonon leptopus (coral vine), from Mexico, has heart-shaped thin green leaves and nearly ball-shaped flowers in delicate pink. It is attractive when growing up a tree or large shrub. It is a bit cold sensitive, but recovers quickly.

Bougainvillea, native to South America, provides long-lasting color throughout

ROSMARINUS OFFICINALIS Evergreen shrub with flat, fragrant leaves and small blue, white, or pink flowers. Some varieties grow to six feet; others are prostrate. Tolerate heat and drought. Zones 7-10.

SALVIA GREGGII Shrubby plant two to three feet tall with clusters of magenta flowers through most of the year. Heat and drought tolerant. Zones 7-10.

SALVIA LEUCANTHA (MEXICAN BUSH SAGE) Spreading shrub to four feet tall with spikes of fuzzy flowers in many shades of blue, purple, and red. Zones 8-10.

SIMMONDSIA CHINENSIS (JOJOBA) Dense, rounded shrub to ten feet tall or more with simple leathery gray leaves, useful as a background or screen. Zones 8-10.

the warm season by virtue of its showy bracts. The flowers are actually rather small and pale. It is often seen as a rampant vine swallowing trees and structures in a cloud of color, but shrubby forms also occur such as 'Raspberry Ice' and 'Rosenka'. Though eventually quite large, to twenty feet, these can also be incorporated as young plants and pruned to be kept in bounds.

Hardenbergia violacea, a tough evergreen vine from Australia, is a dense fast grower and requires little supplemental water. It produces profuse, intensely purple wisteria-like flowers.

Mascagnia macroptera (yellow orchid vine) is an outstanding vine for the desert, with small yellow flowers and winged pods. Frost-sensitive, it will die with first frost, but will recover well. *M. lilacina,* purple orchid vine, is hardy to 15° F.

Maurandella antirrhiniflora (snapdragon vine) is a small delicate vine, but it has loads of dark purple flowers that look like miniature snapdragons. In some areas, it is aggressive and reseeds itself from year to year rather than resisting frost; in other areas it is perennial.

Merremia aurea, a magnificent member of the morning glory family, has attractive wide green leaves and very large (up to three inches) deep yellow flowers that are continuous throughout the summer. They are followed by teardrop-shaped pods. Though frost-tender, this vine produces massive roots that resprout year after year.

Above: Cercidium floribundum. Right: Bougainvillea, Encelia farinosa, Ferocactus acanthodes, Opuntia basilaris.. Opposite: Chamaerops humilis, Aloe striata, Cordyline australis.

Agave americana, Centranthus ruber.

HERBACEOUS PERENNIALS AND ANNUALS Achieving a harmonious combination between most herbaceous perennials and cacti and other succulents requires some effort. Some of the most common perennials, like daylilies or hostas do not work well with succulents—in the case of daylilies because of their form, in the case of hostas because of their cultural needs. Other perennials and annuals are obvious choices—*Gazania rigens* is often used in mass bedding like iceplants and can complement them. Although effort is required to make the combinations of succulents and herbaceous plants work, it is often well spent, providing new colors, textures, and longer seasons of bloom in the succulent garden, as well as a wealth of additional plant material to work with.

When choosing herbaceous plants for the succulent landscape, plan for the long term. Any gardener who has ever spent days taking *Lantana montevidensis* out of an *Agave* bed (and still didn't get it all!) will tell you how important it is to avoid introducing plants that are invasive or spreading. In most cases, experimentation is a good practice; with regard to planting things that may multiply in a cactus bed, it isn't. If you don't know for sure, don't plant it.

Many perennial and annual plants like santolinas and lupines are actually happier in the Southwest than in less extreme climates; it seems that the humidity—and accompanying fungus diseases—that is common in many warm areas is more harmful to plants than the heat.

As with shrubs, most herbaceous plants require more care than succulents. In other types of gardens, annuals and perennials are often planted in tightly marked zones giving a fomal effect. In a succulent garden, they usually look more natural scattered among the other plants. Seeds of annuals may be scattered at the beginning of the rainy season while most perennials can be planted in any but the hottest time of year, if provided sufficient watering to establish before that time. Unlike succulents, annuals and perennials should be watered generously immediately after planting.

The terms "annual" and "perennial" can be a bit confusing. An herbaceous perennial plant is one that dies to the ground each year but whose roots survive to reflower for more than two years (a biennial plant lasts two years). An annual plant dies completely after one season's growth; only the seeds remain. However, many perennials are tender, and do not survive more than a few years; and many plants that are perennials in a mild climate are grown as annuals in cooler climates. And many annuals reseed themselves freely, so they return the following year without replanting.

Abronia villosa, (sand verbena) Trailing, low-growing plant with verbenalike flowers, usually white, pink, or yellow. Grown as a winter annual.

Achillea (yarrow) Ferny foliage and flat corymbs of flowers in white or yellow; selections in many other colors. Full sun; drought and heat tolerant. *A. tomentosa,* a low-growing species, has small heads of yellow flowers and almost ferny-looking foliage. *A. filipendula* has large bright gold flowers, and grows four to five feet tall. Perennial in zones 5-10.

Asclepias curassavica (Bloodflower) Summer-blooming plant to four feet tall with small two-toned orange flowers in clusters. Drought and heat tolerant; annual. Other members of this genus, e.g. *A. linaria,* are perennial and are

Asclepias curassavica.

Baileya multiradiata.

Centranthus ruber.

Chrysanthemum pacificum with
Aeonium haworthii.

Clarkia concinna.

Collinsia heterophylla.

Coreopsis verticillata.

Echium wildpretii.

Eschscholzia mexicana.

Gaillardia grandiflora 'Goblin'.

Gazania rigens.

Gazania linearis with *Lampranthus* and *Drosanthemum.*

Gomphrena globosa 'Strawberry Fields'

Helenium autumnale

Hypoestes aristata.

Nemophila menziesii.

Penstemon parryi.

Phacelia parryi.

also useful in succulent gardens.

Baileya multiradiata Gray green foliage and yellow ray flowers; extremely drought- and heat tolerant. Do not overwater. Perennial in zones 7-10.

Centranthus ruber (red valerian) Blue-green foliage and dull pinkish, red, or white flowers in sparse racemes. Tolerates heat, sun or partial shade, drought. Perennial in zones 5-10.

Cheilanthes and other desert ferns are surprisingly drought and heat tolerant and thrive in rocker crevices even in full sun. Their xeric appearance often belies their affinities.

Coreopsis (Tickseed) Yellow daisy-like ray flowers. *C. grandiflora* forms clumps of dark green foliage and bright yellow double flowers. *C. verticillata* has ferny foliage and single lemon yellow flowers. Perennial in Zones 4-10. *C. tinctoria* is an annual form with bicolored dark red and yellow heads.

Clarkia concinna (red ribbons) Six- to eighteen-inch-tall winter annual with red violet flowers with long, narrow petals. Full sun to partial shade.

Clianthus formosus (desert pea, Sturt pea) Spreading plant to four feet across with unusual red flowers, to three inches long with shiny black blotch at base. Summer annual.

Collinsia heterophylla (Chinese houses) Winter annual, to two-feet tall, with whorls of flowers on pagodalike towers.

Dorotheanthus bellidiformis (Livingstone daisy) Tender winter annual with large showy brightly-colored flowers with dark centers.

Echium wildpretii (tower of jewels) Biennial with a one-foot basal rosette of hairy linear leaves. Bolts in spring to form a six-foot tower, closely packed with spirals of pink flowers..

Eschscholzia californica (California poppy) Freely reseeding winter annual with ferny gray foliage and satiny orange or yellow four-petalled flowers. *E. mexicana* is a closely related species with flowers in white to pink or orange.

Gaillardia grandiflora Three- to four-foot tall plant with daisylike flowers in many

*Above: **Phacelia parryi** with **Cleistocactus strausii**. Left: **Cleistocactus strausii** with California poppies and other wildflowers*

shades of red and yellow, often banded and with darker center. Full sun; drought tolerant once established. Perennial in Zones 5-10. An annual form, *G. pulchella* grows to two to three feet and bears similar flowers year round in mild climates and reseeds freely.

Gazania Low growing, spreading plants with large daisylike flowers in spring and summer. Drought and heat tolerant. Perennial in zones 8-10. *G. rigens* (treasure flower) is useful as a groundcover. Its bright orange flowers are often ornamented with a multicolored blotch at the base of each petal. *G. linearis* has silvery gray hairy leaves and yellow flowers.

Gomphrena globosa Two- to four-foot tall summer annual with flowers in round thistlelike but nonspiny heads. Drought and heat tolerant. Normally magenta, the cultivar 'Strawberry Fields' has bright red heads; 'Alba' has white.

Hedeoma ciliata, a mint relative from Mexico relatively new to cultivation, forms dense cushions with profuse tubular dull red flowers.

Helenium autumnale (sneezeweed) Yellow, red, orange, or copper daisylike flowers with brown centers on tall stems. Full sun, drought tolerant. Zones 4-10.

Lavandula (lavender) Shrubby plants with fragrant foliage and flowers. *L. angustifolia* has gray foliage, is drought-tolerant, and is perennial in zones 4-10 and reseeds in southern California. *L. stoechas* is similar, but has showy bracts atop each spike the same color as the flowers. *L. dentata,* with dentate greener foliage, is hardy in zones 8-10.

Linaria maroccana Winter annual with small but fascinating multicolored snapdragonlike flowers, each with a long spur at the base.

Lobularia maritima, (sweet allyssum) Quick-growing spreading mat with clusters of tiny white flowers with a sweet fragrance. Full sun best, tolerates light shade. Winter annual, reseeds itself.

Lupinus Mostly annuals with purple or purple and white pealike flowers in whorls on erect racemes. *L. densiflorus aureus* has bright yellow flowers.

Melampodium leucanthum (Blackfoot daisy) White daisylike flowers with yellow centers in spring and summer. Needs some water. Short-lived perennial in zones 9-10.

Mimulus aurantiacus (syn. *M. longiflorus*) becomes woody at the base. The sticky herbaceous foliage bears delicate apricot-colored snapdragonlike flowers. Hybrids come in a range of colors: white, yellow, orange, red, and burgundy.

Nemophila maculata (five spot) Winter annual with profuse one-inch, five-petalled flowers, white with a purple spot at the tip of each petal. *N. menziesii* (baby blue eyes) has bright blue flowers.

Penstemon parryi Tall stalks with rose or magenta flowers in racemes and leathery gray-green foliage. Drought and heat tolerant. Perennial in Zones 8-10.

Phacelia Winter annuals, usually blue or purple, sometimes white or pink flowers densely arranged on coiled fiddleheadlike inflorescences.

Phlox subulata (moss pink) Low-growing, spreading plant with small pink flowers. Full sun, drought tolerant but looks better with more water. Zones 5-9.

Portulaca grandiflora (moss rose) Drought and heat tolerant summer annual with one-inch flowers, single with yellow stamens or double, in many shades from magenta to yellow. Needs full sun. Reseeds freely.

Psilotrophe bakeri Mat-forming gray-foliaged perennial covered with yellow dai-

Phlox subulata.

Santolina virens.

Stachys byzantina.

Verbascum bombyciferum.

Zauschneria californica.

Zinnia grandiflora with *Echinocereus triglochidiatus* var. *melanacanthus.*

Festuca ovina var. *glauca.*

Helictotrichon sempervirens. Crassula capitella.

Pennisetum setaceum 'Rubrum', *Aeonium.*

sylike flowers in summer. Hardy in Denver.

Romneya coulteri (Matilija poppy) Tall plant, growing to six feet or more, with crepe-textured white flowers with a yellow ball of stamens in late spring or early summer. Zones 6-10.

Santolina Shrubby plants with finely divided foliage, mounding habit, slender stalks and half-inch hemispheres of minute yellow flowers. Full sun to partial shade, drought-tolerant. *S. chamaecyparissus* has gray foliage; *S. virens* has darker green foliage. Perennial in all zones.

Sanvitalia procumbens Creeping summer annual, to six inches tall, with abundant small bright yellow daisylike heads of flowers, aging orange. Full sun, drought tolerant.

Stachys byzantina (Lamb's ears) Groundcover with silver-gray wooly leaves with lavender flowers nestled in wooly stalks. Full sun or partial shade, drought-tolerant. Perennial in zones 4-10.

Verbascum bombyciferum Bright yellow flowers on spikes to five feet tall or more with felt-covered white foliage. Biennial.

Verbena Popular plants, producing clusters of small flowers in many colors. *V. peruviana* and *V. rigida* (which is usually grown as an annual) are a bit rampant and brightly colored. *V. gooddingii,* an annual native of Arizona, is more subdued in both color and spread.

Zauschneria californica (syn. *Epilobium canum;* California fuschia) Spreading,

Festuca ovina var. *glauca, Kalanchoe blossfeldiana, Aeonium arboreum 'Zwartkop', Dasylirion longissimum, Agave parryi, Beaucarnea recurvata, Aloe plicatilis, Agave americana 'Variegata', and Crassula ovata 'Variegata'.*

shrubby evergreen perennial with gray foliage and bright red tubular flowers
in fall when little else is in flower. Very drought-tolerant.

GRASSES AND GRASSLIKE PLANTS are used as accents in succulent beds more often
than for groundcover. If planted too close together, they will overrun the succulent plants, but their softness can provide a welcome contrast to the more
solid succulents if used sparingly. Spacing will be determined by the ultimate
size of the clump. Those listed here will survive happily with the same watering as succulents.

Chondropetalum tectorum A grasslike plant from South Africa with attractive dark
brown bracts at regular intervals on dark green cylindrical linear leaves in
graceful rosettes; to five feet across.

Festuca ovina* var. *glauca (blue fescue) Clump-forming grass with narrow, silver-
blue foliage. Prefers part shade in hot climates.

Helictotrichon sempervirens (blue oat grass) Mound-forming grass with narrow
light blue foliage; an attractive complement to red flowers or foliage.

***Pennisetum setaceum* 'Rubrum'** (fountain grass) Deep red blades with bottlebrush-
like flowers in spring; this sterile selection will not become invasive like other
pennisetums. Hardy in Zones 8-10.

Xanthorrhoea quadrangulata has a habit similar to *Dasylirion*, and tolerates very dry
conditions.

BULBS are useful additions to the succulent landscape, requiring little space and
adding color at various times of the year, filling niches and flowering through
and above other foliage as few other plants can. While many are winter growing, the opposite of most succulents, those listed here make fine companions
and will tolerate some summer water if provided with good drainage.

Boophone disticha produces a fan of leaves and umbels of reddish flowers. Poisonous.

Crocus goulimyi Typical small crocus flowers in late winter or early spring. Good
in rockery or between stepping stones.

Lycoris radiata Slender dark green leaves, with a pale midstripe are produced in
winter, but spidery red flowers are borne in umbels atop one- to two-foot
stalks in fall.

Oxalis purpurea grows in full sun or shade. A carpet of pink or white flowers and
shamrock leaves in winter, through summer if kept watered. Especially useful
between stepping stones or in the rockery. A dark burgundy-leaved form has
recently been introduced.

Scilla Blue- to purple-flowered with tufts of green leaves in winter. *S. natalensis*
bears flowers on an open raceme to five feet tall. *S. peruviana* has compact
inflorescences less that one foot tall.

Tulbaghia violacea has garlic-scented evergreen tufts of grassy foliage and clusters of lavender flowers much of the year.

Tulipa Some Mediterranean species are summer dormant. *T. clusiana* is red and
white candy-striped; *T. c.* var. *chrysantha* is pure yellow, *T. saxatilis* is pink with
yellow blotches.

Urginea maritima A Mediterranean bulb with onionskinlike layers, emerging
partly above ground. Bears six-foot racemes of white flowers in fall.

Salvia greggii, Aloe dorotheae, Geranium incanum, Stipa tenuissima.

A succulent border can be as varied and rich as any conventional flower border; but with succulents, one has the opportunity of adding color, shape, and texture unimaginable with other types of plants. *Above: Festuca ovina* var. *glauca, Kalanchoe blossfeldiana, Agave parryi, Dasylirion longissimum, Beaucarnea recurvata.*

*Previous pages: Echeveria pallida, Kalanchoe fedtschenkoi, Crassula falcata, Acacia cymbispina, Aloe **x**commutata at the Huntington.*

The mention of a succulent or cactus or desert garden will conjure for many gardeners images of broken pottery and bleached cow skulls. Though some quaint scenes can spring from that stereotype, the homeowner who wants to create new and beautiful landscapes should know that the textures and colors of succulents and their logical companion plants address a wealth of situations, from areas large to small, from normal bedding schemes to the need for contained gardens, from distant property edge to garden focus, from exposed sites in a normal yard to the concrete harshness of swimming pool and tennis enclosure to courtyards of all descriptions. Use of succulents can fit a huge range of styles. These gardens can be dressy and formal or they can stretch along a path with the richness and excitement of the most splendid traditional perennial border. A succulent foundation planting can enhance many styles of architecture and address practical problems of water exclusion and simple security. Succulents are great when you want to be inventive or playful in expressing your own personal style. These plants can easily take the stage as consummate rockery denizens or supreme container subjects. And of course, in all of these situations, they are forgiving of poor conditions and benign neglect.

When you begin considering your new succulent garden, be aware that there are no rules. People who work with succulent landscapes have never felt bound by convention; books have not been written that reduce creativity to formula. This book preserves that freedom, showing examples of different ways people have used succulents to build their own beautiful gardens and condensing some of our ideas as to what is most successful into words and pictures. Beyond those thoughts and some practical how-to information, we encourage gardeners either to work from existing patterns or to strike out in new directions at their own pleasure. Where you start, then, depends on where you are.

The options for landscaping with planters, beds, and even entire gardens logically depends on what one hopes to accomplish. Rejuvenation of an existing succulent planting may be quite straightforward, requiring mainly a few ideas and skills. Beginning with a clean slate, or the intention to remove an old landscape and start over using succulents, leaves much room for discussion. For a complete approach to your property, a basic run through standard landscaping questions should come first:

• What are you planning to accomplish? Are you looking for a completely new landscape, or is there one simple area to be addressed that has certain requirements best met by succulents? Does the display accommodate a collection of plants, rocks, art, etc.? Is the new area to be neutral or focal?

• Are there any particular concerns, such as screening or safety that must be met? Do you demand a flower-filled area, or want to keep a color palette?

• Is there a style or theme particular to the garden you want to build? Will this be a pure succulent planting or will it grade into other types, such as standard xeriscapes, grasses, borders, or even water gardens?

• What is the regional climate and what are the microhabitats for your site? What is your agricultural zone?

• What are your site's special conditions? Is it hilly or flat? What are soil conditions? Is there existing hardscape (walks, terraces, walls, etc.)?

•Is the area in full sun, or are there trees, shrubs, and north-facing locations to consider?
•What are the needs of your family? Are there children? Do you have pets? What hobbies and recreation must be accommodated? Where can you place spiny plants without danger?
•How much money do you plan to spend? Is this a do-it-alone project? Will friends or hired crews be available to help?
•How will you irrigate the plantings?
•How much time will you dedicate to maintenance? Will the garden be an ongoing project, or do you want a completed unit that will be cultivated with little or no future change?
•Does the garden need to look mature on completion? Do you have the time let it grow?
•Where will you obtain the plant material? Is there an opportunity for free acquisition of cuttings or even large or especially useful specimen plants from someone who is clearing a site?

Once you know the answers to most of these questions, design options become more apparent. For larger projects, the next step will likely involve a sketch of the property, if not a full blown landscape plan. Include most fairly permanent structures, features, and larger plants, even if you plan to remove them. It may seem a useless complication to make a drawing. These succulents are so easy, you can plant them, then move them, then move them again and again, *ad infinitum*. But many problems can be predicted and solved on paper, so why would one want to build a garden through complete trial and error? Minimally, a plan will allow you to size up the project and forecast the effort and resources this new garden will require. At its best, the plan can help you build a much better garden that is workable and beautiful.

Observations Even though there are no rules, through considering our most successful plantings, one can see that curators at the Huntington resort to certain patterns of placement and combinations. Lessons are fairly basic:
•We tend to keep our plants together based on scale. Small individual rockery items are not directly combined with golden barrel cactus or huge agaves.
•Repetition is beneficial and not to be considered a cheap ploy. Repeating the same plant, or the same shape, color, and texture brings cohesion to a landscape, large or small.
•Masses of plants are quite beautiful. From one perspective, massing can solve the problem of integrating small plants with large ones. In general, masses can keep a garden from looking too busy.
•Good staging brings much delight. The way you layer and space plants of different potential height and width signficantly affects the overall nature and impact and sense of arrival. It determines the feeling of depth and gives clues as to whether they are viewing from a front, side, or perhaps even back of a garden. It also takes into account the general backdrop, as well as where the garden begins and where it ends.
•Logic can be a good ally. Grouping plants based on some underlying organization, such as native habitat, geographic origin, required conditions, or evolutionaly adaptations may not only provide a theme, but suggests there is a story to be told.

Even a tiny space can accommodate a fascinating array of succulents. The use of containers should always be considered when space is an issue.

Above: Opuntia violacea, Carnegiea gigantea. Below: This group of aeoniums *(A. hierrense, A. arboreum* 'Atropurpureum', *A. haworthii)* is combined with the vivid red and pink flowers of *Lampranthus* and the complementary shapes of the non-succulent *Echium wildpretii.*

Pure displays of succulent plants can be very dramatic. In the right place they are magical, creating scenes of otherworldliness. The *Mammillaria* bed at The Huntington, covered with spinescent cushions, has been compared to the coral reef of an undersea kingdom. The main home entrance at Ganna Walska Lotusland (Montecito, California–see page 83) with its pendulous euphorbias is hauntingly romantic. In Phoenix and Tucson Arizona, one encounters exuberant displays of massive succulents, from the many excellent roadside plantings to striking gardens at the entrances of businesses and homes. For some areas, demonstrated beautifully at the Living Desert (Palm Desert, California), the Desert Botanical Garden (Phoenix) and The Arizona-Sonora Desert Musuem (Tucson), a succulent garden can yield a built focus that grades right into the native landscape.

These gardens are planned around masses (both groups of small or spreading plants as well as diffuse shrubs and small trees) and the well-placed use of specimens. There is often a good amount of exposed rock, soil, or mulch. The plan may actually attempt to create the sense of a desert, or may be completely architectural, playing forms and details against the substrate. There may be another agenda, such as the use of sansevierias at the entrance to EPCOT's Living Seas pavilion to suggest seaweed against an ocean blue wall. Whatever the scheme, this approach tends to produce a strong effect that must either

Left: Sedums and sempervivums in a rock garden. Below: *Mammillaria geminispina* with *Lophocereus schottii* '*Monstrosus*'.

complement your home and other structures or separate itself sufficiently from hardscape so as not to create problems of scale or logic.

Mixed plantings can introduce succulents to almost any garden, regardless of climate or style. Anyone who has wandered the eastern coastal plain or the central prairies knows how natural and stunning opuntias can be against grasses and other herbs. In the Hill Country west of Austin, Texas, one regularly encounters small juniper and oak trees mixed with mesquite and shrubs, having interspersed open areas blanketed by flowering annuals and punctuated with small cacti. The look is natural and handsome, suggesting that succulents can be nicely blended with native southwestern plants, or into more standard xeriscapes that often have the casual appearances of prairie or chaparral. In Kentucky and Tennessee, the cedar glades are characterized by shallow to nonexistent soils and are populated with dwarfed hackberries that have the character of some desert shrubs. Taking a cue from such natural habitats, a gardener can easily provide a natural context for succulents and companion plants by installing a rock outcropping in a sunny place that suggests a localized condition of thin soils.

Rockeries and terraces are special circumstances and opportunities. The possi-

Above: The swordlike leaves of succulent *Furcraea* contrast with *Ceanothus*. *Right:* aloes mixed with calendulas, sweet alyssum, other flowers and conifers.

bilities are wide, limited only by climate, site, and style, availability of rocks, and number of helpers that can be summoned to build the hardscape. Succulents thrive with the great drainage resulting when plants are tucked among rocks. They look quite handsome with a complete backdrop of appropriate stone and real drama can be created through the lifting of specimens that at the same time are brought forward for closer inspection. Throughout the Appalachian mountains, hikers experience this exciting viewpoint along shaded paths when small plants of *Sedum ternatum* are discovered, perched at eye level on rock cuts. The alpine rockery at Denver Botanic Garden is a stunning example of large scale landscaping of this type. A modified version, using succulents, is the Isabelle Greene-designed garden at Longwood Gardens'

famous conservatory, where succulents are artfully interwoven into a rock and xeriscape fabric. Terracing can be incorporated easily in a sloping site, providing excellent opportunities for both sculptural displays as well as the creative use of blanketing groundcovers.

Of course **groundcovers** alone constitute a major succulent resource for the home gardener. They can play highly practical roles, from erosion control on slopes to use as fire breaks in southern California as well as other regions. In circumstances where treading is not a problem, succulent groundcovers, such as *Aptenia* 'Red Apple' can even provide lawn substitutes. It is not uncommon to find local gardeners using these plants for dry parterres, even creating eclectic knot and quilt gardens. In more varied succulent landscapes, the many fine smaller plants available can be used to carpet areas of bare soil, providing cohesion and textural relief, while often creating a living canvas against which to play larger specimens.

Sunny **courtyards, patios, passageways, porches, balconies,** and **window gardens** are often stark because they can be such harsh locations for plants. A garden of succulents in containers not only may bring the best solution for these very exposed microclimates, but can prove to be a design natural. Succulents can meld and contrast beautifully with the hard surfaces of concrete and stucco, brick and terracotta,, stone and sand, glass and plastic, as well as softer mater-

Many succulents thrive as pot plants. See page 208 for more information on indoor potted succulents.

Crassula falcata.

ial such as wood and canvas. They are supreme as textural and sculptural forms against the unrelenting monochrome expanses of concrete flooring and stucco walls (which then function much as the bare soil or rock of a traditional succulent landscape).

Mediterranean and **Southwestern** style courtyards and patios can be greatly enhanced with pale to rich red terracotta pots boasting single specimens of *Agave* or *Echeveria* or even golden barrel cacti, whose forms and colors can mix well with the everpresent and equally forceful *Bougainvillea* or flowering geraniums. The sharp edges of modern concrete and plaster buildings find complementary strength in the powerful mass of *Agave* leaves and *Euphorbia* stems. Succulents are not even restricted to harsh, dry, or desert themes. Sedums and sempervivums are normal components of stone troughs that so finely complement cottages. The brightest and hottest-in-the-summer, coldest-in-the-winter interior window box planters throughout the country are given a sense of tropical luxury when populated with *Pedilanthus, Sansevieria,* and *Schlumbergera.* And single specimens can be mixed with other plant collection trophies, fitting in especially well with the most exotic, from strelitzias to staghorn ferns to South African bulbs. While supporting a great range of themes and styles, these plants are yet succulents, and as such are still very low maintenance, which means not just having low water requirements, but also low production of litter and much reduced need for repotting or replacement as compared to almost any other plant choices for the same circumstances.

Design elements Regardless of the situation or design objectives, the gardener-designer in you will find these succulents are a different breed. In the light of their often nude, sometimes exaggerated forms, old concerns such as texture and color take new meaning. What would Gertrude Jekyll think of a border in which practically every plant provides an arresting "full stop" or a peak season that means every month of the year. Playing with those very elements in your garden is among the challenges and delights that await.

Clearly shape and form are sovereign. Among the cacti and euphorbs are plants of single or branched columnar stems with landscape utility ranging from creating abrupt exclamation points to branched tangles. Shorter versions of these stem succulents yield barrel shapes, small to large. These one finds used individually or, in larger scale settings, spreading into dense low mounds. The plant you choose can yield drastically different effects, depending on the coloration of the stem and the density or color of any armature (spines) or even the presence of hair and scales.

Leaf succulents create different specimen plants, from the rosette shapes of dudleyas and agaves and the rising swords of sansevierias to the stem and ponytail look of beaucarneas, yuccas, and aloes. Smaller-leaved succulents often are used as fine-textured carpeting, with options being quite great, from senecios in the daisy family to the mesembs to crassulas. Comparable to stem succulents, the leaves of these plants yield their own lifelong addition of color to the garden. Considering succulents in general, the color palette comes not

from the flowers, but with the vegetative parts, the leaf and stem. Though that may seem limiting, the blue-silver gardens at Lotusland and Longwood Gardens (Kennett Square, Pennsylvania) and the striking yellow hues of the golden barrel display at The Huntington prove otherwise.

Regardless of size, most leaf succulents also produce inflorescences that stand out in comparison to the foliage. We become accustomed to seeing yuccas and agaves with periodic or seasonal displays that might may be quite astounding. This group of plants is responsible for much of the floral display in succulent landscapes, including such luminaries as the ice plants, the aeoniums, the aloes, and the agaves.

The caudiciforms (woody plants with swollen main stems and smaller side branching) and desert trees and shrubs so often combined with succulents

This front yard, typical of the Arizona style of landscaping, contains opuntias and columnar cacti mixed with creosote bush and red-flowered chuparosa (*Justicia californica*).

open up additional possibilities. These plants, especially the legumes (*Acacia, Caesalpinia, Parkinsonia*) can bring airy textures to fill large areas, providing height and shade as well. They can be the main component, or may even in a reverse manner provide the "full stops" needed to partition a succulent border or segue from one style to another. The desert shrubs can even stand alone, in a pleinair sense washing a smudge of green against an otherwise lifeless pile of rock or concrete. It is these plants that bring the greatest sense of change to succulent landscapes, in that many are seasonally stark and skeletal, ocotillo for example, and have no more perfect visual affinities than in combination with succulents.

Commentary like this could ramble on and on, but the reader has probably seen our point. These are different plants; they may require you to start as a novice regardless of the level of experience you have had with other type of gardening. More than with any other style or type of material, there is a sense of furnishing, rather than planting, a succulent landscape, whether it is a container, a corner or your entire yard. The green and growing items are decorative elements, each having such innate character and individuality that few plants qualify as just filler, like so much *Pittosporum* or *Nandina*. Everything is a special ornament, an object of art. Succulent gardens are not just there, they are crafted and bear the mark of the owner. With succulents, you should sense the freedom to combine and design, to build your own version of a beautiful landscape, a truce between yourself and the elements.

Opposite: Dudleya. Above and below: Agaves in the landscape; above with Euphorbia trigona, usually tender but protected by a large tree; below with a group of succulents and companions.

KEY:
A: *Euphorbia lambii*
B: *Cordyline australis* 'Atropurpurea'
C: *Aeonium castello-paivae*
D: *Doryanthese palmeri*
E: *Euphorbia tirucali* 'Sticks on Fire'

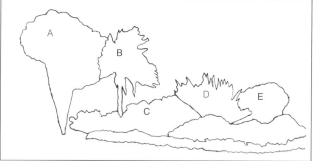

This mixed planting contains *Euphorbia lambii*, *Cordyline australis* 'Atropurpurea', *Kalanchoe fedtschenkoi*, *Tulbaghia violacea*, *Sedum spectabile*, *Doryanthes palmeri*, *Aeonium castello-paivae*, *Euphorbia tirucali* 'Sticks on Fire'

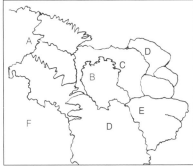

KEY:
A: *Agave attenuata*
B: *Achillea filipendula*
C: *Salvia greggii*
D: *Lavandula angustifolia*
E: *Teucrium majoricum*
F: *Pelargonium graveolens*

This mixed border of herbaceous perennials and annuals is enhanced by *Agave attenuata*, which provides a strong architectural form that unifies the less structured plants around it.

CHOOSING AND IMPROVING THE SITE The two main factors to consider when choosing a site for your succulent landscape beds are sun and soil. To some degree, you can change the site to fit your needs. But much time and aggravation can be saved by finding a site that is suitable for the plants you want to grow–or choosing plants that are suitable for the site you have.

Sun Long term observation of a proposed site will provide information regarding the type of sunlight it receives throughout the day and over the seasons; note whether the site receives direct or filtered sunlight, and whether this sunlight is present for the full day. For most succulents, you will need a good deal of sun; four to six hours per day is considered adequate for success. However, not all succulents and cacti thrive in full sun; some plants, such as *Haworthia, Cyanotis*, and various *Crassula* are native to less extreme conditions and will thrive in the shade of taller plants or trees. (See pages 213 for more information on growing succulents in the shade). And in very hot climates, most plants benefit from some afternoon shade. A shady microclimate, if needed but not already existing, can be created with large specimen plants.

Temperature is somewhat related to sun level, but in most cases it is not only warmth that plants need, but also freedom from the threat of frost. See page 25 for information on hardiness and page 202 for information on growing succulents in cool climates.

Soil Although many succulents will tolerate poor soil and fertile, well-drained soil is essential to the continued success of a landscape bed. Addition of fertilizer will create a lusher look. It is well worth the effort to improve the bed before planting–though this is not a substitute for year-round soil maintenance.

The average soil is made up of sand, silt and sand particles (about 45 percent); air (about 30 percent); water (about 20 percent); and organic matter (about 5 percent). The spaces between the particles in soil allow water and nutrients to travel to a plant's roots; the soil must have enough water and nutrients to supply the plants, and enough space between its own particles to allow water and nutrients to make their way to the roots. Organic matter, the product of decomposing plants gradually forms a black, crumbly substance called humus; it is the "glue" that holds the particles together. Organic matter is also where most of the nutrients that the plant needs are held.

The mineral component of soil is of three basic types: clay, silt, and sand, in order of increasing particle size.

In clay soil, there is a large percentage of clay (the smallest particles), as opposed to sand and silt–water and nutrients have a hard time moving through it. Extremely clayey soils are almost impermeable to water and air; they usually have a high concentration of organic matter. Clay soils are sticky when wet.

Sandy soil has the greatest percentage of sand (the largest particles); water will travel through the soil easily, but the soil will not be able to hold onto the organic matter that the plant requires. Sandy soils are coarse-grained and do not stick together.

Silty soils are intermediate between clayey and sandy.

Loam is a combination of the three—the best mix of sand, silt, and clay to allow the soil to hold organic matter and still leave room for nutrient-laden water to travel to the roots of the plant. The term *friable*, which means easily crushed or pulverized, is often applied to loamy soil; it is the most fertile and easiest-to-work soil type.

You can determine which type of soil is in your garden by looking at it and touching it; if it does not stick together in your hand, and is light brown, it is probably sand. If it is sticky, it is probably clay. Another way of judging soil type is by checking drainage.

DRAINAGE You will note that many succulents require good drainage. Drainage is the ability of the soil to move water so that the roots of the plant do not get waterlogged; if water can't move around in the soil, neither can nutrients. Also, if the water stays in the soil, roots stay wet, which is usually disaster for cacti and other succulents.

To check drainage, dig a hole the size of a one-gallon pot; fill it with water, and see how long it takes to drain. If it drains immediately—in less than two hours—you have sandy soil and will probably need to add organic matter to help the soil hold water. If the water drains between two and four hours, you are blessed with loam. If the water is still standing after four hours, you probably have clay soil—and poor drainage.

There are several ways to correct poor drainage:

1. Add sand and organic matter to the soil. Sand plus clay results in cement; but sand, clay, and organic matter will give you friable soil.

2. Use raised beds, which always provide better drainage and also allow you to mix better soil from elsewhere into your site.

3. Insert a drainage pipe. These pipes, usually plastic, can be purchased at most garden supply or hardware stores and move water to a place where it will do less harm. Dig a trench, about one foot deep and one foot wide that is the length of the pipe. If there is no existing drainage channel at the end of your pipe, dig a dry well. Cover the end of the pipe that starts in your garden with porous material so that it is not clogged by rocks and soil. Place the pipe in the trench, and cover it with gravel. Replace the soil over it. Water will be conducted through the pipe to the dry well.

4. If your problem is serious, or if you think it is worth the investment, talk to a professional landscaper about inserting a drainage system, such as tile, gravel beds, or more elaborate pipe network.

SOIL IMPROVEMENT Good drainage allows water to travel through your soil. This water must carry nutrients with it; if they are not present in the soil, they must be added.

To identify exactly what the soil in your garden needs, there is no substitute for a soil test. A small but representative amount of garden soil is analyzed for nutrient deficiencies and excesses. To get an accurate reading for your entire garden area, take small amounts from several different spots in

To test for drainage, dig a hole the size of a one-gallon pot; fill water and see how long it takes for the water to drain. Below: Testing for drainage. Above: Installation of drainage pipe at The Huntington Botanical Gardens.

VIEWPOINT

SOIL AMENDMENTS FOR NEW PLANTINGS

Normally, we add forest compost to the soil before putting in new plants. If we need particularly good drainage, we sometimes add pumice as well. We also sometimes mix in some of the potting mix that the plant was growing in to make the soil friable.
JOE CLEMENTS
THE HUNTINGTON BOTANICAL GARDENS

For heavy soil, we topdress with six to twelve inches of well-drained soil, and add sulfur or lime to adjust pH to between 6.5 and 8.
DR. MARK DIMMITT
THE ARIZONA-SONORA DESERT MUSEUM

Soil amendments depend on the original soil. Soil should be amended to make it well-drained and friable–but not too friable if you're planting very large succulents because their weight will make them topple if the soil is too loose.
ERNIE DE MARIE
THE NEW YORK BOTANICAL GARDEN

I believe it is best not to amend soils. If amendments are not added extensively and evenly, the plant sits in a "pot" of amended soil, surrounded by non-amended soil and tends to keep its roots in the very restricted amended area. If the soil is extensively loosened before planting, the plant will root comfortably in the native soil. If soil amendments are used, gravel or other coarse material should be added extensively, mounding the soil and maximizing drainage.
KURT ZADNIK
UNIVERSITY OF CALIFORNIA BOTANICAL GARDEN, BERKELEY

For our heavy clay soil, we add a special mixture of compost, gravel, sharp sand, and wood chips. We amend soil more to change its texture and drainage ability than to add nutrients.
CAROL BORNSTEIN
SANTA BARBARA BOTANICAL GARDEN

your garden, mixing them to make a total of about one-half of a cup of soil; mix topsoil and soil one-spade-deep. For a small fee, a full laboratory analysis can be done by a County Extension Office (listed under "government" in your phone book), an agricultural university, or perhaps even a local garden center. The analysis will often be accompanied by recommendations for needed nutrients and their application rates. It usually takes about three weeks to receive a full report; this wait is longer in the spring, when most people get around to testing their soil.

One item that is almost always tested is pH–the level of acidity or alkalinity of your soil. The pH level is measured on a scale of 1-14, with 1 representing pure acid, 14 representing pure alkaline, and 7 being neutral. The pH level indicates the level of negative charges in your soil, and that level greatly affects how the soil can transport nutrients to the plant. For most succulents, a pH level of 6.0-7.0 is best. You can also measure pH level with a simple home kit that can be purchased in garden centers.

In addition to pH, your soil test will tell you whether you need to add organic matter, lime, and/or fertilizer. It will also tell you what not to add. Soil sampling and testing is, over time, a money saver. By knowing exactly which additives are needed, you can save quite a bit by not using unneeded or excessive additives.

Soil building is not an overnight process; significant improvements usually take three to four years. Once nutrient and pH levels reach normal range, soil will need only minor adjustments. Although there are many ways to fix soil quickly, these are generally more expensive than soil-building practices and are sometimes harmful to the environment. Take your soil tests in the fall, so you will have time to employ a soil-building fix; take them regularly, year after year, until your soil stabilizes at an acceptable level.

Soil additives Organic matter: If your soil is low in organic matter it will often have a high pH level. Organic matter can be added with any of several products that are on the market, including peat moss, packaged manure, or commercial compost, available in bulk either in bags or bales, ready for immediate use and usually "weed-free." Compost is one of the safest and most effective ways to improve the pH and general condition of your soil and help the environment at the same time. Compost is decomposed plant material that adds nutrients to the soil while improving its overall composition. It is safer and usually less expensive than chemical fertilizers, but not as fast-acting or as efficient in correcting specific nutrient deficiencies.

Agricultural lime: Lime is an essential additive to acidic soils, as it will help raise the pH to levels that many plants require. It is slow-acting and should be tilled into the soil sixty to ninety days before planting. Agricultural lime is available as dust or pellets; pellets are preferable because they are easier to measure and apply, though lime dust is less expensive. If your soil has a high magnesium level, be sure to avoid dolomitic limestone; get calcareous limestone ($CaCo_3$) instead.

Fertilizers: Granular or pelletized fertilizers are generally used as "starter" fertilizers for your plants and seedlings. These are applied two days to one week prior to setting out plants.

Different kinds of fertilizers are available for different growing needs. The nutrient content is identified by a series of three numbers. The first number represents the percentage of nitrogen (N) in the mixture. The second tells the percentage of phosphorus (P), and the third the percentage of potassium (K), or potash.

Nitrogen is the fastest-reacting part of the fertilizer mix and promotes rapid growth of foliage and stems. Phosphorus promotes root growth; it does not move around within the soil, so it should be mixed deeply or it will not reach the roots. Potassium releases relatively slowly and is most useful to root crops. A good general starter mix for a wide range of plants is 8-8-8 or 10-10-10. Higher mixtures such as 13-13-13 or 20-20-20 could burn young plants and seedlings.

Fertilizers also contain trace elements, such as copper and zinc. Plants need only minute amounts of these elements, and they usually do not have to be added; but they are important to your plants' development, and if your soil test indicates that they are lacking, they are easy to add. A soil analysis should tell which nutrients you do not need to add, as well as those you need to amend. For example, if your soil already has high amounts of phosphorus present due to years of adding a general fertilizer mix, or native soil fertility, you should now add a mixture without phosphorus in it such as a 15-0-15 mix.

WHAT TO LOOK FOR WHEN CHOOSING PLANTS

You will want only the healthiest of plants to go in your carefully prepared bed. When shopping, inspect plants carefully for insects, e.g., mealy bugs, white fly, aphids or mites, insect damage and disease which may manifest as stunted, distorted growth, mottled leaves or scarring. Smaller plants are usually easier to establish in the garden, but check for number of branches or offsets if a plant is slow-growing. Good color (not necessarily green in the case of succulents!) indicates good cultural practices. Make sure plants are not pot bound or conversely, that they are well-established if grown from cuttings. If possible, avoid recently collected plants that have no roots. Don't forget to match plants with the conditions under which they will be grown.

When choosing plants, bigger isn't always better; although smaller, the *Agave multifilifera* on the right (far left picture) has a better form and is therefore more desirable than the one on the left. In the near-left picture, a scarred *Echinopsis* 'Flying Saucer' is unsightly and not as attractive as the unscarred specimen; but the scarring will not effect the plant's growth adversely.

Handling plants during propagation (or any time) can be dangerous. Wear proper protective gloves and eyewear, and hold the plant will folded paper, tongs, or strips of fabric. Always sterilize tools used in propagation to avoid transmitting viruses; wash hands or gloves frequently.

PROPAGATION

Because most succulent plants used in the landscape are easily propagated, mass plantings need not mean a huge financial outlay. Vegetative, or asexual, propagation by division and cuttings is probably the easiest and quickest way to mature plants. Vegetative propagation results in plants with the same characteristics of the original plant. For best results, it should be undertaken when plants are beginning active growth. This could be winter or summer, depending on the species. Initially, cuttings should be protected from all harsh conditions: hot, direct sun, temperature extremes, or too much or too little water. Sexual propagation by seed will result in large numbers of plants with the possibility of variation among them. Generally, spring is a good time to sow seed, although there are exceptions. Grafting is a special technique useful in the landscape not so much for obtaining large numbers of plants as for creating unusual forms, making tender plants more hardy or slow-growers faster. As with cuttings, periods of active growth, particularly of the understock, are the best times to attempt grafting.

Precautions Since propagating plants requires handling them, you must take care to protect yourself from painful spines or toxic sap. Wear snug-fitting latex examining gloves. The tight fit repels spines much like a properly inflated bicycle tire resists puncture. Gloves are available in boxes of one hundred in three different sizes. Cloth or leather gloves soon become embedded with broken spines and so are not suitable for handling some finer-spined plants such as opuntias. However they are essential protection against heavier spines of barrel cacti and the like. (Some gardeners disagree, stating that latex gloves are very uncomfortable and are easily punctured; these gardeners recommend heavy leather gloves.) Handle cacti with tongs, large forceps or a newspaper folded into a long strip or band. Use burlap bags rolled like the newspaper, carpeting, or a length of old garden hose or heavy rope, for especially large specimens. The sap of euphorbias is toxic—and sometimes squirts several feet—so when cutting them, wear goggles and gloves and avoid contact with skin or any mucous membrane. Use a vegetable oil-soaked cloth to wipe off the oil-soluble sap. Then wash thoroughly with soap and water after working with them. A reported antidote to euphorbia sap is the juice of *Aeonium lindleyi* which is used to bring relief when applied to irritated skin or even in the eyes. Contact with some agaves may cause skin irritation. Wear long sleeves and gloves when handling them. Rinse with cool water and wash with soap if irritation develops. Never cut succulents with a chain saw.

When conducting vegetative propagation or grafting, be sure to sterilize cutting tools in between plants and wash hands or gloves frequently, especially if you have touched the open cut. This will help prevent transmission of disease organisms, particularly viruses, which enter through wounds in the plant. Tools may be sterilized by dipping in isopropyl alcohol, a 10% clorox solution for ten minutes, or by baking for fifteen minutes at 350° F. We use our razor blades just once and then place them in the "razor dump" to be sterilized later in the oven. Latex-gloved hands may be dipped in the alcohol

DIVIDING HESPERALOE PARVIFLORA

1. The plant to be divided will yield several divisions that can be planted outdoors in a mass planting.

2. Loosen potbound roots by rolling the container and banging on it.

3. Remove the entire plant from the pot when it has been loosened.

4. Using your hands, begin separating the rootball; don't worry if some of roots seem to be tearing.

5. If the roots are stubbornly tangled, use pruning shears to make the final division.

6. The original plant has been divided into five section. Each division has at least some of healthy roots.

Soft, non-spiny succulents, such as aeoniums, can be cut with razors.

which is handier than washing them all the time.

Division Propagation by division is the process of dividing or removing offsets from the parent plant, either by hand or with a sharp knife or shears. In neither case is the parent plant destroyed. Roots, if not already present, will develop when the offsets are placed in growing medium. (Our growing medium or potting mix is two parts forest humus, two parts pumice, and one part builder's sand, with a trace of superphosphate and cottonseed meal.) Vigorous divisions may be planted directly in the landscape bed, but small or weakly rooted plants should grow on in individual pots or a flat, depending on how many there are. Before potting, trim with a clipper broken roots and any which are too long for the flat. Protect newly divided plants from extreme conditions as you would for cuttings.

Cuttings Propagation by cuttings refers to cutting of stems or leaves. Depending on the plant being propagated, stem cuts may be made with clippers (ground covers, small aloes), long serrated knives (large columnar or globular cacti), or single-edged razor blades (plants from the *Crassulaceae* family). In most cases, the minimum requirement is that the cutting have two nodes (the slightly swollen spot on the stem where leaves usually emerge): one for shoot growth, the other for root development. It is customary to cut the stem one-quarter inch below the node intended for roots, and, if it is a medial cut (one cut from the middle of the stem so that it lacks the tip or apical meristem), one-quarter inch above the top node. Insert the base of the cutting in growing medium enough so that the lower node is covered and the cutting will still stand up. The medium should be kept moist but not soggy. A technique we sometimes use for a handful of stick-like cuttings or just one or a few individual columnar cacti is called "half-potting." This is a regular pot filled less than half-way with potting mix into which the cuttings are inserted. This method reduces the chance of rot before roots are able to form, but will require transplanting soon after growth begins or the plants will become overcrowded. This method also provides support for topheavy cuttings against the side of the pot.

An apical cutting, a stem cutting which includes the tip (as well as a node), will result in a perfect specimen plant, whereas a medial cut will always show the place on the stem where it was cut, as will the base of the parent plant. So the latter two, if they are cacti, for instance, will be ruined as specimen plants, but their usefulness lies in their ability to grow offsets which subsequently can be removed as apical cuttings, i.e., perfect specimen plants. Leafy or branching succulents may hide the cut with no detrimental effect to the plant's appearance.

For whole leaf cuttings on some plants, such as echeverias and some haworthias, leaves must be removed very carefully and completely so that all of the leaf is removed from the stem because it is from the basal, bud portion of the leaf that roots and shoots emerge. Nestle leaves in growing medium in a flat or other shallow, well-draining container, either on their sides or with the basal portion lightly covered with growing medium, which should be kept

TAKING CUTTINGS OF CLEISTOCACTUS

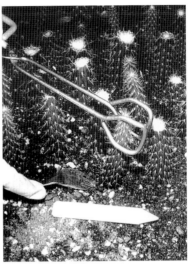

1. When taking cuttings of cactus, grasp with tongs, then cut with sharp, sterilized pruning shears.

2. Place cuttings in a flat with medial cuts aligned with tips; allow one week for callusing if this process is necessary.

3. After callus has formed, place the cuttings in a prepared flat of tamped-down medium. Dig a small hole with a fork or similar tool. Insert cutting and retamp mix to support cutting

TAKING CUTTINGS FROM EUPHORBIA AMMAK

1. Grasp the plant with a folded newspaper; use gloves and eye protection. Note the milky latex dripping from the plant. Remove the top six inches or more. Use gloves and eye protection.

2. Half-potted cuttings of *E. ammak* and *E. abyssinica* placed in a larger pot for support.

3. A compact rootball has formed after several months. The small volume of soil retained enough moisture to stimulate root development but not enough to encourage rot.

STEM CUTTING FROM KALANCHOE MARNIERANA

1. Stem cuttings will be taken from this leggy *K. marnierana*.

2. To restart, clump a group of cuttings.

3. Repot the clump of cuttings in the proper potting medium. Uncallused cuttings may be watered in and will form new roots in about a week or two. The same process can be used to renew a landscape bed.

LEAF CUTTINGS

X*Graptoveria* 'Opalina' with roots and shoots.

Haworthia magnifica.

Echeveria lilacina.

moist but not soggy. Some plants, such as sansevieria, can be propagated from partial leaf cuttings. Others, like kalanchoe, produce offsets when the midrib of the leaf is severed at several points or sometimes while still on the plant without any special treatment.

Some plants require that their cuttings callus before being placed in growing medium, otherwise they are prone to rot. Callusing is achieved by exposing the cuts to air, for anywhere from twenty-four hours to three months or more depending on the time of year, the weather, and the type and size of plant. Good air circulation and protection from direct sunlight is essential. Achieve these by laying the cuttings, without crowding, in a flat which both sits on and is covered by flats with a very open mesh. With some cuttings, particularly cacti, it is difficult to tell the top from the bottom on the medial cuts. Orient them in the callusing flat, as you are cutting them, in the same direction as the tip cuttings. Some taller or softer cuttings may need to be supported upright in an empty pot to callus to avoid distortion by bending as the cells in the shaded side elongate.

Callusing.

Seeds Seeds can be purchased from mail order catalogs or set and collected from your own plants. Setting of seed may occur naturally or you may want to purposely cross-pollinate select plants yourself, using your finger, an artist's paint brush, tweezers, or a stiff wire, bristle or cactus spine to transfer pollen from one flower to another. It is a good idea to record parentage in case something truly new and exciting results. Fruits are generally ripe and ready to harvest when they turn dry and/or brown; some split open so you need to keep watch on them to prevent loss. An extreme example is euphorbia, whose ripe fruits burst open forcefully, shooting their seed far and wide, so it is necessary to cover the plant with a screened box or wrap the fruits in strips of cotton, nylon netting or adhesive tape to trap the flying seed.

There are as many ways to sow and grow seed as there are gardeners, but we sow our seeds close together on top of our regular potting mix, covered to the depth of the diameter of the seed by clean, coarse silica sand. Use a container, i.e., a pot or flat, appropriate to the amount of seed. Containers are then misted daily with plain water up to and through germination. It is important never to let the surface dry out. We begin watering with liquid fertilizer as needed (approximately once a week under our conditions) after the first set of true leaves has appeared. Transplant to individual pots or growing flats when large enough to handle or when they have outgrown their space. Damping off is a problem that often afflicts young seedlings. Some growers treat with fungicide but clean culture and proper growing conditions can help avoid this.

Euphorbia grandicornis fruits are wrapped in nylon to prevent them bursting open and shooting out their seeds.

Grafting Grafting is the process of uniting one plant cutting, the scion, to another rooted plant, the understock. Usually, globular, crested, or pendent scions are grafted onto columnar understock, but sometimes a globular understock is used when the purpose of the graft is to create a hardier root system and the understock is not seen. Another purpose of grafting is to create unusual, even whimsical forms.

techniques

Mammillaria geminispina (crest) makes a spectacular and unusual potted specimen. The large surface in contact with the soil makes such a specimen prone to rot. Grafting in onto a stock which elevates the crest above the soil (see opposite page) is a technique for introducing such novelties into the landscape.

Stock and scion must be botanically compatible, e.g., euphorbias to euphorbias, or one cactus to another; at a minimum, plants chosen for grafting should be from the same family (there is only one instance of successful grafting between two succulent families). Often, grafts of plants from different tribes or subfamilies are successful. It is a somewhat painstaking procedure that meets with varying success.

Using a sterile, sharp blade appropriate to the size of the plant, make a clean, horizontal cut to the top of the stock on which the scion will rest. It is sometimes necessary to trim away the epidermis around the shoulders of the cut so that when it dries the stock does not pull away from the scion. Next cut the scion horizontally and place it on top of the stock, lining up the interior vascular rings. Apply pressure firmly, but not too tightly, by placing two large rubberbands across the top of the scion and underneath the pot of the understock, at right angles to one another. Rubberbands or strips of nylon stocking may also be attached to spines emerging from the sides of the understock. If milky euphorbia sap gets in the way, spritz it away from both the scion and the stock with water from a spray bottle. When handling euphorbias, remember to take the safety precautions mentioned at the beginning of this chapter.

A union will usually take place in twenty-four hours if it is to take place at all. After that point, the bands can be loosened, but care should be taken to avoid jostling the plant for several weeks until active new growth begins.

In this example of grafting, *Echinocactus horizonthalonius* was grafted as a pinhead-size seedling onto *Pereskiopsis* to hasten growth.

Here, the crest of *Monvillea spegazzinii* has reverted to its original form; the reverted portion must be removed to maintain the rest of the crest.

GRAFTING MAMMILLARIA GEMINISPINA ONTO ECHINOPSIS

1. Select a crest of the *Mammillaria* plant to graft.

2. Remove the head of the grafting stock (*Echinopsis*).

3. Bevel the edge of the grafting stock by trimming away the epidermis around the shoulders of the cut so that when it dries the stock does not pull away from the scion.

4. The grafting stock (*Echinopsis*) and the scion (*Mammillaria*), both cacti, were chosen for grafting because they are physiologically compatible.

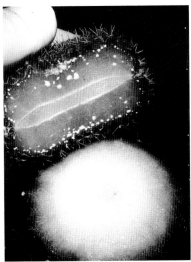

5. Align the vascular tissue of the plants. The *Echinopsis* shows a circle of vascular tissue where it was cut. The *Mammillaria* shows a more elongated elipse of vascular tissue. The circle and the elipse are aligned for maximum overlap.

6. Using rubber bands or nylon strips, anchor the scion into position.

DIVIDING AN AEONIUM BED

1. A bed of leggy 'Aeonium 'Pseudotabuliforme' in need of replanting.

2. Cuttings are taken—up to six inches of stems with rosettes—with sterilized pruning shears or knife and stored in a shady area.

3. The bed is cleared of all debris and old plant material; soil is turned over to loosen any clods.

4. Soil amendments—in this case compost—are added to the soil.

5. The amendments are incorporated into the soil by turning it over with a shovel.

6. With a trowel or similar implement, a hole is made deep enough to cover nodes at the base of the cutting and support them. The freshly cut aeoniums are replanted, and the soil tamped down around them.

PLANTING

If you have already planned your garden on paper, spacing has already been considered. Proper spacing will vary with individual plants, so it is necessary to be familiar with their growth habit. Specimen plants should be given enough room to reach their mature size. Bedding plants should be close enough so that they will fill in an area in time but not so close that they are competing for space before they are properly established. Mature height, water and light requirements, and flower and foliage color will also be spacing and design factors.

It is always a good idea to examine the soil and amend it if necessary before planting. Add soil amendments to the top of the soil, and turn over the soil with a spade or spading fork. Even if soil is not amended, it should be turned over at least one spade deep to make it loose and friable. Some gardeners advocate double digging, a method of turning over the soil to a greater depth (place the first level of soil to the side of the trench while turning over the next level; then replace the soil) but this is not usually necessary for succulents unless the soil is extremely compacted.

As to the actual planting, a general rule of thumb is to plant as deeply as the plant was growing. However, some plants may be planted more deeply if they are top heavy or leggy. Adventitious roots will generally form, but in the case of fleshy, columnar cacti, for example, there could be an increased risk of rot. Dig a hole half again as big as the root ball, remove the plant from its pot or flat taking care not to damage the stem, and untangle the roots to the extent that they will grow out into the soil and not stay massed in the shape they are presently in. Fill the hole with soil and tamp so that there is a firm connection between the soil and the roots. If planted during the growing season, plants can be watered in immediately or within a week and may need extra shading for a week or two. Non-leafy specimens which would take considerable time to recover from sunburn, like most euphorbias and cacti, may be covered with several layers of cheesecloth and uncovered one by one every few days. Companion plants, like desert shrubs or herbaceous annuals and perennials do not have the resiliency of succulents, and should be watered in immediately.

At Desert Botanical Garden in Phoenix, succulents planted in spring or summer must be shaded to prevent sunburn unless the precise orientation of the plant is known and repeated. Succulents planted in the fall rarely need this treatment. Gardeners there allow transplants to dry for a week or two in a shaded area; where that is not practical (for large cacti), transplants are not watered for the first week or two after planting to allow damaged roots to callus.

Often, it is necessary to move a plant because it has overgrown its old site, or simply because you want to put it in a different place. With small, unarmed plants, this is a fairly easy procedure. Dig the plant up, with its roots, and plant as for any seedling. With a large and/or spiny plant, the operation becomes more difficult. Use ropes and a stretcher to remove and move the plant; see photo sequence on the following pages.

TRANSPLANTING A GOLDEN BARREL CACTUS

NOTE: Moving a large, spiny plant is a difficult and possibly dangerous operations. It requires two people, both wearing protective clothing and eyewear.

1. In preparation for planting, a new hole is dug and pumice is added. The new hole is about the same size as the rootball.

2. The golden barrel cactus is dug up from its previous site with shovels; care is taken to keep the roots as intact as possible.

3. A stretcher is prepared to receive the large plant. Be sure it is strong and rigid enough to hold it.

4. The plant is rolled onto a prepared stretcher and secured with rope.

5. The plant moved to its new site.

6. At the new site, the plant is lassoed with a heavy rope.

7. Using the stretcher and the heavy rope, the plant is placed into the hole.

8. The rope is used to position the plant properly while the soil is filled in around it.

9. Using the handle of a shovel, the soil around the plant is leveled and tamped down. The plant is held with the rope so that the soil directly under it can be leveled.

10. A final tamping. Watering in at this time is not necessary and can, in fact, be fatal.

11. The area around the newly planted golden barrel cactus is raked again for neatness.

VIEWPOINT

IRRIGATION PRACTICES

We irrigate on a regular basis. Succulents might be able to survive without regular irrigation, but they would not thrive. Since our goal is a garden, and not a natural desert landscape, we provide additional water through overhead irrigation systems on a weekly or biweekly basis in spring and summer. We even water the winter growers, not because they need the water, but to cool them off in the most intense heat of summer.
JOE CLEMENTS
HUNTINGTON BOTANICAL GARDEN

We don't irrigate our desert garden, except for once per month–to simulate desert rainfall–in the hot, dry desert months and occasional spot watering by hand when necessary. This garden is intended to replicate nature, and achieve the look of the desert.
CAROL BORNSTEIN
SANTA BARBARA BOTANICAL GARDEN

We've installed an in-ground drip-irrigation system that uses less water, waters the plants more thoroughly where they need it, and is convenient for our large number of plants.
MARY IRISH,
DESERT BOTANICAL GARDEN

Since succulents have extensive, shallow root systems, I think sprinklers are most effective. There is no need to wet more than six inches deep unless the soil is deep and gravelly.
DR. MARK DIMMITT
ARIZONA-SONORA DESERT MUSEUM

ROUTINE CARE
Watering

It is commonly thought that succulents require little or no water. However, it is more accurate to say that they have evolved to survive on sporadic water when necessary. There is no question that they will be more lush if they receive adequate water.

When considering irrigation (and fertilization) practices at Huntington Gardens, the question that is often asked is: Do you want a desert or a garden? Allowing plants to survive on available rainfall will yield a natural–i.e. sparse–landscape. If your goal is to have a thriving garden, not one that is just getting by, regular watering is recommended.

During the growing season (usually spring and summer) regular means weekly or biweekly for the beds and deep monthly waterings for specimen plants. Winter water will be determined by rainfall and temperatures.

Many gardeners believe that watering should be done in the morning, to allow the plants to dry before nightfall and so to avoid fungal problems. But many gardeners water at night. Some justify this by saying that it rains at night in the desert because this is when pores are open and carbon dioxide is being taken from the air. a more practical reason to water at night is that it's a more convenient time for many people. In extremely hot climates, some people have found that light reflects off water at midday, burning the plants; we've never found this to be a problem, but if you garden under a brutal sun, watch for it. Most succulent plants are able to absorb the water when they need it, making time of day a fairly unimportant factor.

If you live in an area where available water is filled with harmful minerals or chemicals, consider installing a reverse osmosis system that removes these. For most areas, this is not necessary; succulents are usually able to tolerate most tap water.

Determining when succulents need water is somewhat of a challenge at first. Succulents don't wilt like most plants do except under the most extreme drought conditions. By that point, most small feeder roots have died and provide a site for potential rot unless plants are watered carefully.

In general, when plants are actively growing, they should never be allowed to go bone dry. Probe the soil with a metal rod or dig a small hole with a trowel or shovel to a depth of several inches to determine if there is moisture below the surface. The surface of a well-drained soil may dry within an hour of watering, but deeper moisture, especially under mulched areas, may remain for weeks depending on soil texture and the weather. Also, the surface may dry during the heat of the day but will be moistened again overnight by capillary movement of water from below. The only way to know how much water lurks beneath the surface is to check by probing.

Most plant roots grow within the top foot or so of soil and with many succulents in the top few inches. The shallower the roots, the more prone to drying out they are. Deeper watering–to a depth of a foot or more–will stimulate deeper root growth and therefore greater drought resistance; these depths are insulated from the extremes of drought and temperature. Moreover, deep watering can be done less frequently, saving water in the long run. Again, the only way to know how deeply water is penetrating is to probe the area in question after water has had time to soak in.

Gravel mulch, rocks, or other hardscape (paved walkways, patios, etc.) may initially keep the soil beneath from becoming moistened, but, by the same token, will prevent it from drying out once water has penetrated. Roots may grow into these moist pockets to sustain plants during dry periods.

It is not water that causes rot, but the fungi it encourages. Well-oxygenated soil will afford healthy root systems that can resist fungal infection. Coarse-textured well-drained soil is the key to this. Gravel mulch can also help by keeping a succulent's body elevated above the soil.

If rot does occur, it will usually appear around the base of the plant. If caught in time, the rotted portion can be removed and the top can be rerooted, like a cutting. Sometimes, even if the rot is not entirely removed but the plant is allowed to dry out, it will form callus around the rotted portion and new roots will be produced through it. This process should be allowed if only a small portion of healthy tissue remains.

Several types of irrigation systems are available for home gardeners; each has its advantages and disadvantages. An overhead system is usually inexpensive and easy to operate; but it uses more water than other systems, and a lot of this water is lost in runoff. A drip irrigation system with emitters installed at the base of plants or a microperforated hose (sometimes called a soaker hose) uses less water, but does not provide the overall coverage of overhead waterings. Some drip systems require installation, which limits new planting in the garden. Innovative new water-saving equipment with more efficient and/or adjustable heads that deliver water with greater accuracy or with precision timers and automatic water sensors that turn the system on and off exactly as needed are on the market.

Fertilizer Along with watering goes fertilizing. During the growing season, a dilute (one-quarter strength) solution of a general fertilizer (10-10-5, 12-5-5 or similar formula) should be applied every month or two. (For the most efficient use of fertilizer, water first and then fertilize.) Using a dilute solution

Left: Overhead irrigation. *Below:* Drip irrigation with soaker hose.

provides more even growth than less frequent applications of recommended strength solution. Depending on your irrigation system, this can be applied through the drip system or by hand with a hose-end sprayer or a siphon mixer. At The Huntington, gardens are prewatered before the dilute fertilizer is used; this saturates the ground and allows the fertilizer to be spread more efficiently and deeply. Time release fertilizers may be used but are not as precise. Fertilizer need not be applied when plants are dormant or about to go dormant, as in the fall. Again, these recommended times do not apply to plants that actively grow in the winter; these plants seem to have lower nutrient requirements. It should be noted that fertilizing may forestall for a time the need to renovate the soil, but cannot substitute for soil-building additions of organic matter. Also, smaller specimens and groundcovers may have greater nutrient requirements than larger; sometimes spot fertilization is indicated.

Weeding is best done manually, either by hand or with a hoe, before weeds mature and set seed. If flowers or seed have already set, dispose of weeds in a closed container. A sign in our office reads, "Give a weed an inch and it will take a yard."

Mulching is recommended because it helps retain moisture in the soil, reduce weeds and prevent crusting of the soil surface, and it can be attractive as well. Inorganic mulch, like gravel, does not break down but will need refreshing occasionally to retain its good looks. Choose a size and color that complements the plants in the bed. Organic mulches have the advantage of improving soil fertility and texture but are not recommended because they have been found to cause rot.

Grooming In a succulent landscape, grooming consists of removing spent flower stalks, yellowed leaves and old flowers. Pruning, as is generally thought of in the garden, is often replaced with cutting back and re-rooting leggy plants, for example, aeoniums and certain kalanchoes. Some bedding plants, for example, lampranthus, get old and need to be replanted every two years or so. This is where propagating techniques come in handy. Make cuttings and then replace the old plants with the fresh cuttings for an unscraggly new look. Pinching out growing tips will cause branching as with other plants.

Transplanting should be undertaken when plants are actively growing and given enough time to acclimate to their new position in the garden before going dormant. Be sure to match plant needs with existing conditions. (For a discussion of moving plants, see propagation section.)

WINTER PROTECTION

The best defense here is to choose plants that are hardy in your area. Climate zones for the United States are available from the USDA (or see page 24). There will also be microclimates in your yard–areas that are protected by walls or building, for example–that you can take advantage of for the more tender plants you wish to grow. Otherwise, during periods of cold, cover the tender ones with paper bags, newspapers or blankets. At Desert Botanical

Plants that are only marginally hardy in your area have a better chance of surviving the winter if placed in a protected area. This coldframe, in New Jersey, is covered with plexiglass when the temperature drops below freezing.

FERTILIZING

Concentrated fertilizer can be distributed with a proportioner. The simplest and least expensive is a hose-end siphon mixer which distributes at a rate of 16 to 1 approximately. This makes for convenient measuring; a concentrate of one cup (sixteen tablespoons) per gallon will come out of the watering end of the hole at the recommended distribution of one tablespoon per gallon; one-quarter cup per gallon will yield one-quarter strength fertilizer. Fertilizing with one-quarter strength fertilizer with every watering is optimal for container grown succulents.

GROOMING

Grooming of old flower stalks can improve the appearance of plants.

Dead leaves should be removed from the base of echeverias to reduce hiding places for bugs.

VIEWPOINT

FERTILIZATION

Monthly application of fertilizer during the growing season is most effective. Most desert soils need only nitrogen unless heavily irrigated. If chlorosis is a problem, lower soil pH to less than 8.
DR. MARK DIMMITT
THE ARIZONA-SONORA
DESERT MUSEUM

Less is more in succulents. One balanced feeding for plants in the ground at the beginning of the growing season is adequate.
MARY IRISH,
DESERT BOTANICAL GARDEN

For pot plants, fertilization begins with first growth in early spring and should be done regularly (every other watering) using a good organic fertilizer at 20 to 25 percent strength. Frequent feedings at one-quarter strength are much better for pot plants than one or two large does per year. Fish emulsion is good, as is a low nitrogen fertilizer somewhere in the 2-5-4 range.
KURT ZADNIK
THE UNIVERSITY OF CALIFORNIA
BOTANICAL GARDEN, BERKELEY

Osmocote time release fertilizer pellets work well if one does not want to fertilize often. Be careful not to get them stuck in cactus spines.
ERNEST DE MARIE
THE NEW YORK
BOTANICAL GARDEN

We fertilize once per season with Liquinox 12-5-5, applying a dilute liquid mixture with a hose. We don't apply the fertilizer to agaves or cereus. Occasionally we also fertilize once per winter with 0-10-10.
JOE CLEMENTS
THE HUNTINGTON BOTANICAL GARDEN

Unless you want an absolutely lush garden, fertilizer need not be applied more than two or three times per season. More frequent fertilizing will mean more pruning, weeds, and work–and may put some plants in danger of winter damage.
GARY LYONS

Certain pests attack specific groups of succulents. For example the yucca weevil (above) attacks yuccas and agaves, which are in the same family; certain agave species are quite susceptible to their boring larvae when introduced into an area where they are rampant.

Aloe are susceptible to a species of mite, called aloe mites (which are very different from spider mites). These microscopic pests feed on the leaves of aloes, sucking their juices, and cause distorted, cancerous-looking growth.

Garden, the vulnerable tips of columnar cacti are protected with styrofoam cups. Remove and replace protection as needed (daily). Plants that are watered and fertilized properly are less susceptible to extremes of cold. However, in extreme climates cool, wet soils often lead to greater frost damage; soil should be kept on the dry side in winter. Generally, succulents are dormant during the cold season and require no fertilizer and little if any water.

DISEASES AND PESTS

To reduce the incidence of diseases and pests as much as possible, start your garden with healthy, vigorous plants planted in a well-prepared bed. Do not introduce a sickly plant into the landscape. Nurse it along in isolation if you must have it. Keep your plants healthy with the good cultural practices already mentioned. In addition, practice good sanitation which will eliminate shelter for undesirable insects and decaying vegetation for fungi. Avoid overcrowding so that there will be good air circulation. Chemical controls are best avoided but should they become necessary, try the least measure first before moving to stronger treatments. Always read and follow the label instructions as to use and safety precautions! Store unused portions in their original containers out of reach of children and pets.

ORGANIC GARDENING In the past few decades a vast and successful effort has been made to find new ways to garden without using harmful chemicals. The approach, called organic gardening, is directed at the soil and at the measures taken to control pests.

The soil is built up through the addition of organic materials, especially compost. The addition of compost, homemade or store-bought, and other organic material such as peat moss, green cover crops, and bone meal makes the soil so fertile and productive that petrochemicals are not needed.

Pest problems are handled through a practice called Integrated Pest Management (IPM), developed by the Council on Environmental Quality. IPM is defined as "maximum use of naturally occurring pest controls, including weather, disease agents, predators, and parasitoids. In addition, IPM utilizes various biological, physical, chemical controls and habitat modification techniques. Artificial controls are imposed only as required to keep a pest from surpassing tolerable population as determined from accurate assessments of the pest damage potential and the ecological, sociological, and economic costs of the control measures." In other words, gardeners must make reasonable assessments of how much damage a particular pest will do. If the pest is just munching on foliage, let it be. If controls must be taken, nonharmful ones should be tried first. Only in extreme cases is chemical warfare waged–and then in the most nonharmful ways possible.

The weapons in the IPM arsenal include:

•Careful monitoring to identify problems before they become widespread.

•Beneficial insects, such as ladybugs, praying mantises, and some nematodes, which feed on garden pests. Some of these reside naturally in your garden; others can be bought and placed there.

• Bacteria such as Bt (*Bacillus thuringiensis*) that attack garden pests. These bacteria can be bought by the pound and dusted on the plants; strains have been discovered that breed and attack many common pests.

• Insecticides such as rotenone, pyrethrum, and sabadilla and insecticidal soaps.

• Hand-picking pests off foliage wherever they are seen in small numbers.

Despite these efforts, there are some common pests that you will encounter from time to time:

Aphids are small sucking insects with tiny "exhaust pipes," ranging in color from green to gray to black, which feed on tender new growth, often flower stalks and buds. These can be removed with a sharp spray of plain or soapy water. Control is important because they are the primary vector of viruses.

Mealybugs are sucking insects that look like small cottony masses and may appear on stem, spines, or roots. These may be sprayed with soapy water, daubed off with a cotton swab dipped in alcohol, or removed from spines with tweezers. Dilute alcohol with water (35 percent alcohol) to avoid damage to plant.

Scale are gray to dark brown "armored" sucking insects that are usually found on stems. Scale are persistent and may require repeated treatment as for mealybugs.

Ants tend and defend honey dew-producing insects like aphids and scale and therefore should be kept to a minimum in the garden.

Snails and slugs eat leaves and leave unsightly slime trails. These may be picked by hand at night and killed or given to a friend with chickens or ducks. Poison baits are also available, but use with caution around pets. Sanitation and periodic checks under potential hiding places are the best defense against these pests.

Spider mites. Certain leafy succulents (adeniums for example) are susceptible to spider mites. These inconspicuous pests usually go unnoticed until damage is done. Their sap-sucking habits result in a yellowish speckling over the surface of the leaf while in heavy infestations, the fine silk produced by these spider relatives covers the leaves in cobwebs. Commercially available miticides are usually effective, but the best protection against spider mites is a well ventilated environment. Bathe the leaves with Safer's and provide more air movement

Viruses in cacti and succulents are just beginning to be studied. Symptoms may or may not be present but include distorted growth, discoloration, or corking (in *Kalanchoe*). Plants in the Crassulaceae family are often susceptible. Presently, there is no treatment for viruses, so the best defense is choosing healthy plants and keeping insect vectors, particularly aphids, to a minimum.

Fungal diseases are secondary diseases which cause rot and are due usually to injury, wetness, and cold. To save a rotting plant, cut away all the diseased tissue and allow the remaining tissue to callus or heal before replanting as described under "Cuttings" on page 182. Good sanitation, care in handling, and a proper watering regime will keep fungal disease in check.

Spider mites.

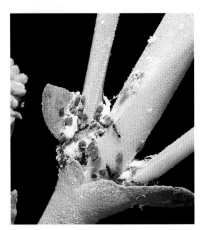
Mealybugs and ants.

Virus-infected aeonium.

Sedums and sempervivums grow
among grasses and other perennials in
the rock garden of the United States
Botanic Garden.

COOL CLIMATE SUCCULENTS

Most people think of succulent plants as suitable only for warm climate gardening. Few could imagine a garden full of succulents that can be created and grown successfully in the northeastern United States. Actually, many traditional gardens in cold climate areas already include a number of hardy succulent species, such as sedums and sempervivums. Some adventurous gardeners have even built special gardens exclusively for hardy succulents and compatible plants, often with outstanding success. Experimental growing of additional succulent species in the open ground each year leads invariably to new recommendations for hardy succulent gardening. Moreover, recent expeditions to areas with cold winter climates in South Africa, Lesotho, Patagonia, and other locations have greatly enriched the diversity of plant species available to gardeners in cold winter climates. The selection of commercially available winter-hardy succulent species and gardens devoted mainly to these plants will certainly increase markedly in the next decade.

COLD HARDY SUCCULENTS IN THE WILD Learning about the areas in which these plants were found and the conditions under which they grew in their native habitat will help you evaluate potential hardy succulents suited to the conditions (temperature, rainfall patterns and amounts) in your own area.

The mountains of Europe and Asia are home to several succulent plant genera, especially of the *Crassula* family. Included are myriad species and hybrids of *Sempervivum* and *Sedum,* and a host of lesser known but attractive genera such as *Orostachys, Jovibarba, Rhodiola*, and *Rosularia.* Some of these plants live in areas with rather high annual rainfalls, but are found growing in crevices among rocks where drainage is excellent. Others grow in areas with a pronounced dry season. European and east Asian species tend to be more tolerant of wet conditions and high humidity than central Asian species, which are adapted to drier winters and less humid summers than those of most of the northern United States. Of course, gardeners in areas with cold, dry winters (such as in parts of the north central and western states) may be successful with some of the species that are difficult to grow in northeastern or midwestern states.

The Rocky Mountains and Great Basin areas of the U.S. produce a number of succulent species worth growing in the eastern states if some provision can be made to protect them from excessive dampness, particularly in winter. These species typically are resistant to both extremes of heat and cold, but the deleterious effects of excessive rainfall or humidity are often more of a problem in the eastern states. Included in this group are garden-worthy cacti of the genera *Opuntia, Coryphantha,* and *Echinocereus,* as well as other hardy genera. A large number of compatible (from both an aesthetic and cultural viewpoint) plants which are not succulent in the strictest sense but useful in succulent gardens are also found in this area: *Yucca, Astragalus, Cheilanthse* (desert ferns), *Penstemon,* and others.

The southwestern states and Mexico contain a great many succulent species, but most of these are not hardy in the North. A few do survive, if given protection from winter moisture. South America contains regions with cold winters, notably the Andean plateau (*altiplano*) and the southern reaches of Argentina and Chile, including Patagonia. The *altiplano* has very dry winters in most areas, or deep snowfall in others, so the plants are not adapted to the extremes of winter wet and the freeze-thaw cycles of most of the northern United States. Nevertheless, gardeners are experimenting with such cacti as *Echinopsis* and such oddball succulents as the rosulate violets in gardens. Over time, new plant introductions from these regions will provide a number of useful species for succulent gardens in cold areas of the U.S.

South Africa is without doubt the richest area of the world in numbers and diversity of succulent plant species, but most of the succulent flora is not sufficiently coldhardy to be grown outdoors year-round in northern U.S. However, horticulturists are discovering that many of the species found in the highveld (the high plateau of grasslands) of the Transvaal and the Drakensberg mountains of Natal are coldhardy, and efforts to introduce new species from these regions are currently underway. Along with the interior regions of the Cape and the country of Lesotho, these areas experience extreme cold and heat, with very variable amounts of rainfall each year. Winters are normally quite dry (except in parts of the Drakensberg, where snow falls quite frequently). Two members of the ice plant family (*Delosperma cooperi* and *D. nubigenum*) are becoming important coldhardy succulents in American horticulture and it is expected that additional members of this family will soon be commercially available. People are even experimenting with "living stones" (*Lithops lesliei*), found in some areas of the highveld. A few species of *Crassula* and even *Aloe* from the area merit trials as potential coldhardy garden plants.

HARDY SUCCULENT GARDENS In nature, most succulent plants experience an extended period of drought at some point during the year. In the eastern and midwestern states, high humidity and rainfall are the most severe limiting factors in successful succulent gardening. However, provisions can be made to compensate for excessive rainfall. In choosing an outdoor site for a succulent garden, select an area in which the soil is very well drained, or amend the site to allow for rapid drainage. Sandy soils, such as those found on coastal islands, usually do not hold water for long periods of time and may be suitable for planting with little preparation. More often, the site contains heavy soils, which need to be amended to provide optimal drainage. Gravel and course sand are useful mineral amendments which allow the soil to dry more rapidly.

Rock gardens Preparing a rock garden is perhaps the best way to create a garden for coldhardy succulents. This involves choosing a rocky site or placing rocks so that shallow pockets are created among the rocks. These soil pockets should dry rapidly after a rainfall, providing a suitable microhabit for succulent species that would otherwise rot. Crevices also restrain certain rapid growing plants, such as sempervivums, preventing them from crowding out other plants. Creating overhangs with rocks allows moisture from sensitive species to be placed in areas that are protected from direct rainfall. Planting on the slopes created by a rock garden (or in natural or manmade rock

This New Jersey rock garden, created by Dr. Jerry Barad, is composed mostly of succulents, including coldhardy sedums and sempervivums, and other species that are wintered indoors and planted outdoors in spring.

crevices) enhances drainage, especially for rosette-forming plants that often lie flat on the rock, at an angle that deflects rainfall away from the center of the rosette. By creating appropriate microenvironments, the skillfull gardener can grow a variety of interesting hardy succulents.

Other gardens One can also select succulents that do well in any reasonably drained soil. Typically, these plants will also do well (or better) on a slope or in a rock garden, but they are tolerant enough to use in wetter garden situations. Many of the sedums and sempervivums come to mind, and there is even a cactus native to the eastern states (*Opuntia humifusa*, syn. *O. compressa*) that will grow in ordinary garden loams. However a succulent garden is created, it must be in a site with as much direct sun as possible. Few succulent species thrive in deep shade in the northern states. Remember that direct sunlight in the northern states is not nearly as strong as it is in most natural succulent habitats. Even succulents that grow in northern latitudes almost always grow in open, sunny habitats, often at high altitudes where sunlight is more intense.

A wide variety of tender succulent plants can also be used temporarily in almost any sunny garden. For example, the colorful rosettes of some aeoniums and echeverias can be used as highlights in an annual flower border. In this situation, the plant is treated as an annual, or it may be lifted before inclement weather arrives and placed indoors, or propagated from cuttings. However, plants grown in outdoor soils may harbor pests such as nematodes, so careful inspection is advised. Potted plants may also be summered in soilless areas on patios and decks, often much to their benefit. Almost any succulent plant can be grown outdoors this way, and they are easy to move indoors before frost. Succulents with interesting architectural features, such as large pachypodiums with thick spiny trunks and bold foliage are displayed to maximum advantage in such situations. The plant benefits as well, often growing much better than if it were kept indoors all year. Any indoor plant will burn if placed in direct sun outdoors, so be sure to acclimate it first by placing it in a shady location. Just like many people, plants that have been indoors all winter adapt to summer sun by gradual exposure.

PLANTS FOR COLD CLIMATE SUCCULENT GARDENS

The following is a list of coldhardy succulents and annuals species suitable for growing in cold climates. (Some of these are mentioned in Chapter 2 as well; see index for additonal information where noted).

Agave Hardy agaves provide dramatic contrast in a garden with their spiked rosettes of stiff foliage. Two of the hardiest species are *A. utahensis* and *A. parryi.* Planting agaves under overhangs or in vertical crevices should be tried where wet winters occur. See Chapter 2.

Calyptridium C. umbellatum is a pretty succulent-leaved plant found in the mountains of the West. Small rosettes produce tiny magenta flowers during the summer. It is known as pussypaws because of the appearance of dense flowering spikes produced on stems which lie around the plant. Propagation is best done by seed, which is produced freely by established plants. Seed is obtainable from some rock garden and native plant seed firms and societies.

Coryphantha C. vivipara grows in the western states up into Canada! It is a beautiful little cactus with large pink flowers. Protection from winter wet is the main difficulty encountered in growing it in the eastern states, but it is extremely coldhardy. See Chapter 2.

Crassula C. strigosa from the Drakensberg is worth trying as a groundcover. Small white flowers are produced above the succulent leaves in summer.

Delosperma D. cooperi produces magenta flowers all summer over short masses of succulent leaves. It is perfectly hardy in New York City, even during the harshest winters. *D. nubigenum* is even hardier, forming a flatter mat of succulent foilage than *D. cooperi.* It produces abundant bright yellow flowers in spring. Like most members of the ice plant family, the flowers of delospermas open only in direct sunlight. See Chapter 2.

Dorotheanthus D. gramineus and *D. bellidiformis* are annual succulents from sandy areas near Capetown, South Africa. Both produce brilliant flowers in shades of white, purple, magenta, and pink. *D. bellidiformis* also flowers in pastel tones. These small leaf succulents do not flower for very long, but they provide a carpet of color before really hot summer weather sets in. Grow both from seed.

Echinocereus E. viridiflorus, E. triglochiodiatus, and *E. pectinatus* are three wonder-

Though not coldhardy, echeverias make lovely annual accents in cool climates.

Echinocereus viridiflorus.

ful examples of coldhardy cacti in this genus. *E. viridiflorus* produces yellow-green flowers on small globular plants. Much larger and more colorful flowers are produced on *E. triglochidiatus* and *E. pectinatus*, usually in shades of red and magenta, respectively. Both are variable plants, but *E. pectinatus* is easier to handle than the well-armed *E. triglochidiatus*. See Chapter 2.

Jovibarba *J. allionii* resembles a small *Sempervivum,* to which it is closely related. Bright green "hens" quickly produce a large brood of "chicks" which surround the mother plant. This is a good plant for crevices among rocks.

Lewisia Lewisias include some of the most colorful flowerings succulents. *L. redidiva,* the bitter root of the Rocky Mountains, produces striking pink water-lilylike flowers from the bare earth in spring. However, the thick root rots easily if exposed to constant dampness during its late summer rest period. Plant lewisias in well-drained gritty soils. A layer of gravel around the crown of the plant also helps to prevent rot. Lewisias are best grown from seed sown in spring under cool temperatures or purchased as small potted plants.

Opuntia *O. humifusa* grows in the eastern U.S. and tolerates higher rainfall than most cacti. Yellow flowers and edible fruits are produced by this "prickly pear" cactus during the spring and summer respectively. *O. phaeacantha* is a larger plant with flowers in many shades of yellow, pink, and even red. It appreciates a well-drained soil and sunny location and is very coldhardy. The large flowers are produced over a long period by this well-armed prickly pear cactus. *O. imbricata* is one of the "jumping cholla" cacti, so called because its long, extremely spiny stem sections easily detach from the plant onto passing animals or humans. When the unfortunate carrier of the cholla extricates itself, the discarded stem will root and grow into a new plant. Chollas lend height and texture to the succulent garden, but do not plant them where small children or passersby might encounter them. All prickly pear cacti are easily propagated from stem sections ("pads" if wide and flat, "joints" if elongated and cylindrical). Merely lay them down where they are to be grown, or start some in pots. Handle all the species with care, for the characteristic small hairline spines found on them are often more irritating and harder to extract than the much larger typical cactus spines which are also usually present. See Chapter 2.

Portulaca *P. grandiflora* is a common and easily grown annual from South. America. It grows in any sunny location with decent drainage, and flowers best on poor soils. Stunning flowers open in sunshine in brilliant shades of red, purple, orange, yellow, and pink. White and pastel shades are also sometimes available. Double-flowered forms look like small roses, hence the common name "moss rose." Portulaca looks especially nice in rock gardens and growing among grass in dry sunny locations, and it will self-sow and spread. Plants and seeds are readily available in most garden centers.

Sedum *S. spurium*, the dragon's blood sedum, is a rapid grower and profuse bloomer, producing masses of pink or red flowers in summer. *S. acre* will grow in shade, but the yellow flowers are more abundantly produced in sunny locations. It is good for difficult situations, but can become aggressive, so must be controlled if it is not to overrun other plants. Unlike these creeping species, *S. spectabile* is an upright grower with tuberous roots and thick, gray-green leaves. Large, flat-topped masses of pink flower are produced in late summer and fall. This plant tolerates shade well, and can be grown in a perennial border. Many other sedum species and hybrids are available commercially. See Chapter 2.

Sempervivum The well-known houseleek or hens-and-chicks is an easily grown plant, ideal for rock gardens or even as an edging plant in a sunny border. Some species, such as *S. arachnoideum,* bear attractive wooly hairs which cover the plant. All sempervivums produce many offsets, and some can become aggressive in the garden. Planting in crevices delimited by rock inhospitable to root growth helps, but one must still watch for the "tumblers", little ball-shaped offsets that roll right over the rocks into neighboring soil pockets! However, because they grow so thickly, established sempervivum colonies require only infrequent weeding, so they are an ideal low-maintenance plant.

Yucca Yuccas are not succulent plants, strictly speaking, but they do grow in dry locations and are adapted to resist drought by means of their tough leathery leaves. They make excellent accent plants in the garden and produce huge panicles of attractive white flowers. *Y. filamentosa* grows easily in eastern gardens, which is not surprising since it is native to the Southeast. As with many native plants of the South, it is hardy far north of its native range. Unlike several western plants, this *Yucca* does not grow long stems. It is an easy and dramatic plant to grow in a low-maintenance garden.

ERNEST DE MARIE, THE NEW YORK BOTANICAL GARDEN

A tiny selection of the thousands of cacti and other succulents that can be grown easily indoors.

BRINGING THE DESERT IN–SUCCULENTS INDOORS

Succulents, including cacti, make wonderful indoor plants, especially in areas where they cannot survive outside. In general, frost sensitive succulent species make better houseplants than winter hardy succulents, since many winter hardy succulents require extremely cold winters to perform well. Succulent plants do not demand much attention, making them ideal for the indoor gardener with limited time. No plastic bags or plant sitters are necessary when going on long vacations. Merely water well and enjoy your trip, because your plants are unlikely to notice whether you were gone for a week or a couple of months!

When you get back, there are a few things to remember about the cultivation of indoor succulents to achieve best results. Sun is required for most indoor succulents, the more the better. Ideally, this means a large unobstructed south-facing window, but for many succulents, such as haworthias, a good eastern exposure will also suffice. Artificial light, preferably fluorescent, will enable dedicated plant enthusiasts to grow many succulents in the darkest of areas. Succulents grown under artificial light must be placed near the tubes, within two to six inches or so. They should not be very large or tall, because they will not receive enough light intensity far away from the tubes. However small cacti and dwarf (especially rosette-forming) succulents are ideal light garden plants. Watering rules are fairly straightforward: when in doubt, don't. More plants die indoors because of too-frequent watering than from any other cause, and succulent plants can be even more sensitive to this problem than other types. Water well and frequently during the plant's active growth season, allowing the soil to dry thoroughly between waterings. Exceptions to this rule are noted in the list of plants that follows. Less frequent or no watering is needed when the plant is not growing, which is usually in winter for most species. If the plant begins to shrivel, it may be signalling a need for a drink. However, nearly all succulent species are adapted to cope with occasional, sudden, and prolonged periods of drought stress, so a few weeks without water, even during the growing season will not harm most succulents if they are not routinely treated this way. Water-soluble fertilizers applied during the growing season benefit most succulents. Follow the instructions on the package, but use at one-half to one-quarter the recommended strength for best results.

Soil mixes for growing indoor plants should be well-aerated, since growing roots require oxygen. Soil behaves differently in a pot than outdoors, so changes need to be made to compensate for the different physical properties of containerized soil. Actually soil itself is not recommended for indoor plants. In pots, soil becomes too compact and hard, reducing air available to roots. In addition, outdoor soils are loaded with weed seeds, plant diseases, and pests which easily get out of control in pots. Even earthworms, so beneficial in outdoor gardens, damage roots by excessive tunneling though the soil when trapped in pots. The best mixes for indoor plants contain little or no soil. A good basic mix for many indoor plants, succulents included, would be two parts peat moss, two parts perlite, and one part sterilized soil, plus one table-spoon each of dolomitic limestone and bonemeal per bushel. Grit can be added to make the mix heavier, so larger plants can be stabilized, or it may be used as a surface dressing. Perlite does have the obnoxious habit of floating to the surface of the mix when watered, but well-established root systems will hold it in check, and a light covering of grit or fine gravel can be used to hide it. Also be sure to moisten perlite before handling it, as its dust is hazardous if inhaled. There is actually no one recipe for the best mix; what works best under your conditions may differ from what is best for another person. If available in your area, pumice and/or turface may be used in place of, or mixed with, perlite. "Instant" soil mixes also can be used, or amended as needed. In The New York Botanical Garden, nearly all the plants in the Desert Collection grown in pots are in a mix consisting of three parts Metro-Mix 360 (a soilless mix) and two parts perlite, plus dolomite and bonemeal in small quantities. This includes such different plants as rare impatiens species, salvias, aloes, euphorbias, cacti, and even lithops! Different watering schedules enable such a wide variety of plants to coexist in pots of the same mix within the same greenhouse.

Temperatures should mimic what the plants prefer in the wild, but need not be extremely cold or hot. Night temperatures should drop ten degrees or more (Fahrenheit) for most succulents, especially in winter. This drop enhances flower bud formation in many succulents, including cacti. Cooler night temperatures also improve the growth of most succulents.

Pests and diseases are best prevented by good sanitation and careful inspection of any new plants. If pest populations become rampant, and organic methods have not worked, control is possible with fungicides and insecticides, but be sure the product is labeled for use on indoor plants, and follow directions *to the letter*. Some pesticides damage certain plant species, but not others, so limit the use of any product you are not familiar with. Among the more sensitive succulent plant are echeverias, pachypodiums, tillandsias, and sedums. Horticultural oils, soaps, and growth regulators are generally less toxic to people than other pesticides, but may still damage certain plants, especially if temperatures are high or directions are not followed.

When selecting plants to grow indoors, choose those that grow well in the conditions you can offer. If you like to keep your apartment a toasty 70° F, on cold winter nights, it would not be wise to grow most flowering cacti. If you have little or no sunshine, sansevierias would be a better choice than euphorbias for you.

SUCCULENTS FOR INDOORS The selection of succulents that can be grown indoors is enormous, so what follows is a compilation of a few particularly easy and/or choice species that grow well indoors. Emphasis is placed on smaller succulents, since they fit best into most people's living arrangements.

Aloe contains a number of lovely species and hybrids that do well indoors. Aloes also do well under lights. Recommended species include *A. albiflora* (dark foliage and white bell-shaped flowers), *A. bellatula* (a small plant that

PLANTS FOR SECURITY

For urban dwellers, a windowsill garden full of large, prickly succulents may confer a degree of protection against burglars. Given a choice, would *you* willingly choose to crawl through a window full of well-armed euphorbias or opuntias? Apartment dwellers should remember, however, to keep their fire escape windows accessible from inside. For example, a table behind the windowsill might be on wheels, so it can be rolled away when needed in an emergency. Precautions to allow emergency egress do not necessarily mean that it need be easier for unwelcome persons to enter through the same windows.

Small cactus can be beautifully displayed in a dish garden. This is an excellent way to grow plants with similar cultural needs and enhance a table or windowsill in bright light.

Select an attractive container such as a terracotta bowl or rustic box, making sure that it does not leak or that it sits on a saucer to catch any runoff. Put gravel or coarse charcoal in the bottom half of the container and fill the rest of the container with a suitable cactus potting mix. Choose plants that will remain small and that will thrive under the same conditions, such as jade, chin cactus, beavertail cactus, aloe, and *Haworthia*. Even small specimens of cactus that grow large can be used with the intention of moving them out of the dish garden as they grow too large. When placing the plants, use design principles of mixing textures, shapes, and sizes to achieve an attractive combination. Plants can be put close together for an instant impact or spread farther apart to accommodate their growth. Situate the roots so the plant is firmly planted and will easily support itself. Add design elements desired, such as decorative stones or driftwood. Finally, topdress the soil with attractive gravel and water the plants lightly. After moving the dish garden to its display spot, watch carefully for a few days to make sure the plants are settling in.

produces rather large orange tubular flowers on one-foot-long spikes), *A. vera* (also known as *A. barbadensis*, the "burn aloe"–an easy houseplant to grow, and useful for its soothing sap, but rarely flowers indoors); *A. bakeri* (compact creeeping habit, lots of orange flowers), *A. rauhii* (small rosettes of spotted leaves and spikes of orange red flowers), *A. viguieri* (similar to *A. rauhii*, but with larger foliage lacking spots), *A. ciliaris* (a vining aloe, grows easily, but may be shy to flowers indoors–needs room for best results), *A. sinkatana* (small clustering rosettes of spotted leaves and capitate inflorescences of yellow or red flowers) and *A. aristata* (compact rosettes and colorful large pink or orange flowers in spring or summer, excellent for a cool windowsill). Many other aloes are frequently available in the trade, but most will eventually grow too large for the average windowsill, or may be more difficult to grow well. Examples includes *A. striata* (coral aloe), which has attractive rosettes of pin-striped leaves, but gets too big for most indoor situations, and *A. variegata*, a beautiful small species with white marked leaves, which somtimes rots if watered heavily in summer, its dormant period.

Agaves are usually too large and vicious for indoor settings, but some smaller-growing species make attractive plants for sunny locations. Among the best are *A. victoriae-reginae* (especially the compact form), *A. nizandensis* (small, attractive, but brittle striped leaves and no spines), and *A. bracteosa* (unarmed attractive foliage, but eventually it gets very big). *A. attenuata* is unusual in that it grows a long stem topped by a rosette of fleshy unarmed leaves. Young plants of many other species make good houseplants. However, clipping off the especially wicked terminal spine on each leaf is suggested for people concerned about the possibility of injury to themselves or others.

Beaucarnea includes the popular "ponytail palm", *B. recurvata*. A swollen base is topped by one or more branches bearing gracefully drooping long leaves. Nearly foolproof, it will eventually grow large, but takes many years to do so.

Cacti as houseplants do best in full sun. Tall growing columnar types such as *Cereus* will need to be pruned or restarted from large cuttings, as they eventually outgrow their allotted space. Opuntias are attractive windowsill plants, especially *O. basilaris* (beavertail cactus) and *O. microdasys*. If you have a very sunny window and wish to discourage intruders, try species with colorful, prominent, and sharp spines such as *O. invicta*. *Mammillaria* includes some of the best cacti for indoors. Most are quite attractive small plants, and some produce quite spectacular flowers. Recommended species include *M. bombycina* (attractive white wool and freely-produced small cream flowers), *M. elongata* (clusters of cylindrical stems studded with red berries), *M. zeilmanniana* (attractive magenta flowers) and *M. senilis* (ball-shaped plant covered with soft white hairs, red flowers in spring). *Echinopsis* flower well if kept cool in winter, otherwise they produce loads of offsets instead of flowers! All bear spectacularly large, often fragrant, flowers, which last only a short time. Other good flowering cacti genera are *Rebutia, Notocactus, Parodia,* and *Coryphantha*.

Crassula ovata is the popular jade plant, which is easy to grow in a location that receives some sun. *C. orbicularis* resembles a small wide-leaved green spider plant, producing a large number of offsets at the end of delicate stolons. Almost any *Crassula* will make a nice houseplant, but do not overwater those from the western Cape of South Africa during the summer, which is normally their dry season.

Echeveria peacockii is a beautiful small lavender-tinted blue-green plant with orange flowers. *E. setosa* is one of several species with attractive hairy leaves. The many other echeverias suitable for the home produce rosettes of very attractive foliage topped with spikes of "candy corn" flowers.

Euphorbias often grow large, but a number of species and hybrids make highly successful indoor plants. *E. milii* and its hybrids deserve special mention, producing attractive red, pink, orange, yellow, white, or bicolored flowers in sunny locations. Keep *E. milii* fairly warm and water frequently if you want the plant to retain its foliage. Otherwise, the plant sheds most of its leaves, leaving spiny branches with tufts of leaves and flowers at the ends. *E. pedilanthoides* looks like a delicate bonsai with red flowers. It is a very attractive species for warm locations. *E. decaryi* has thick leaves on gnarled stems, and grows well under lights. It prefers warmth and more water than most other euphorbias. *E. obesa* is often grown as a curiousity, as it resembles a green baseball! It needs sun to grow well, and can be propagated from offsets that form on old plants. *E. grandicornis* has attractively shaped stems well-armed with large spines. It grows large, but is easy to renew from cuttings . Do not place this heavy, exceedingly well-armed plant in a window you may need to use in an emergency exit.

Faucaria is one of the easier genera of the ice plant family to grow indoors. They produce yellow (rarely white) flowers over mounds of soft, toothed foliage during the summer. *F. tigrina,* tiger's jaws, is the most commonly available species, bearing large yellow flowers in the center of softly toothed rosettes.

Gasteria bicolor var. liliputana is a tiny plant with glossy leaves and spikes of pink flowers in spring. *G. carinata* var. *verrucosa* has interesting textured leaves covered with numerous small white "warts." All the smaller gasterias make good houseplants. Keep an eye out for the recently described species *G. ellaphieae, G. baylissiana,* and *G. glomerata.* All three have very attractive foliage and fairly short spikes of colorful flowers.

Haworthias seem made for indoor situations. All species are small enough to grow indoors, and most are easy to grow. Bear in mind that they are often shallow-rooted, and may periodically lose their roots when in pots. Should this happen, remove the dead roots and any dead foliage, dry for a few days, and replant in a fresh medium. Generally, the softer, pale-leaved species such as *H. cymbiformis* prefer more water and shade than hard-leaved darker colored species such as *H. attenuata.*

Plectranthus hilliardiae produces large tubular blue flowers on a compact, fleshy-leaved plant. *P. ernestii* has smaller foliage on thick stems with swollen bases. It produces large amounts of small lilac flowers all summer. Both upright and prostrate growing forms are in cultivation.

Gasteria liliputana.

Sansevieria trifasciata 'Golden Hahni'.

Sansevieria trifasciata is one of the most commonly grown indoor plants, and with good reason. Except for severe cold, it will tolerate almost any abuse heaped upon it—if you cannot succeed with the snake plant, consider plastic plants. It is probably the most reliable houseplant for warm, dry, shady locations. There are many mutations of this species, often with yellow or white markings. If grown in adequate sunlight and given plenty of water and fertilizer, your snake plant will produce unusual white wispy flowers on long spikes in the spring. The flowers are very strongly perfumed at night. Most other sansevierias are also easy houseplants. Particularly lovely if you come upon them are *S. aethiopica, S. aubrytiana, S. parva,* and *S. kirkii* (especially var. *pulchra*), all of which have attractive foliage and are unarmed. Many other species, quite a few not even named yet, are in cultivation, but beware of species such as *S. bagamoyensis* and *S. phillipsiaa,* which have sharp points at the ends of tips.

Sedums are good for windows with cool nighttime temperatures. The Mexican species which are usually too tender to grow outside in most of the U.S. make particularly attractive houseplants. *S. morganianum* is the well-known burro's tail. It produces cascading branches loaded with fat whitish gray-green leaves, which promptly form roots and shoots when they fall off. *S. hintonii* has attractive white hairs covering the leaves. It does not grow large, and should not be overwatered. *S. frutescens* can get too big for most windows, but is easily renewed from cuttings. It resembles a small tree with a fat peeling trunk. Small white flowers are produced among the narrow, fleshy leaves.

Stapeliads make fascinating houseplants for warm, bright locations. *Stapelia* includes the largest-flowered species, which flower freely in summer if happy. The large, intricately patterned flowers are real showstoppers, but don't get too close if you are not prepared for their "fragrance." There is actually one species with pleasantly scented flowers (at least to some people), *S. flavopurpurea*. Other stapeliads such as *Huernia, Pectinaria, Caralluma* and *Orbeopsis* also make easy houseplants, but all have unpleasantly scented flowers, except for *Caralluma quadrifida,* which produces rose-scented flowers.

Trichodiadema species will flower all summer in sunny indoor spots. The bristly crystalline leaves are attractive, as are the magenta flowers, which open in sunshine.

ERNEST DE MARIE, THE NEW YORK BOTANICAL GARDEN

SUCCULENTS FOR SHADE

Popular opinion has it that all succulents need full sunshine to survive. While it is true that many succulents in coastal California grow and flower better in full sun, a gardener with a shaded location need not despair.

Actually, in more brutal climates–like the low desert of Arizona or interior southern California–shade is actually needed. Very few plants will tolerate the strong sun in these climates and light shade, particularly afternoon shade is preferable for almost all plants. This includes the smaller cacti like notocacti and mammillarias as well as most of the aloes, euphorbias, and other shade plants. The shade should not be dense or total, but the protection of a high tree or shrub is a definite advantage. In addition, overhanging branches can provide several degrees of frost protection for more tender species. The exception to this rule is the ice plant family; most members of this group, like *Lampranthus* and *Delosperma* will not open their flowers unless in full sun.

Plants that thrive in shade are following their native habits. Most succulents found in the wild grow in the shade of desert plants or in the protection of cliffsides. They are able to get enough sun in those locations to perform photosynthesis, and the shade makes it easier for them to conserve water.

In southern California, most succulents do prefer sun for four to six hours per day. But there is also a large selection of plants that will tolerate or even prefer less light. Most haworthias and gasterias are shade-loving, and therefore serve beautifully as underplantings for less shade-tolerant plants. Some aeoniums, bulbines, kalanchoes, sedums, senecios, and sempervivums also perform admirably in shade. Even many aloes, agaves, and echeverias will grow well in quite shades locations. In many cases, though, the tall-growing species of these genera serve as primary specimens, providing rather than receiving the shade.

Plants grown in shade need different care than those grown in full sun. They usually require a bit less water, since it does not evaporate as quickly in those conditions. They should also be planted more closely, since they are not like to grow as rapidly. Fertilizer should be withheld or provided only sparingly lest plants grow thin, weak, and etiolated.

If your site is very shady, consider containerized plants. These can be moved in and out of the sun as needed and the extra drainage and confined root space provided by a container can keep the plants from growing too rapidly. .

One other important point: if shade is provided by large trees that produce a great deal of litter, spiny succulents are not recommended. Cleaning fallen leaves and branches from well-armed cacti is a chore no one enjoys. Less spiny choices include sansevierias–which are very happy in shade–aeoniums, kalanchoes, and senecios, which allow leaf litter to filter to the ground, creating mulch.

Sansevieria subspicata growing in the shade of an oak tree (*Quercus agrifolia*).

SOME SOURCES

American Horticultural Therapy
Association
362A Christopher Avenue,
Gaithersburg, Maryland 20879
800-634-1603

Canadian Horticultural Therapy
Association
c/o Royal Botanical Garden
PO Box 399, Hamilton, Ontario,
Canada, L8N 3H8
416-529-7618

ENABLING GARDENS

Being forced to stop gardening is one of the worst fates that can befall a gardener, but the inability to get down on one's hands and knees owing to arthritis, a bad back, a heart problem, the need to use a wheelchair–or the normal aches, pains, and fatigues of advancing age–is no reason to stop gardening. By using a few different gardening techniques, modifying tools, following new criteria in the selection of plants, and tapping into the many resources available for information and help, no one should ever have to stop gardening.

Begin by thoroughly and frankly assessing your situation.
• How much time can you devote to gardening?
• Do you need crutches, a cane, or wheelchair to get around?
• Can you get up and down from the ground without assistance?
• How much sun or heat is wise for you?
• Can you bend at the waist easily?
• Is your coordination impaired? balance? vision? ability to hold tools?

Consult your doctor, occupational or physical therapist, and most importantly speak to a horticultural therapist.

Horticultural therapists are specially trained in applying horticulture in therapeutic programs for people with disabilities and older adults. They have developed specialized gardening tools and techniques that make gardening easier for every situation.

Once you've decided how much you can and want to do, the garden can be planned. For example, people with relatively severe mobility impairments should have firm, level surfaces an easy distance from the house and should use containers or raised beds to bring soil up to a comfortable working height–usually somewhere around two feet high with a maximum width of thirty inches if worked from one side and sixty inches if both sides of the container or bed are accessible. People with more mobility can work with easily worked, light soils mounded to eight to ten inches above grade and should use lightweight, long-handled tools. Smaller containers can be hung within easy reach on poles or fences, and an overhead structure can be used to support hanging baskets on ropes and pulleys so the baskets can be lowered for care and then replaced to an out-of-reach position.

Important considerations when planning the garden layout include:
• Start small: keep it manageable
• Use or create light, easily worked soils so less force is required to work them either by hand or with tools
• Keep all equipment and tools in accessible places
• Arrange for a nearby water source–soaker hose or drip irrigation, perhaps–to minimize the difficulties in watering
• Use mulches to cut down on weeding

acuminate: gradually tapering to a long pointleaves with a long, tapering point.

adventitious: when plant organs emerge from unusual positions, such as when roots are produced by leaves or stems, or buds are generated by leaves.

areole: a compact cushionlike structure of cacti from which spines and flowers are produced.

alpine: plants that grow on mountains at high elevations where it is too cold for trees to grow.

alternate: leaves that occur singly along the stem, rather than in pairs or whorls.

angiosperm: a flowering plant.

annual: a plant whose natural life expectancy is 1 year or one season; it grows from seed, blooms, produces new seed, and dies.

anterior: the under side of a leaf

anther: the male reproductive part of a flower where pollen is produced.

aphid: any of several kinds of small, sucking insects that usually congregate on new growth; they are readily controlled by insects predators, insecticidal soap, botanical insecticides, or traditional pesticides.

apical: at the tip; toward the apex.

arborescent: of treelike habit.

arboretum: a place where trees are cultivated for scientific and aesthetic purposes; a tree garden.

armed: provided with defense by means of thorns, spines, prickles, or barbs.

asexual: plant propagation by bulbs, cuttings, or tissue culture.

attenuate: tapering gradually to a narrow point.

autotrophic: organisms that derive their energy from converting inorganic materials into organic molecules. Green plants are photosynthetic autotrophs that convert sunlight energy into sugars.

axil: the angle formed between the upper side of a leaf and the stem to which it is attached. **Axillary** growth occurs at that point.

betalains: an assortment of chemical compounds contained within members of the cactus family, ice plant family, and a few other related families responsible for the vivid pinks, reds, and magenta colors often found in the flowers of these groups.

biological control: a method of taking advantage of natural predators and parasites as nontoxic controls of garden pests.

biome: a major category of habitat type based on overall, large scale climate patterns and the general appearance of vegetation in that habitat. Thus, all deserts around the world are in the same biome.

blade: the broad part of a leaf.

botany: the science of plants, their classification and study.

bract: a leaf at the base of a flower, or elsewhere on the inflorescence, usually differing in size or shape from ordinary leaves; sometimes large and showy, colorful, and petal-like.

bristle: a stiff, sharp hair on a plant.

bud: a growing point enclosed by rudimentary, usually small, leaves. Buds either produce foliage or flowers.

bulb: the resting phase of some plants; they are composed of leaves (often fleshy) formed into a rounded, underground mass that protects the developing short, thick stem inside.
bulbil: a small, aerial bulb with fleshy scales produced in the axil of a leaf.

caliche: a dense, compacted soil layer rich in calcium carbonates, a hardpan.

callus: the thickened, undifferentiated tissue mass that forms when plants are wounded; it prevents water loss or infection during the healing process.

calyx: the often green, leaflike structures (**sepals**) that enclose and protect the flower bud before opening. The calyx is usually present as a cup at the base of the flower after opening. Some plants have highly colored calycxes that rival or outshine the petals.

capitate: head-shaped, or collected in a compact cluster.

caudex: the woody or fleshy basal stem of a plant with otherwise thin stems and leaves. Adj.: caudiciform.

cell: the basic structural, functional unit of life; all living things are composed of cells.

cespitose: growing in tufts of dense clumps, forming mats.

chaparral: a community of shrubby plants in the southwest that are adapted to dry summers and wet winters.

chlorophyll: the green pigment in plants that absorbs light energy in photosynthesis.

ciliate: having margins fringed with tiny hairs.

clone: n. a plant produced by asexual reproduction; it is genetically identical to its parent. v. to propagate asexually (by cuttings, typically) in order to obtain a plant identical to the parent.

cordate: heart-shaped.

corolla: the petals of a flower.

corymb: a broad, flat-topped flower cluster.

crenate: having leaf margins cut into even, rounded notches or scallops.

crispate: having curled or rippled leaf margins.

cultivar: a horticultural variety that has originated and persisted under cultivation.

cuttings: pieces of stems, leaves, or roots cut from a plant and placed in a rooting medium to grow a new plant.

cyathium: an inflorescence typical of Euphorbia. Several male flowers are grouped into a small bowl surrounding a single female flower. (Alternatively, male and female flowers can be borne on separate plants.) Each cyathium typically has one or more glands which may be showy.

cyme: a usually flat-topped inflorescence in which the central flowers open first.

damping off: a common name for a number of soil-borne fungal diseases that cause seeds to rot or seedlings to collapse.

deciduous: plants that lose their foliage every year, with the loss triggered either seasonally or by growing conditions (drought).

decumbent: lying down but with the tip ascending.

dentate: a leaf with sharply pointedy teeth that project outward.

dichotomous: bifurcating regularly and repeatedly, with the two branches of each fork being equal.

diffuse: of open growth habit, with loose or spreading branching.

dioecious: unisexual plants, with male and female flowers borne on separate individuals.

dissected: leaves deeply cut into numerous narrower segments.

distichous: with leaves arranged in two vertical rows along the stem.

dormancy: a resting phase for plants, during which they have no active growth.

dorsal: the back or outer surface of a leaf.

double: having the number of flower petals greatly increased.

ecotype: those individuals that are fitted to survive in only one kind of environment occupied by the species.

endemic: native to a particular restricted geographic region.

epidermis: the outermost layer of cells (exposed to the environment) in all organs with primary growth only.

epiphyte: a plant that grows perched on another plant but does not derive nutrients from it.

etiolated: blanched and elongatedor discolored plant parts caused by growth without sufficient light.

farinose: covered with a mealy powder.

fimbriate: fringed with longer or coarser hairs as compared with ciliate.

flora: all the plants native to a particular area, such as the flora of North America, or the flora of the Cape Province of South Africa.

floriferous: producing lots of flowers.

foliage: leaves.

furrowed: leaves having longitudinal channels, ridges, or grooves.

gene pool: Genes are the genetic information carried on from generation to generation. The gene pool is the sum of all the genetic information contained within an interbreeding population.

genus: the taxonomic term for a group of species that share certain structural characteristics in common.

germination: the process by which a seed sprouts to develop into a young plant.

glabrous: having a smooth surface without hairs.

glaucous: of a bluish gray to bluish white color based on a waxy or powdery, frosty-looking bloom.

glochid: a tiny barbed spine or bristle.

grafting: attaching a cutting from one plant to a stem of another, typically hardier, more insect or disease resistance, or faster growing relative for the purpose of improved propagation.

habit: the growth form or general characteristic appearance of a plant. Shrub and epiphyte are growth habits.

hardiness: the capability of a plant to withstand sub-freezing temperatures without protection. Hardiness does not refer to a plant's disease or pest resistance.

hirsute: having coarse, rough hairs.

hispid: having stiff, bristly hairs or tiny spines.

horticulture: the art and science of cultivating useful or ornamental plants.

humus: the well-decomposed part of organic material found in mineral soils.

hybrid: the offspring of a cross between plants of different varieties, species, or genera.

indigenous: native, not exotic.

inflorescence: the flowering part of a plant.

keel: the central ridge along the underside of a leaf.

lanate: woolly.

lanceolate: shaped like the head of a lance, tapering from a rounded base to an acute apex.

latex: milky sap produced by some succulents, including euphorbias and asclepiads.

leaching: washing or draining away by percolation of water, like rain water washing away nutrients from the soil.

lignify: to become woody.

linear: long and slender with essentially parallel sides, as a linear leaf.

mealybug: a small, white, cottony-looking insect that infests both new and old plant growth; they can be controlled by spraying with insecticidal soap.

microclimate: the climate of a small area of the garden, as the sunny, shady, or dry part.

monocarpic: flowering once, then dying, as some agaves.

naturalized: a plant that has grown and spread randomly, as though native.

nocturnal: active at night; night-blooming flowers are nocturnal.

node: the place on the stem where a leaf is borne.

nomenclature: the Latin names of plants and the terminology that describes them.

obovate: egg-shaped, broader toward the apex.

offset: a short, lateral shoot or small bulb at the base of the mother bulb by which some plants naturally spread or can be propagated.

opposite: leaves that are borne in pairs opposite one another along the stem.

ovate: egg-shaped, broader at the base.

panicle: a loosely branched, pyramidal flower cluster; each branch of the panicle is often a raceme or corymb.

papilla: a small, nipple-shaped protuberance.

pectinate: comblike .

pedicel: the stalk of an individual flower.

peduncle: a stalk supporting a single flower or flower cluster.

pendent: drooping.

persistent: leaves that remain attached to the stem rather than falling off.

petiole: the stalk of a leaf that attaches it to the stem.

photoperiod: the relative lengths of alternating periods of light and dark that affect the growth and maturity of some plants, controlling flowering or leaf drop in some plants.

photosynthesis: the process by which plants convert light energy into chemical energy. Carbon dioxide and water are used to produce sugars that the plant uses for its growth, and oxygen is released as a byproduct.

pinnate: leaves that resemble a feather in structure, with parts arranged along both sides of an axis.

pistil: the female organ of a flower.

plicate: leaves that are pleated lengthwise like a fan.

pollen: produced by the male reproductive parts of a flower, the anthers, each pollen grain contains the male's genetic information. The sperm that eventually fertilize eggs in the ovary are derived from pollen.

pollination: the transfer of pollen from an anther to a receptive pistil.

prickle: a small, weak, spinelike point arising from the bark or epidermis of a plant, rather than from wood.

procumbent: trailing or lying flat but not rooting.

prostrate: lying flat on the ground, as in prostrate stems.

pubescent: fuzzy, covered with soft down or hairs.

punctate: having a surface marked with dots or pits.

raceme: an unbranched stalk bearing numerous flowers, each borne on an individual stem (pedicel).

recurved: curved downward or backward.

rhizome: an underground stem.

rosette: an arrangement of leaves radiating from a central point, usually at ground level; characteristic of many aloes and agaves.

scabrous: having a rough surface, due to short stiff hairs, scales, or other small protuberances.

scale: a large group of small insects covered with shield-like scales that stick tightly to plants. Control by releasing predatoryial or parasitic insects or spray with insecticidal soap.

scandent: climbing.

scape: a leafless stem (peduncle) that emerges from the ground and bears one or more flowers.

sepal: the individual modified leaves, usually green, that make up the calyx. They protect the flower bud until opening.

serrate: saw-toothed margin.

shrub: a woody plant, generally smaller than a tree, which produces several stems from the base rather than a single trunk from the base.

spike: a usually unbranched flowering stem that bears multiple blooms directly attached (without pedicels) along the upper portion of its length.

spine: a stiff, sharp-pointed outgrowth of a stem or leaf.

stalk: 1. main stem of a plant supporting leaves and flowers. 2. pedicel of a flower or peduncle of a flower cluster, petiole of a leaf.

stamen: the male reproductive part of a flower composed of the anther and a supporting filament.

stigma: the tip of the pistil, or female reproductive part of a flower, that receives pollen.

stipules: a pair of usually leaflike lateral appendages found at the base of the petiole of some leaves.

stolon: a horizontal stem that gives rise to a new plant at its tip, as in some *Sempervivum* species.

stomata: tiny openings in leaves or some green stems through which carbon dioxide is taken in by a plant and oxygen and water vapor are released.

subshrub: a perennial plant that has a woody base but with herbaceous shoots that die back annually.

tender: not tolerant of freezing temperatures. (The opposite of hardy.)

tepal: when petals and sepals cannot be clearly distinguished, they are collectively referred to as tepals.

terete: circular in cross section, but usually tapering at both ends.

terminal: growing at the tip of a stem.

thorn: a sharp, rigid, woody spine.

tomentose: densely covered with matted woolly hairs.

transpiration: the loss of water vapor from the leaves.

tubercle: a knoblike projection.

umbel: a rounded flower cluster, with each individual pedicel originating from approximately the same point.

undulate: having a wavy margin or surface.

variegated: regularly or irregularly marked with different colors, often yellow or white due to lack of chlorophyll.

vegetative propagation: propagation by asexual means, such as cuttings or offsets.

ventral: the front or upper surface of a leaf.

viscid: sticky

whorled: having three or more radiating leaves or flowers emerging around a common diameter at a single node.

xeric: adapted to an etremely dry environment.

xeriscape: a landscape designed with drought-tolerant plants.

xerophilous: flourishing in or able to withstand a hot, dry environment.

xerophyte: a plant structurally and physiologically adapted to live and grow with limited water.

SOURCES

Cactus and Succulent Society of America, Inc.
PO Box 35034
Des Moines, Iowa 50315

The Cactus File
Cirio Publishing Services, Ltd.
24-25 Shamrock Way
Hythe, Southampton 5045 6DY
United Kingdom

SOURCES

Abbey Gardens
4620 Carpenteria Avenue
Carpenteria, CA 90313
805-684-5112

Arid Land Greenhouses
3560 West Bilby Road
Tucson, AZ 85746
602-883-9404

B&B Cactus Farm
11550 E. Speedway Blvd.
Tucson, AZ 85748
602-721-4687

Buena Creek Gardens
418 Buena Creek Road
San Marcos, CA 92069
619-744-2810

Cactus and Succulent Society of America
Seed Depot
27821 S.E. Sunray Drive
Boring, OR 97009

Clyde Robin Seed Co., Inc.
PO Box 2366
Castro Valley, CA 94546
415-785-0425

Desert Nursery
1301 South Copper
Deming, NM 88030
505-546-6264

Glendale Paradise Nursery
11249 Wheatland Avenue
Lakeview Terrace, CA 91342
818-899-4287

Greenlee Nursery
301 E. Franklin Avenue
Pomona, CA 91766
714-629-9045

Grigsby Cactus Gardens
2354 Bella Vista
Vista, CA 92083

Living Stones Nursery
2936 North Stone Avenue
Tucson, AZ 85705
602-628-8773

CONTRIBUTORS

Main Garden:
THE HUNTINGTON BOTANICAL GARDENS
1151 Oxford Road
San Marino, California 91108
818-405-2160

Consulting Gardens:
James Henrich
Denver Botanical Garden
909 York Street
Denver, Colorado 80206

Mary Irish
Desert Botanical Garden
1201 North Galvin Parkway
Phoenix, Arizona 85008

Virginia Hays
Ganna Walska Lotusland Foundation
695 Ashley Road
Santa Barbara, California 93108

Dr. Ernest de Marie
The New York Botanical Garden
Bronx, New York 10458

Carol Bornstein
Santa Barbara Botanical Garden
1212 Mission Canyon Road
Santa Barbara, California 93105

Kurt Zadnik and Sean Hogan
University of California Botanical Garden
Centennial Drive
Berkeley, California 94720

LEAF SHAPES

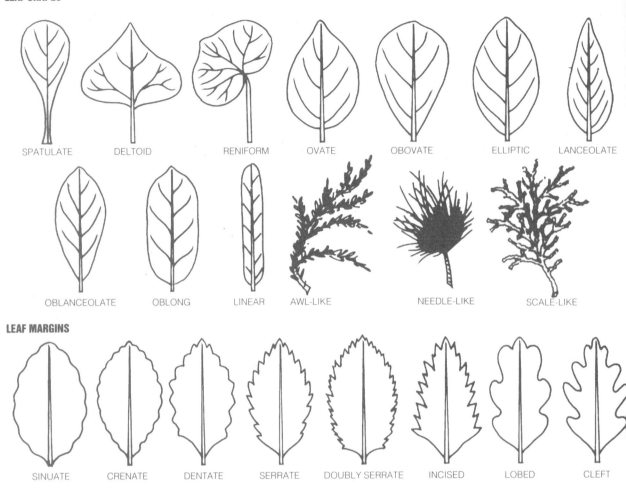

SPATULATE DELTOID RENIFORM OVATE OBOVATE ELLIPTIC LANCEOLATE

OBLANCEOLATE OBLONG LINEAR AWL-LIKE NEEDLE-LIKE SCALE-LIKE

LEAF MARGINS

SINUATE CRENATE DENTATE SERRATE DOUBLY SERRATE INCISED LOBED CLEFT

LEAF ARRANGEMENTS AND STRUCTURES

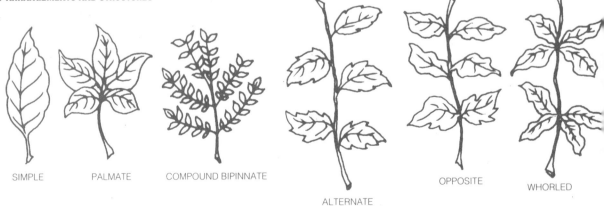

SIMPLE PALMATE COMPOUND BIPINNATE ALTERNATE OPPOSITE WHORLED